The End of Sc

JAMES R. OTTESON
Wake Forest University

CAMBRIDGE
UNIVERSITY PRESS

32 Avenue of the Americas, New York NY 10013-2473, USA

Cambridge University Press is part of the University of Cambridge.

It furthers the University's mission by disseminating knowledge in the pursuit of education, learning, and research at the highest international levels of excellence.

www.cambridge.org
Information on this title: www.cambridge.org/9781107605961

© Cambridge University Press 2014

This publication is in copyright. Subject to statutory exception and to the provisions of relevant collective licensing agreements, no reproduction of any part may take place without the written permission of Cambridge University Press.

First published 2014

Printed in the United States of America

A catalog record for this publication is available from the British Library.

Library of Congress Cataloging in Publication data
Otteson, James R.
The End of Socialism / James Otteson.
pages cm
Includes bibliographical references and index.
ISBN 978-1-107-01731-3 (hardback) – ISBN 978-1-107-60596-1 (paperback)
1. Socialism. I. Title.
HX73.O86 2014
335–dc23   2014015721

ISBN 978-1-107-01731-3 Hardback
ISBN 978-1-107-60596-1 Paperback

Cambridge University Press has no responsibility for the persistence or accuracy of URLs for external or third-party Internet Web sites referred to in this publication and does not guarantee that any content on such Web sites is, or will remain, accurate or appropriate.

The End of Socialism

Is socialism morally superior to other systems of political economy, even if it faces practical difficulties? In *The End of Socialism*, James R. Otteson explores socialism as a system of political economy—that is, from the perspectives of both moral philosophy and economic theory. He examines the exact nature of the practical difficulties socialism faces, which turn out to be greater than one might initially suppose, and then asks whether the moral ideals it champions—equality, fairness, and community—are nonetheless important enough to warrant attempts to overcome these difficulties, especially in light of the alleged moral failings of capitalism. The result is an examination of the "end of socialism," both in the sense of the moral goals it proposes and in the results of its unfolding logic.

James R. Otteson specializes in political philosophy, the history of economic thought, and political economy. He is the author of *Adam Smith's Marketplace of Life* (2002) and *Actual Ethics* (2006), the latter of which won the 2007 Templeton Enterprise Award. He is also the editor of *The Levellers: Overton, Walwyn, and Lilburne*, five volumes (2003). His most recent book is *Adam Smith* (2013). Otteson is executive director and teaching professor in the School of Business at Wake Forest University, a research professor in the department of philosophy and in the Center for the Philosophy of Freedom at the University of Arizona, and a senior scholar at the Fund for American Studies in Washington, DC.

San Diego Christian College
Library
Santee, CA

For my children
And for the other young souls on
whom civilization will depend

Contents

Preface

Not many people today call themselves, or describe their positions as, socialist. There are a few redoubtable figures—including the initial inspiration for this book, the late G. A. Cohen—but their small numbers might make one wonder why one should bother writing a book addressing them. The answer is that although few people call themselves socialists, a large proportion of people endorse policies—and indeed, a political worldview—that is what I will call *socialist-inclined*. Socialist-inclined policy is that which tends to prefer *centralized* over *decentralized* economic decision making. It also tends to distrust granting local people or communities a wide scope to organize themselves according to their own lights, especially when their decisions conflict with larger, preferred corporate or social goals. It tends to prize material equality over individual liberty and is willing to limit the latter in the service of the former, and it tends to hold that self-interest is either morally suspect or can be eradicated from (or at least significantly diminished in) human behavior by the proper arrangement of political, economic, and cultural institutions. A great number of people, regardless of party affiliation, fall somewhere along those continua in the directions of socialism. The argument of this book applies, therefore, to all those policies, beliefs, and positions that are socialist-inclined, even if not avowedly "socialist."

As a theory of what traditionally was called political economy, socialism is not properly a theory of ethics (let alone metaethics), but neither is it simply a set of policy prescriptions. It is instead a system of social organization that is inspired by moral concerns but limited by both politics and economics. It aims to inform our social institutions in a way that is properly moral, but at the same time integrated with the facts of both our political situation and our economic reality. Like any other system of political economy, it must meet moral muster: it must, that is, aim to comprehend—or at least comport with—our most important moral aspirations. Yet because it aims at reform of our actual institutions, it cannot ignore the political, economic, and even cultural realities we face. If socialism were to issue in policy recommendations that were politically or economically unsustainable, or that were impossible to implement given central and enduring facts of human nature or of the human condition, or that could be maintained only by morally repugnant means, then these would count against it. They would count against any other system of political economy too.

What I propose to do in this book is to examine the case for socialism as a theory of political economy—in other words, not based purely on its moral aspirations or intentions, or only on whether it "works"—but on whether its moral commitments are the right ones *and* whether the policy prescriptions it entails are practicable.

Proceeding in this way implies criticisms of two other potential methodologies. On the one hand, if one's political philosophy takes no reckoning of its real-world practicability, perhaps on the grounds that such questions belong to some discipline other than philosophy—economics or political science, perhaps—then it has not yet risen to a level warranting serious consideration for reforming actual institutions. On the other hand, if one's policy prescriptions fail to acknowledge a reliance on or reflection of proper moral values, then they, too, do not yet warrant serious consideration. It is only when the connection between morality and policy are not only acknowledged but integrated that one develops a theory of political economy worthy of assessment. Paraphrasing Immanuel Kant, theory without experience is mere intellectual play, whereas experience without theory is blind.

In the following chapters, I therefore examine both parts of the socialist enterprise. But I do so in reverse order. After first describing my use of the term "socialism" (and "capitalism" as well), I then evaluate socialism's feasibility. Before we can know whether the attempt to instantiate a system of political economy is worth the effort, we need to have an honest reckoning of the difficulties involved, and we need to have a reasonable estimate of both the potential costs and the potential benefits. It turns out that socialism faces formidable obstacles to its implementation and would incur substantial costs. The obstacles and costs are more daunting than one might have expected. Yet being difficult or costly to implement does not by itself defeat a proposed system of political economy, because the proposed system might reflect moral values important enough to justify the attempt regardless. Thus the second part of the book examines the moral values served by, or intended to be served by, socialism and asks whether they warrant the effort despite the difficulties. My examination shows that socialism's moral values are worthwhile in the abstract but lose their attractiveness as they become more specific, as they must to translate into policy. The conclusion I draw, then, is that socialism is a difficult and costly system of political economy that the specific conceptions of its moral values do not justify. That constitutes the end of socialism, then, in both senses of the word *end:* an attempt to implement it will inevitably end in heavy costs to its community, and the philosophical case for socialism ends in failure. Or so I shall argue.

Disclaimer

I have written this book not only for specialists but also for educated lay readers, and in so doing I have sought to strike a balance between addressing the concerns of scholars and remaining intelligible to readers not steeped in the scholarly debates. I realize that this strategy risks disappointing both audiences. Because no book can satisfy all audiences or address all concerns related to its topic, however, I have therefore tended to err on the side of nonspecialist audiences when making the necessary choices about how to frame discussions or which topics not to address. For those wishing to pursue the arguments further or more systematically, I make frequent reference to other sources and discussions.[1] But my goal is to contribute to a larger public conversation about the benefits and liabilities of socialism (and, to a lesser

---

[1] Please see Gaus 2011, however, which heroically provides perhaps the most complete discussion and justification for a liberal social order that one book possibly can.

extent, capitalism). The United States, like much of the Western world, stands now at a crossroads; which direction it goes will affect not only its current but also its future prospects, including for generations not yet born. To them, and in the sincere hope that they will live lives of freedom, peace, and prosperity, this book is dedicated.

Acknowledgments

In writing this book, I have benefited from reading the work of and having conversations with many people. They include historical figures such as Aristotle, Frédéric Bastiat, Adam Ferguson, Hume, Kant, Locke, Marx, Mill, Albert Jay Nock, Rousseau, and Adam Smith. They also include contemporaries (or near-contemporaries) such as Armen Alchien, Elizabeth Anderson, Richard Arneson, Bradley Birzer, James Buchanan, Art Carden, Henry Clark, Ronald Coase, G. A. Cohen, Harold Demsetz, Douglas Den Uyl, Ronald Dworkin, Richard Epstein, Gerald Gaus, Ryan Hanley, Friedrich Hayek, Max Hocutt, Daniel Klein, Will Kymlicka, Mark LeBar, Loren Lomasky, James McCawley, Deirdre McCloskey, Michael Munger, Robert Nozick, Maria Paganelli, Mark Pennington, Steven Pinker, Benjamin Powell, Douglas Rasmussen, John Rawls, Richard Richards, Russell Roberts, David Rose, William Ruger, Michael Sandel, Debra Satz, David Schmidtz, Peter Singer, Jason Sorens, Thomas Sowell, Cass Sunstein, John Tomasi, and Peter Vallentyne. A special note of thanks goes to some extraordinary students, including Noah Greenfield, who read and commented on the entire manuscript, as well as Josh Halpern, Shmuel Lamm, Mikey Stone, and many other students at Yeshiva University and New York University with whom I discussed ideas in this book. Two anonymous reviewers for Cambridge University Press provided numerous insightful and valuable suggestions, which I have incorporated liberally. I express my sincere gratitude to them all. Of course, I am responsible for any errors.

I would also like to thank my editor at Cambridge University Press, Robert Dreesen, for his encouragement and support. Thanks also go to Beatrice Rehl of Cambridge University Press, who first convinced me I should work on this project.

I gratefully acknowledge the following institutions that provided invaluable and generous support during the time it took me to write this book: the Earhart Foundation, the Fund for American Studies, the Hertog Foundation, and the William E. Simon Foundation.

Above all else, I would like to thank my family—my beloved Katharine, Victoria, James, Joseph, and George—for their love, patience, and unfailing support. In this, as in everything else, they are the *sine qua non*.

What Socialism and Capitalism Are

Introduction

The place to begin any systematic discussion of capitalism and socialism is by specifying what we mean by the terms. Each has meant different things to different people, and each of them has considerable baggage—mostly negative. Today, the term "capitalist" is usually meant as a pejorative epithet, carrying with it the connotation that someone is greedy and selfish, uncaring toward others, and probably indifferent (or worse) toward values such as fairness and equality. Similarly, being a "socialist" means allying oneself with unrealistic utopian schemes and failed or dictatorial political experiments.

Yet two recent events have thrust both terms back into public discussion: the election of Barack Obama as president of the United States in 2008 and the global economic recession that began around the same time. President Obama's election has brought with it numerous claims not only that he himself is a (perhaps closet) socialist, but also that his policies, while nominally liberal, are really socialist at heart. Those who claim this do not mean it as a compliment. And the global recession is seen by many as a failure—and thus an indictment—of capitalism, perhaps even its death knell. Both sets of claims, as well as responses and counterclaims, are easy to find. They are often unproductive, however, in part because people mean so many different things by the terms they use. Yet there can be little hope of fruitful discussion, much less unity, if people cannot agree on the definitions of the central terms they use.

Some recent defenders of versions of capitalism have argued that because the term is so widely misunderstood and has so many negative connotations, we should abandon it and go with something else: commercial society, free enterprise society, market society, innovation society, and so on.[1] Perhaps the logical complement to socialism is not "capitalism" but "individualism"; since the word "socialism" seems to emphasize the primacy of the community or society over the individual, then "individualism," which reverses the preference, might be what is called for.[2] Socialism has come to refer, however, not just to social or cultural claims but also to economic and political claims. Thus, "capitalism" seems the better opposing choice because it, too, seems to encompass not only economic but also political and even cultural institutions. There are other considerations one might make about the choice of terminology, but, as Caesar said when he crossed the Rubicon, *alea iacta est*—"the die is cast." The terms "capitalism" and "socialism" have, for better or worse, become the preferred terms, and so I shall use them.

Definitions

Socialism's traditional definition is the public ownership of the means of production. That definition reflected the central method for achieving socialism's goals at a time—late nineteenth and early twentieth centuries—when "means of production" were almost exclusively things like factories and land. Owning them enabled the reorganization of society's political economy in the service of socialism's ends. By the dawn of the twenty-first century, however, the digital age has utterly transformed economic production. What constitutes "means of production" has now broadened to become indefinitely open-ended. Accordingly, the socialist inclination has had to adapt to the times. Rather than owning the means of production outright, it now typically proposes to regulate, canalize, or "nudge"[3] people's behavior and redistribute portions of their productive output in preferred directions. The principal values that motivate socialism have been—and

---

[1] See, for example, Clark March/April 2012 and McCloskey 2010.
[2] See Hayek 1945.
[3] This term comes from Thaler and Sunstein 2009.

remain—equality, community, and fairness (properly defined, of course). Whether serving those ends requires owning the means of production depends on historical circumstances. What will always be required for socialism to serve its ends, however, is to *centrally organize political-economic decision making.* Without that, there is no socialism; with it, the fairness, equality, and community of socialism can, it is hoped, be achieved.

By contrast, socialism's antithesis—capitalism—has at its core *decentralized* political-economic decision making. Its preferred values might be justice, liberty, and individuality (again, properly defined), but it holds that allowing individuals or voluntary groups of individuals to make political-economic decisions for themselves with little state interference is what enables the realization of the values it holds dear. Thus, the socialist-inclined position tends to favor planned patterns of social order—or the correction of unplanned patterns—according to principles and authority centrally derived and administered, whereas the capitalist-inclined position tends to favor unplanned or "spontaneous" patterns of social order that are deferential to what individuals and voluntary groups decide to do and skeptical of what third-parties might like to mandate or nudge them to do. I argue that this is the real difference between socialism and capitalism.

My working definition of socialism, then, is a system of political economy that prefers centralized political-economic decision making to achieve its ends. Other things being equal, the more fully an economy is centralized—whether through outright ownership or through the more common means today of command-and-control policies of *dirigisme*—the more fully is the economy socialist. Capitalism, by contrast, is a system of political economy that prefers decentralized political-economic decision making to achieve its ends. The more decentralized an economy is in this sense, the more capitalist it is.

It is important to emphasize that my goal is to describe a cluster of features that versions of these two competing systems of political economy share. Because their respective features fall along continua, it is quite possible that some particular positions or policies (or figures or political parties) will fall partially in one and partially in the other, or that persons of good faith might disagree about how to categorize a particular position, policy, and so on. For that reason, it will often be useful to think of *socialist-inclined* and *capitalist-inclined* policies or positions, which indicate the tendencies of the particular policies or positions under discussion.

Elaboration

We can flesh out the natures of, and differences between, socialism and capitalism by considering three separate aspects: their respective (1) conceptions of human nature, (2) central values, and (3) public policies entailed, or at least suggested, by (1) and (2).

Human Nature. In each pair of the following aspects of human nature, socialist-inclined policy tends to advocate the first characteristic and capitalist-inclined policy advocates the second:

1. altruistic vs. self-interested
2. cosmopolitan vs. localized
3. unconstrained vs. constrained

Although socialism does not deny that human beings are motivated by self-interest, it nevertheless believes in human *altruism* in one, or in some combination, of the following ways: people are at least as altruistic as they are self-interested; people can, under the proper institutions, develop altruistic motivations that dominate self-interested ones; or people should act out of altruism—if not always, then much more than they do when under (quasi-) capitalist institutions. Moreover, socialism holds out as an ideal that people can come to view others as equally worthy of their concern, regardless of physical, or perhaps psychological, nearness. Some, like Peter Singer, view this as a matter of expanding the concentric circles of our sympathy, perhaps until they encompass all human beings—a universal brotherhood of man, as it were.[4] Finally, socialism holds that human nature is not as *constrained* as others often take it to be; under different institutions, or with different experiences, human nature might be significantly different from what it currently appears to be.[5] That means that socialism

---

[4] See Singer 2011a. Singer wishes to expand the circle to include some nonhuman animals as well. See his 2011b: chap. 3.

[5] I take this terminology from Sowell 2007a. Steven Pinker accepts Sowell's distinction between "unconstrained" and "constrained" visions of human nature, but prefers the terms "utopian" and "tragic," respectively; see Pinker 2002: chap. 16. See also Haidt 2012.

is able to face the criticism that its prescriptions are inconsistent with human nature by responding: perhaps with human nature *as it currently* appears, but not necessarily *as it might be* constituted.

By contrast, capitalism tends toward the latter in each of the three aspects. Thus, it does not deny that human beings act out of altruism, yet it nevertheless holds one or some combination of the following theses about *self-interest:* human beings are fundamentally or predominantly self-interested; people's self-interest is a "natural" fact about them that cannot be eradicated by changing institutions; or there are some, perhaps many, arenas of human interaction in which acting from self-interest is not only allowable but even proper. Moreover, the objects of people's concern are naturally, and often properly, *localized* in the sense that they are part of people's individualized familiarity. They tend, that is, to deal with people, places, and facts known and familiar to people personally, rather than with global or other large-scale entities. Some, like Adam Smith, frame this position by conceiving of human concern for others as a scarce resource that must be husbanded to be effective—and can thus be dissipated by spreading too thin or invoking indiscriminately.[6] Finally, as suggested by its conception of self-interest, capitalism presumes a more constrained vision of human nature, holding that human motivation and other important putative facts about human nature are more enduring and thus more immune from attempts at institutional engineering than other positions might suppose. As Bryan Caplan recently put it, instead of conceiving of human beings as something like clay that institutions and experiences can shape, capitalism conceives of them as more like pieces of hard plastic: concerted pressure can bend them somewhat, but they snap back into their original shape once released.[7]

An early but important qualification regarding these characteristics—altruistic vs. self-interested, cosmopolitan vs. localized, and unconstrained vs. constrained—is that they represent end-states along continua. Most positions fall somewhere along the continua rather than fully instantiating one of the ends. In his recent discussion, John Tomasi includes "[n]ew liberals, modern liberals, liberal democratic

---

[6] See Smith's *Theory of Moral Sentiments* 1982: 137–43. Hereafter, this work is referred to as "TMS."

[7] See Caplan 2011: chap. 3.

theorists, prioritarians, sufficientarians, egalitarians of various stripes, or—at their most enthusiastic—high liberals" as all falling in the category he calls "left liberals."[8] Although one might argue about whether and to what extent any of those positions are properly called socialist, it can nevertheless be fruitful to think of them as not only tending toward political-economic centralism but also as falling on various places along the continua indicated—tending toward altruism, cosmopolitanism, and an unconstrained vision of human nature (all properly qualified, of course), rather than the reverse. On the other side of his spectrum, Tomasi includes "[c]lassical liberals, economic liberals, anarcho-capitalists, right-libertarians, or (as some insist) *real* liberals" under the heading "libertarian" (xi). I suggest thinking of these positions as falling somewhere along the continua indicated earlier, but tending in the other direction: toward decentralism, as well as self-interest, localism, and constrained human nature.

Values. Consider these potentially conflicting values:

1. Equality vs. liberty
2. Community vs. individual
3. Cooperation vs. competition

Socialism does not hold (as a descriptive claim) or endorse (as a normative claim) that equality, community, or cooperation are the *only* values or should *always* dominate their respective partners; similarly for capitalism on the other side. The claim, rather, is that socialism holds *equality* to be one of the most important moral and political values, whereas capitalism holds *individual liberty* to be the same. I present them here as opposed because, conceived in their respectively proper ways, they can easily conflict: instantiating socialism's preferred conception of equality may entail curtailing some of the individual freedoms capitalism champions, and, for its part, instantiating capitalism's conception of individual liberty may allow inequality along dimensions that worry socialism.

Similarly, while not denying altogether the importance of individuals, socialism tends to privilege the *community* or the society—its aims, purposes, and value—over those of the individual when the

[8] See Tomasi 2012: xiii.

two conflict. Marx referred to this as taking proper recognition of man's "species being," which for him involved commitments to certain universal social and moral perspectives rather than individual perspectives.[9] By contrast, capitalism tends to take the side of the individual over that of the society when the two conflict. It holds that individuals are not only the fundamental units of social analysis, but that insofar as the community or the society exists, it is as an abstraction, not a reality, and thus it has no interests or purposes separate from those of individuals. Friedrich Hayek goes so far as to argue that the term "social justice" is, for this reason, a literally meaningless term—like "a moral stone."[10]

Finally, socialism tends to value cooperation above competition. One of its central and abiding criticisms of capitalism is that its extreme rewards for success and punishments for failure encourage an almost ruthless competition among people. By contrast, as Michael Newman puts it, socialism is "based on the values of solidarity and cooperation," which include "a relatively optimistic view of human beings and their ability to cooperate with one another" (2005: 3). Socialism values working together out of a joint spirit of other-regarding service, whereas capitalism values the initiative, innovation, and sense of accomplishment embodied in individual—and therefore competitive—striving. G. A. Cohen claims that socialism envisions human life as based on "communal reciprocity," which he defines as an "antimarket principle according to which I serve you not because of what I can get in return by doing so but because you need or want my service, and you, for the same reason, serve me" (2009: 39). By contrast, according to economist Frank Knight, "the [capitalist] competitive economic order must be partly responsible for making emulation and rivalry the

---

[9] See Marx's essay "Alienated Labor" (*Selected Writings*, 1994: 58–68). See also Will Kymlicka's essay "Marxism" (2002b). Rousseau makes a similar claim in his short essay, "Luxury, Commerce, and the Arts," in which he prioritizes the good of the community above that of the individual. Indeed, Rousseau claims that as modern commercial society began to privilege the individual, "the State soon perished" (in Clark 2003: 395).

[10] See Hayek 1978: 78. I think Hayek goes too far here. Granting that "society" or "community" has no material existence in the way human beings do, people still have both individual purposes *and* communal or corporate purposes—things they would like to achieve on their own or for themselves, as well as things they would like for their communities to achieve or accomplish. For discussion of this aspect of Hayek's thought, see Schmidtz 2012.

outstanding quality of the character of the Western peoples who have adopted and developed it" (1997 [1935]: 39).

It is not that the socialist wants no competition and the capitalist wants no cooperation. The socialist understands that competitive mechanisms may sometimes be required to determine proper allocations of scarce resources; the capitalist argues that the free enterprise system indeed depends on widespread cooperation. But the socialist conceives of his preferred cooperation as *outcome-equality coopera- tion,* where all rise or fall together. Marx captures the socialist position in his 1848 *Manifesto of the Communist Party:* "the free development of each is the condition for the free development of all" (1994: 176). Adam Smith, a century earlier, described his preferred "obvious and simple system of natural liberty" as one in which "man has almost constant occasion for the help of his brethren" and in which "it is by treaty, by barter, and by purchase, that we obtain from one another the greater part of those mutual good offices which we stand in need of."[11] For Smith, then, the preferred conception of cooperation is *agent-equality cooperation,* where the cooperating parties are allowed equal freedom to consent or not. Given, therefore, the reliance of both socialism and capitalism on both cooperation and competition, per- haps the best way to understand this dichotomy is by considering their respective answers to the following question: All else being held equal, should we endorse institutions that promote joint decision mak- ing whereby people's material fortunes tend to rise or fall together, or those that promote individualized decision making whereby peo- ple take localized responsibility for their own material fortunes? All else being equal, socialism inclines toward the former, capitalism the latter.

One other important aspect that distinguishes the socialist con- ception of cooperation from the capitalist is the extent to which the people cooperating know each other. Cohen argues that cooperation should take place only when the cooperating parties know each other personally.[12] This informs his claim that under socialism each person serves others not because of what she can get from them, but because

---

[11] In Smith's *The Wealth of Nations* 1981 (1776), pp. 687, 26, and 27, respectively. Hereafter, this work is referred to as "WN."

[12] Cohen's claim here might seem to restrict the degree to which his position can be considered "cosmopolitan." But Cohen might argue that if we can expand our objects

they need her help (2009: 38–45). I can serve your needs only if I know what they are, and I can know what they are only if I know quite a bit about you. The capitalist order, by contrast, relies on cooperation among people who do not know each other well, even among complete strangers. Take the computer on which I am writing this book: I have no idea where its parts were made, who made them, what people who made it were paid, or what alternatives were available to them aside from their contribution to this computer. To bring this computer to my desk required the efforts of literally thousands of people, the vast majority of whom are totally unknown not only to me but to each other as well. This is cooperation based not on personal knowledge, on personal bonds, or on personal affections; it is instead cooperation based on mutual self-interest across vast networks of unfamiliarity. The personal bonds that dictate socialist cooperation therefore involve a critical tradeoff, which we will explore more fully later, between the extent of cooperation and standards of living. Socialist theory is willing to sacrifice some of the gains that capitalist trade effectuates in order to ensure that people cooperate with the proper sense of joint purpose and mutual need-serving. Capitalist theory, alternatively, is willing to sacrifice the socialist demand for mutual need-serving based on personal familiarity in order to enable the far-flung cooperation among strangers that maximizes prosperity.

Policies. Socialism's and capitalism's respective conceptions of human nature and of value lead, finally, to the endorsement of public policies that distinguish them substantially. Two areas of policy in particular are implicated:

1. Public or common property vs. private property
2. Regulated exchange vs. free exchange

For socialism, the preference is for public or common property over private property, and for regulating economic exchange and decision making over allowing free exchange and decision making. Socialism's position on property was announced already in Marx's *Communist Manifesto*, which claims that a proper Communist revolution "cannot be effected except by means of despotic inroads on the rights of [private]

---

of concern to include all people in our community, then the "personal" can come to encompass the entire community.

property," and articulates, as the first of its ten measures required for that revolution, "[a]bolition of property in land and application of all rents of land to public purposes" (Marx 1994: 175). Not all positions that tend in the socialist direction demand the abolition of private property, but they tend at least to be skeptical of it; hence socialists are not unwilling to endorse restrictions on private ownership—not only the "means of production," which was Marx's main concern, but also land and other assets—as well as limits on the property's potential uses. And while capitalists, or at least some of them (like Adam Smith), are willing to consider the benefits of public or common ownership of some property, they nevertheless maintain a strong preference for private ownership. John Locke captures both the preference for and the slight reservation about private property in his 1690 *Second Treatise of Government*: "Whatsoever then [a person] removes out of the State that Nature hath provided, and left it in, he hath mixed his *Labour* with, and joyned to it something that is his own, and thereby makes it his *Property* [...] at least where there is enough, and as good left in common for others" (§27, p. 288). Locke argues that, even given that God "hath given the World to Men in common" (§26, p. 286), it nevertheless is possible for individual people to gain private and exclusive title to some parts of the world formerly held in common. Yet there are limits to this appropriation, limits that constrain what we might otherwise believe, using Locke's language, we have a "natural right" to possess. Despite these acknowledgments in the opposite direction, as it were, the socialist and the capitalist maintain a clear preference for public or common property and for private property, respectively—a preference robust enough to indicate an important economic principle that will round out the general description of each.

The socialist's preference for public property entails a concomitant preference for regulated economic exchange and decision making. This is actually a two-step preference. The initial step after endorsing public property is toward *centralized decision making*: if we all own, say, our nation's natural resources in common, then we should all decide collectively how to employ them. But that, it turns out, is a logistical impossibility. It is not possible to get everyone's literal permission before a decision is made about how to employ any natural resource. As Locke points out, "[i]f such a consent as that were necessary, Man had starved, notwithstanding the Plenty God had given him" (*Second*

Treatise, §28, p. 288). In practice, then, the claim that property is held in common implies that some group, a subset of the whole—selected, perhaps, by some form of proper democratic procedures—decides for all of us. That is what I mean by *centralized decision making*. What is not meant is precisely what happens in the free-enterprise system of capitalism, namely *decentralized decision making*. If property is held privately, it implies two things in particular: (1) private jurisdiction over the property, which means that the relevant private owner is the one who gets to decide what happens to the property; and (2) excludability, which means that the private decision-making entity gets to say "no trespassing" to others. If our society is based on a regime of private property that includes these two features, then decisions about what to do with the property—whether to use, sell, or trade it; whether to develop or improve it and, if so, how; what the terms of any agreements would be; and so on—would be up to the private owner(s). Because that owner has decision-making jurisdiction, others would have no authority to coerce him into doing something with his property other than what he decides.[13] An acknowledgment of such a prohibition on the authority of a third party to interpose into first- and second-party decisions regarding the latters' property implies, then, an economic order that is decentralized.

Summarizing Socialism and Capitalism

Capturing several of the elements presented here, Michael Newman argues that "the most fundamental characteristic of socialism is its commitment to the creation of an egalitarian society"; moreover, "all socialists have therefore challenged the property relationships that are fundamental to capitalism." Socialists "emphasize community, cooperation, and association" and are "preoccupied by the massive inequality" that capitalism allows. Finally, Newman claims that "socialists have always rejected views that stress individual self-interest and competition as the *sole* motivating factors of human behaviour in all societies and at all times. They have regarded this perspective as the

---

[13] I use the word "coerce" deliberately as meaning either the use of force or the threat of force. See Stigler Spring 1971. An injunction against coercion does not entail, adapting J. S. Mill's language, an injunction against remonstrating, reasoning, persuading, or entreating the property owner. See Mill 1997 (1859): 13.

product of a particular kind of society, rather than an ineradicable *fact* about human beings" (2005: 2–3; Newman's emphases).

By contrast, Milton Friedman defines "competitive capitalism" as "the organization of the bulk of economic activity through private enterprise operating in a free market" (2002: 4). Deirdre McCloskey writes: "I mean by 'capitalism' merely private property and free labor without central planning, regulated by the rule of law and by an ethical consensus" (2007: 14). And Joseph Schumpeter, in his 1942 *Capitalism, Socialism, and Democracy,* compares socialism and capitalism in this instructive way:

> Commercial society is defined by an institutional pattern of which we need only mention two elements: private property in the means of production and regulation of the productive processes by private contract (or management or initiative). [...] By socialist society we shall designate an institutional pattern in which the control over the means of production and over production itself is vested with a central authority—or, as we may say, in which, as a matter of principle, the economic affairs of society belong to the public and not the private sphere. (1947: 167)

Here is Adam Smith describing what he called "the obvious and simple system of natural liberty":

> Every man, as long as he does not violate the laws of justice, is left perfectly free to pursue his own interest his own way, and to bring both his industry and capital into competition with those of any other man, or order of men. The sovereign is completely discharged from a duty, in the attempting to perform which he must always be exposed to innumerable delusions, and for the proper performance of which no human wisdom or knowledge could ever be sufficient; the duty of superintending the industry of private people, and of directing it towards the employments most suitable to the interest of the society. (WN, 687)

The Morality of Socialism and of Capitalism

Let us conclude this introductory chapter by briefly indicating the moral values that proponents of socialism and capitalism respectively believe their preferred systems serve. In each case I take a single figure as a paradigmatic representative: G. A. Cohen for socialism; Adam Smith for capitalism.

Socialism's Morality. The late G. A. Cohen was a distinguished political philosopher in All Souls College, Oxford who made important contributions to many areas of political philosophy, including evaluation and criticism of libertarianism, defense of a kind of egalitarianism, and, most germane here, defense of socialism. *Why Not Socialism?* (2009) was Cohen's last book and was therefore in some ways his final statement defending his lifelong commitment to socialism. It is, therefore, a good place to begin.

In *Why Not Socialism?* Cohen argues that socialism is a system of political economy that is morally superior to capitalism, and therefore, despite the practical challenges involved, it should be the ideal that guides and informs our policy.[14] He makes this claim on the basis of two specific moral principles. The first is "an egalitarian principle" of "socialist equality of opportunity," which "removes obstacles to opportunity from which some people suffer and others don't, obstacles that are sometimes due to the enhanced opportunities that the more privileged people enjoy" (12–13). Cohen emphasizes that this egalitarian principle "is not only *equalizing,* but also a *redistributing,* policy" (14), since it

seeks to correct for *all* unchosen disadvantages, disadvantages, that is, for which the agent cannot herself be held responsible, whether they be disadvantages that reflect social misfortune or disadvantages that reflect natural misfortune. When socialist equality of opportunity prevails, differences of outcome reflect nothing but difference of taste and choice, not differences in natural and social capacities and powers. (17–18)

For Cohen, and for socialism more generally, the central motivation and first virtue is equality. There are disagreements about how exactly to understand the preferred equality—Cohen himself discusses, in addition to his preferred "socialist equality of opportunity," "*bourgeois* equality of opportunity" and "*left-liberal* equality of opportunity," both of which he finds lacking (14–17)—but it seems safe to posit as a first characteristic of anything we might call "socialist" a serious, deep, and *moral* commitment to equality.[15]

---

[14] All quotations from this book are located on the page indicated in parentheses. All italics are in the original. It should be noted that Cohen intends his book to offer "a compelling *preliminary* case for socialism" (1), not the final, definitive word, even if he does also claim that his "preliminary case stacks up on further reflection" (ibid.). See also his more detailed *Rescuing Justice and Equality* (2008).

[15] Michael Newman writes: "In my view, the most fundamental characteristic of socialism is its commitment to the creation of an egalitarian society" (2005: 2).

Cohen's second moral principle is "a principle of community," in which "people care about, and where necessary and possible, care for, one another, and, too, care that they care about one another" (34–5). He argues that this principle of community has "two modes." The first is "the mode that curbs some of the inequalities that result from social-ist equality of opportunity" (35). This community principle extends even further the equality he argued socialism embraces. Cohen's rea-soning is based on the belief that if A is significantly wealthier than B, then A and B will have such vastly different life experiences that they will be unable to "enjoy full community" with one another (35). Cohen argues that, however strict it might have seemed, his first principle of socialist equality of opportunity will nevertheless allow inequalities to arise owing to people's varying tastes and choices. Because this can endanger "full community," however, Cohen concludes that the former inequalities must be "tempered" by a robust commitment to commu-nity. And this commitment will lead us to strive to further equalize the already flattened outcomes allowed by his first principle.

The second "mode" of Cohen's principle of community "is a com-munal form of reciprocity" (38), which is "the antimarket principle according to which I serve you not because of what I can get in return by doing so but because you need or want my service, and you, for the same reason, serve me" (39). It is important to see that this "socialist" conception of reciprocity is not distinct from the standard economic conception insofar as it relies on the needs of the potential exchang-ers. Adam Smith claimed that "it is not from the benevolence of the butcher, the brewer, or the baker, that we expect our dinner, but from their regard to their own interest. We address ourselves, not to their humanity but to their self-love, and never talk to them of our own necessities but of their advantages" (WN, 26–7). Thus Smith claims explicitly that in the kind of market exchanges he envisions, each potential exchanger does, in fact, consider—or "address"—the other person's interests. How, then, is Cohen's socialist principle different? By denying that each potential exchanger should take *his own* inter-est into account as well. On Smith's account, A and B consider each other's interests and see whether there might not be a point at which there is an *intersection of preference:* A's preference for something B has is sufficiently high, and B's preference for something A has is suffi-ciently high, that there is a point (or at least one point) at which their preferences intersect, enabling an exchange. On Cohen's account, by contrast, what is sought is rather a *threshold of possibility:* A has a preference (or need) for something that B has but does not need as much as A does, and they therefore exchange; there is nothing further to be negotiated or investigated because when one person's sufficiently great preference (or need) reaches the threshold of another person's ability to provide what the former desires or needs, that is (or should be) enough to generate the exchange. In other words, if it is possible for B to give to A what A needs—perhaps with the rider that in so giving B would not thereby make herself worse off than A—then B should do so.

Cohen argues that this notion of communal reciprocity further distinguishes itself from market-based reciprocity: whereas the latter does not value cooperation for its own sake, but only as a means to the end of serving one's own interests, the former "relishes cooperation itself" (42). Cohen believes that the "marketeer" engages in reciprocal exchanges only because, and only to the extent that, it serves his own interest (42–3). Although the socialist has an "expectation that (if you are able to) you will also serve me," this expectation is nevertheless "noninstrumental" because the socialist gives "because you need, or want" and then "expect[s] a comparable generosity from you" (43).

Now, Cohen also claims that the socialist will "find value in both parts of the conjunction—I serve you and you serve me—and in that conjunction itself" (43). This means for him that socialist "communal reciprocity is not the market-instrumental one in which I give because I get, but the noninstrumental one in which I give because you need, or want, and in which I expect a comparable generosity for you" (ibid.). There is a puzzle here, however. If I am giving to you "because you need," my giving still seems instrumental—a means to the end of serving your need. Furthermore, Cohen argues that he expects you to serve him as well; the fact that you would serve him out of generosity is irrelevant to the fact that he expects it of you. Perhaps, then, we should take his claim to be that, despite the fact that each of us serves the other with an eye toward getting something in return, we also value the act of exchanging itself, or the reciprocity in itself. That seems plausible, if odd for Cohen to claim since it would not distinguish socialist reciprocity from capitalist reciprocity. Adam Smith, for example, not only recognizes but builds on what he takes to be human

beings' natural sociality, the psychological (and economic) need they
have to associate with others. Consider the first sentence of Smith's
Theory of Moral Sentiments: "How selfish soever man may be supposed, there are evidently some principles in his nature, which interest
him in the fortune of others, and render their happiness necessary to
him, though he derive nothing from it except the pleasure of seeing
it" (TMS, 9). Similarly, when explaining the impulse behind the "divi-
sion of labour, from which so many advantages are derived," Smith
claims that it is the "consequence of a certain propensity in human
nature [...] to truck, barter, and exchange one thing for another," a
propensity he speculates might "be the necessary consequence of the
faculties of reason and speech" (WN, 25). But the faculties of reason
and speech are, for Smith, social faculties that develop in conjunction
with, and through, interactions with other people.[16] Hence, although
Smith accounts for market exchanges by appeal to mutual self-interest,
he couches it in terms of humanity's natural sociality, and even goes so
far as to suggest that we do indeed "relish" these exchanges for their
own sake (TMS, 41).

Capitalism's Morality. I take Adam Smith as my exemplar of
capitalism. I do this for several reasons, despite the fact that Smith
himself never used the term "capitalism" (or "capitalist").[17] First, he
is widely regarded as the "founding father" not only of the discipline
of economics generally but also of capitalism in particular.[18] Second,
his investigation and defense of what we now call capitalism remains
probably the most influential of any such discussion, and in my judgment it remains one of the most sophisticated.

Smith offers three central moral arguments in favor of decentralized
political economy: (1) it leads to increasing overall prosperity, (2) it
fosters community, and (3) it reflects moral equality. The first of these
arguments, which is perhaps his least controversial, is itself based on

---

[16] See Otteson 2002a.

[17] Smith uses the terms "capital" and "capitals," but both he and his contemporaries
would have used something like "commercial society" to refer to the system of polit-
ical-economy later called "capitalism." Although the first usage in English of "capitalism" was apparently in Thackeray, Marx popularized the term in the nineteenth
century. See Marks 2012 for discussion of the history of the term.

[18] See Muller 2003: esp. chap. 3. For a review of Smith's contribution to and influence
on the subsequent discipline of economics, see Skousen 2009.

a chain of further arguments and claims about the human condition; I propose, however, to pass over discussion of it for now because we will examine it in detail later. Let us instead briefly address the other two claims, which might strike one as counterintuitive.

First, regarding community, consider this remarkable passage from Smith's *Wealth of Nations:*

> The woollen coat, for example, which covers the day labourer, as coarse and rough as it may appear, is the produce of the joint labour of a great multitude of workmen. The shepherd, the sorter of the wool, the wool-comber or carder, the dyer, the scribbler, the spinner, the weaver, the fuller, the dresser, with many others, must all join their different arts in order to complete even this homely production. How many merchants and carriers, besides, must have been employed in transporting the materials from some of those workmen to others who often live in a very distant part of the country! How much commerce and navigation in particular, how many ship-builders, sailors, sailmakers, rope-makers, must have been employed in order to bring together the different drugs made use of by the dyer, which often come from the remotest corners of the world! What a variety of labour too is necessary in order to produce the tools of the meanest of those workmen! [...] [I]f we examine, I say, all these things, and consider what a variety of labour is employed about each of them, we shall be sensible that without the assistance and cooperation of many thousands, the very meanest person in a civilized country could not be provided, even according to, what we very falsely imagine, the easy and simple manner in which he is commonly accommodated. (WN, 22–3)

This is a celebration for Smith. It represents not the total independence demanded by eighteenth-century philosopher Jean-Jacques Rousseau—who envisioned a kind of solitary, almost orangutan-like, existence as the ideal for humans—but neither is it the atomism that some critics of capitalism describe. It contemplates instead a set of social institutions that can allow us to transcend the confines of our small-group instincts by engaging in far-flung cooperation. Smith envisions markets allowing us to "serve" one another even when we do not love one another, even when we do not know of each other's existence. That implies an extensive *inter*-dependence—which is a real, if different kind of, community.

And *inequality?* Capitalism does indeed allow, even perhaps require, inequality. Because people's talents, skills, and values vary, because people's desires and preferences vary, and because of sheer luck, some people will be able to generate more wealth in a free enterprise system than others will: inequality will result.

For Smith, however, allowing these inequalities reflects a respect for individual dignity. When Smith famously writes, "[i]t is not from the benevolence of the butcher, the brewer, or the baker, that we expect our dinner, but from their regard to their own interest. We address ourselves, not to their humanity but to their self-love, and never talk to them of our own necessities but of their own advantages" (WN, 26–7), some hear *selfishness*. But Smith saw in the dynamics of such exchanges not selfishness but *respect*. Perhaps that sounds counter-intuitive, but consider that such transactions cannot take place without mutually voluntary consent—which itself requires each person to respect the other's schedule of value and not presume to impose her own. Each person is then dependent on the other, but neither must obey the other. For Smith that reflects an equality of moral agency—each is equally entitled to consent, or to withhold consent—that is not diminished if some come in time to possess more than others. Consider, by contrast, that if we decide we should, or are entitled to, prevent others from engaging in mutually voluntary cooperation, we presume for ourselves not an equal but a superior moral agency, and we hold the moral agency of those others to be inferior to ours.

Conclusion

The key difference between socialist-inclined and capitalist-inclined political economy is the extent to which the former relies on centralism and the latter on decentralism. In addition, socialism tends to favor a picture of human nature that is altruistic, cosmopolitan, and unconstrained whereas capitalism's picture is self-interested, localized, and constrained. Whereas socialism tends to value equality, the community, and noncompetitive cooperation, capitalism tends to value liberty, the individual, and competitive cooperation. And whereas socialism tends to prefer public or common property and regulated exchange, capitalism favors private property and free exchange.

Yet these are descriptions in theory: How do they work out in practice? Specifically, what challenges does the centralism involved in socialist-inclined policy face?

PART I

SOCIALISM'S PROBLEMS IN PRACTICE

A common view holds that socialism is superior in principle to capitalism. It may be impractical or difficult to implement, but it offers a morally inspiring vision, if only we could live up to its ideals. If it turns out that at least some measure of capitalism is required to produce the goods, so be it; but the operation of markets should be limited and canalized according to our considered moral judgments. As socialism's moral judgments are superior to those informing capitalism, it is socialism's morality on which we should draw to correct the excesses, exploitations, failures, or other negative consequences of, as Michael Sandel puts it, "market triumphalism" (2012: 6–8 and passim). Edward Skidelsky and Robert Skidelsky make a similar point, although from the other side, as it were, when they speak of the "Faustian bargain" modern commercial societies have made. They see in the bargain a willingness to accept morally suspect, even "repellent," motives like selfishness and greed in exchange for the increased economic productivity that markets enabled (2012: chap. 2).[1]

Most people who advocate any version of socialism acknowledge that it faces practical difficulties. G. A. Cohen, for example, devotes an entire chapter in his book *Why Not Socialism?* to its alleged "infeasibility." There are many ways that thinkers address these practical difficulties, but perhaps the main way is by recognizing, and then accepting, a tradeoff. The tradeoff they accept is that between wealth

---

[1] The Skidelskys argue that, as in Faust's bargain with the devil, the concessions we have made to the capitalist order will eventually catch up to and ruin us.

and morality: we are willing to give up on some of our wealth—even
if only some of the wealth of some of our wealthiest—if it serves, or
better promotes, ends that we judge morally worthy. For example, if
we think that material equality is important, or that great disparities
in material possessions are worrisome, then we might be willing to tax
some people's wealth and redistribute it with the aim of raising the
least among us, even at the acknowledged cost of (somewhat) lowering the wealthiest among us. If the objection to this is raised that
it might lead to marginally lower standards of living, perhaps in part
because the wealthiest may be marginally less willing to engage in
wealth-producing activity, the response is usually to bite the prover-
bial bullet: we will accept slightly lower standards of living if it means
slightly less inequality.

The difficulties of implementing the economic and political policies
recommended by socialism are large, however, and the costs associated with the willingness to trade off wealth against equality are often
underestimated. Part of the reason these costs are underestimated is
that they are often hidden and thus difficult to see, whereas the potential benefits of redistributive policies are by contrast much easier to
see. That means that the tradeoff people claim they are willing to make
often does not reflect a full accounting of the situation faced. Once a
full, or at least a fuller, accounting is constructed, however, the tradeoff looks much less inviting. In fact, the negative consequences turn
out to be so large that it is not clear that the tradeoff is worth making
after all.

The costs involved with socialist redistribution stem largely from
the limits of human knowledge. That might seem paradoxical—how
can a limit, which sounds like an absence, create real costs?—but the
paradox is resolved once we appreciate the mismatch between what
we believe we know and what we in fact know. Socialist-inclined policy, which relies on centralized political-economic decision making,
requires for its effectiveness an enormous body of knowledge, as well
as the abilities to analyze, assess, and comprehend it, neither of which
does anyone possess. Thus the policies, in practice, operate on the
basis of incomplete knowledge, which greatly reduces the likelihood
of their achieving their aims. The limits of what we do, and even can,
know generate costs by failing to incorporate crucial facts about better
ways to use scarce resources, better ways for people to cooperate, and

better ways to achieve people's ends. Note that I said *better* ways, not *the best* ways. It turns out that we do not know what the "best" ways are—no one does, even if we often mistakenly believe we do. We live in a world of incomplete knowledge and thus second-best alternatives. What we need to be able to do, therefore, is to make improvements, even if those improvements are not the best that can be imagined in theory or in a hypothetical world. Centralized decision makers unfortunately cannot reliably achieve these improvements because they simply do not possess much of the knowledge necessary to do so.

Another practical obstacle socialism faces is what I call the Day Two Problem. It has two related aspects that concern problems created by substantial centralized redistribution of wealth. After any centralized redistribution takes place, people return to buying, selling, trading, leasing, lending, borrowing, exchanging, donating, and gifting their property, their land, their labor, their love, their concern, their knowledge, their futures, their reputations. That means that new inequalities immediately arise. These inequalities might be not only more of what existed before, but new kinds of inequalities, in new directions, and along new margins. The Day Two Problem is what to do *then*—that is, what to do after these new inequalities have arisen, most of which will have been unintended and many of which will have been unforeseeable because they result partly as reactions to the previous redistributions.

A final prefatory note: the challenges to establishing a socialist order discussed in this Part are, while "practical," nevertheless ultimately moral as well. We call them "practical" because they concern difficulties involved in the implementation of a socialist political economy. They confront issues of tradeoffs, opportunity costs, and efficient use of scarce resources, which some are inclined to dismiss as merely materialistic and thus unrelated to, even beneath, the things that really matter in human life—the "moral" matters. Yet every particle of capital that exists and is able to be allocated, redistributed, or exchanged has been generated by the labor of human beings.[2] There is no spontaneously created capital; all of it is the result of human agency. When we undertake to reallocate, redistribute, channel, or restrict it, we therefore undertake to affect human behavior, human

---

[2] The phrase "particle of capital" comes from Sumner 1883.

decisions, human lives. As with any other way we might propose to affect human lives, then, we must first take proper care to ensure we do so in ways that minimize any damage we might cause, and only then, second, maximize any benefit we might generate. Practical problems may deal with economic considerations, but economics addresses itself to human behavior. And when one is dealing with human beings, morality must not be far away.

2

Knowledge and Planning

Introduction

In the first half of the twentieth century, a series of economists led by
Ludwig von Mises and Friedrich Hayek discovered and demonstrated
a problem facing socialist economic planning that became known as
the "knowledge problem."[1] A socialist economy by hypothesis allows
little or no private decision making about how to use capital, and it
restricts, perhaps all the way to zero, the operations of economic markets. It may do this either by owning the means of production outright
or, as is more common today, by a policy of dirigisme that centrally
controls the use and activity of nominally private property. Whatever
good—moral or otherwise—that the socialist economy is designed to
achieve, its lack of decentralized decisions about how to use property
in markets leads to the absence of proper *prices*—and this fact has surprisingly far-reaching consequences.

Prices Real and Artificial

Prices arise when people make localized bids for exchange: person
A says to person B, "I will give you my x for your y." Person C says
to B, "I will give you $x + w$ for your y." Person A will not top that
offer so B and C strike a deal and a price precedent of $x + w$ for y is
established. There is nothing intrinsic, inherent, or transcendent about

[1] See Mises 1990 (1920) and Hayek 1948.

23

a price; it is merely what someone in a particular circumstance is willing to sacrifice for something. A person weighs the proffered good or service against his schedule of value and the other opportunities available to him and thence makes a decision. One person's decision is not necessarily determinative of—or even relevant to—anyone else's because each person has his own schedule of value, opportunity costs, and so on. Yet when this process is repeated hundreds or thousands of times, patterns emerge from the decisions people make and these patterns come to reflect facts and information—i.e., knowledge—that they have but that others do not. To take an example from Adam Smith (WN, 76), suppose a clothier has just heard of the death of an important person in a nearby town; he therefore anticipates that black cloth will soon be in higher demand, so he makes extra purchases of the required proper cloth. To make sure he gets it, he has to offer a price slightly higher than normal. Now, the weaver from whom he buys might not know of the death, but he does not need to: the higher demand is reflected in the slightly higher price now offered for his cloth. He takes this as a signal to buy more dye and wool, and the slightly higher demand gets reflected in price adjustments all along the way. The price mechanism is thus really a knowledge mechanism: it incorporates, in one package, numerous factors of availability, local situations, people's desires, costs, and so on.[2]

It is important to see that these factors are *real* factors—not made up or imaginary—because they arise from facts about people and about people's actual situations. I could decide I want to sell my labor at $1 million per hour if I would like, but the deafening sound of crickets would quickly remind me that my wishes do not determine external reality: other people do not value my labor at $1 million per hour. It is not that there is no one who could conceivably afford it, or groups of people or governments who could amass enough money to afford it. Rather, my labor is not worth the cost to them when compared to what they could otherwise do with that money. This is why prices set by decentralized bargaining are real in a way that prices set by a centralized authority are not.

Because people's situations change, however, prices—if allowed to change according to people's decisions and situations—will adjust to

---

[2] See Hayek 1945.

reflect these changes. They might "gravitate" (Smith's term[3]) toward an equilibrium, but because human life is not static—think of the constantly changing weather as but one factor continuously and unpredictably affecting human decisions—there will never be a time when prices spontaneously settle on one level and then never move. The only prices that do not move are those that are not allowed to move; in that case, however, they soon cease to reflect people's actual situations and incorporate people's localized knowledge. They become aspirational or wishful but not real. That is precisely what happens in the socialist economy, which explains why socialist economic calculation becomes not just difficult but impossible, and why socialist economies inevitably end up with shortages and oversupplies.

Planning and Cheese Making

Suppose you are the director of an Allocation Branch of government[4] and you operate in the context of public ownership of resources and the means of production. Suppose further that you have a team of experts at your disposal, and the scope of your jurisdiction includes considerable natural and labor resources. You also have sufficient authority to enact your decisions about your nation's economy in policy. Let us narrow the focus and concentrate on just one commodity— say, cheese—and one firm—Cheesemaker, Inc. Now, there are many kinds of cheese. Some of them take a long time and careful human monitoring to produce; others are easier to produce and can be completed with automated technology. How much total cheese do we want? How much cheese of each kind? Should resources be invested in hiring more manual labor or in more automated technology? Should Cheesemaker specialize in producing just one kind of cheese or should it produce many kinds—and, if the latter, which ones? Where should Cheesemaker locate its operations? Should it divide its operations among several locations? Should it incorporate other aspects of its extended business—milk procurement, shipping, crate manufacturing, health insurance, and so on—into its own operations or should other firms handle those tasks? In the absence of market prices—in the

[3] See, for example, WN, 77.
[4] As described by Rawls 1971: 276.

absence, that is, of knowing how much these various alternatives cost and what their likely proceeds would be, which are reflected in the relevant prices—it is impossible to answer these questions in a way that matches the realities people face. Prices allow one to make calculations based on profit and loss, which here are proxies for good (efficient) uses of resources and bad (inefficient) uses of resources, respectively. Without prices, you would just have to guess. You might guess that people will want a lot of bleu cheese, and so you accordingly outfit Cheesemaker to produce a lot of bleu cheese. But you cannot know whether the resources you will put into production of bleu cheese— resources that you therefore would not be able to put into, say, sharp cheddar—will satisfy people's wishes. You may end up with too much bleu cheese, not enough sharp cheddar, or any of thousands of other combinations that are exceedingly unlikely to match what people's actual wishes will be.

One may reply that there are other, perhaps even more important, things than efficiency and hence other (and perhaps more important) considerations that ought to be brought to bear in deciding where to expend our scarce resources. Fair enough; indeed, that is surely true. But that does not resolve the problem that the lack of prices in socialist economies raises. Without people being able to offer and accept (or refuse) their goods and services to one another according to their individual assessments of their own local circumstances, real prices do not arise. That means there are no data—no numbers—on which to make economic calculations. All we would have to go on is our guesses and expectations, informed by our hopes, dreams, wishes, aspirations, convictions, and biases. Now, the knowledge problem does not by itself constitute an argument against making decisions about resources on the basis of such criteria, but it does entail that if one wishes to substitute these criteria for the signals indicated by prices generated by people's actual decisions in market settings, one will have to acknowledge the high probability that there will inevitably be too much of some things produced and not enough of other things produced: oversupplies and shortages.

This is exactly what has, in fact, happened in socialist countries. The Soviet Union was created in 1922 across a vast area with rich natural resources and people with many different kinds of skills. And yet, by the time of its ignoble demise in 1991, it had thousands of tanks moldering in the countryside and bridges and roads no one used (oversupplies) while there was not enough bread or toilet paper or potable water (shortages). One might argue that the Soviet Union's moral and political goals justify its material sacrifices, but the over-supplies and shortages—and the nearly systematic mismatch between what people needed, wanted, and desired on the one hand and what the government's central decision makers could provide on the other hand—are both explained and predicted by the knowledge problem.

Despite its straightforwardness and seeming empirical valida-tion, however, the knowledge problem has suffered a bizarre fate in the history of political economy. Although it has now become part of the widely accepted wisdom of the discipline of economics, it has nevertheless failed to make much headway in political philosophy, where arguments for socialist-inclined policy tend to proceed on the basis of considerations like justice or fairness or equality with little notice or mention of the difficulties involved with the economic cal-culations that such polices face. This suggests that the problem needs reconsideration. In what follows, I consider four applications of the knowledge problem—central planning, personal values, equality, and community—that flesh out the scope of the problem, paying particular attention to issues concerning socialism. The challenges are deeper and more pervasive than one might expect, and together they constitute formidable, perhaps even fatal, practical obstacles to socialism.

Decentralized Planning: Of Woolen Coats and Pencils

Early in *The Wealth of Nations*, Adam Smith includes a striking par-agraph describing a day-laborer's "woollen coat." Here is the para-graph, reproduced in full:

Observe the accommodation of the most common artificer or day-labourer in a civilized and thriving country, and you will perceive that the number of people of whose industry a part, though but a small part, has been employed in procuring him this accommodation, exceeds all computation. The woollen coat, for example, which covers the day-labourer, as coarse and rough as it may appear, is the produce of the joint labour of a great multitude of workmen. The shepherd, the sorter of the wool, the wool-comber or carder, the dyer, the scribbler, the spinner, the weaver, the fuller, the dresser, with many others, must all join their different arts in order to complete even this homely production. How many merchants and carriers, besides, must have been employed in transporting the materials from some of those workmen to others who often live in a very distant part of the country! How much commerce and navigation in particular, how many ship-builders, sailors, sail-makers, rope-makers, must have been employed in order to bring together the different drugs made use of by the dyer, which often come from the remotest corners of the world! What a variety of labour too is necessary in order to produce the tools of the meanest of those workmen! To say nothing of such complicated machines as the ship of the sailor, the mill of the fuller, or even the loom of the weaver, let us consider only what a variety of labour is requisite in order to form that very simple machine, the shears with which the shepherd clips the wool. The miner, the builder of the furnace for smelting the ore, the feller of the timber, the burner of the charcoal to be made use of in the smelting-house, the brick-maker, the brick-layer, the workmen who attend the furnace, the mill-wright, the forger, the smith, must all of them join their different arts in order to produce them. Were we to examine, in the same manner, all the different parts of his dress and household furniture, the coarse linen shirt which he wears next his skin, the shoes which cover his feet, the bed which he lies on, and all the different parts which compose it, the kitchen-grate at which he prepares his victuals, the coals which he makes use of for that purpose, dug from the bowels of the earth, and brought to him perhaps by a long sea and a long land carriage, all the other utensils of his kitchen, all the furniture of his table, the knives and forks, the earthen or pewter plates upon which he serves up and divides his victuals, the different hands employed in preparing his bread and his beer, the glass window which lets in the heat and the light, and keeps out the wind and the rain, with all the knowledge and art requisite for preparing that beautiful and happy invention, without which these northern parts of the world could scarce have afforded a very comfortable habitation, together with the tools of all the different workmen employed in producing those different conveniencies; if we examine, I say, all these things, and consider what a variety of labour is employed about each of them, we shall be sensible that without the assistance and cooperation of many thousands, the very meanest person in a civilized country could not be provided, even according to, what we very falsely imagine, the easy and simple manner in which he is commonly accommodated. Compared, indeed, with the more extravagant luxury of the great, his accommodation must no doubt appear extremely simple and easy; and yet it may be true, perhaps, that the accommodation of an European prince does not always so much exceed that of an industrious and frugal peasant, as the accommodation of the latter exceeds that of many an African king, the absolute master of the lives and liberties of ten thousand naked savages. (WN, 22–4)

The extensive cooperation required to bring even this "homely" product to the lowest day-laborer is remarkable. Smith claims indeed that it "exceeds all computation." It is all the more remarkable because it is completely unplanned. That does not mean that the people involved had no plans; of course they did. But no one planned the whole thing. Each person who had a hand in the achievement of this feat had only her own local aims in mind. And yet something much larger than what any of them intended emerged. Perhaps not a single one of those hundreds, even thousands, of people have met, or even heard of, the particular day-laborer who eventually wears this coat.

A similar story was presented by Leonard Read in his 1958 essay, "I, Pencil." Read's claim was that no one—literally no single person—knows how to make even as simple a thing as a pencil. A person can know the outlines, like what the main materials are, where they come from, and so on, but what no single person knows is all the relevant, and necessary, details required to bring the production of an actual pencil to fruition. How many truck drivers are required, and which ones? How long should it take them to get the product from there to here? What is a good price for this material, and this one, and this one? How many factory workers do I need, and for how long? Is this person reliable enough to entrust with this crucial task? Should a distribution center be built here, here, or here—or not at all? The questions go on and on: the moment one starts tracing out the links in the long chains of labor, materials, and cooperation that combine to bring this pencil into your hand, one realizes that the questions about the details seem to have almost no end. That is why no single person can answer them all.

The general manager of one of the plants of Faber-Castell—the largest pencil manufacturer in the world, producing some two billion pencils per year—will know an awful lot about what goes into the production of pencils, certainly more than you or I. But even the general manager can master only a handful of the links in the long chain, which reaches across continents and over months of time and involves tens of thousands of people—most of whom are complete strangers to one another. Faber-Castell has fourteen production locations on four different continents, employs some 7,000 people worldwide, and divides the labor involved in constructing pencils according to materials derived from, and labor supplied in, these various countries. Which person working for the company knows all of the company's workers? Which person knows even ten percent of the workers? And which person knows even one percent of the people who supply its employees with the goods and services—fuel, coffee, education, food, clothing, love, support, and so on—they need to in order to perform their duties for Faber-Castell? The answer to these questions is: no one.

One thus begins to have a sense of the enormity of the body of knowledge exploited by the people involved in the creation of a pencil, and thus the enormous improbability of any single person—or even group of persons, however smart—being able to assemble and process it. And that is only one company, in one industry, providing a relatively simple product. In 2008, the United States had some 31.6 million businesses across thousands of industries employing some 120 million people.[5] Imagine how much knowledge a person would have to possess to organize them centrally.[6] The problem is even worse than that, however, because those businesses, industries, and people are constantly changing. Even if one could somehow assemble all the relevant knowledge today, what happens tomorrow? The intelligence of the centralized decision makers we are imagining is irrelevant. Suppose they are literally the smartest people in the world—they have the highest IQ, the most prestigious degrees, the best training. Still, the knowledge they do have is dwarfed by the magnitude of what they do *not* know.

The Totalizing Fallacy. In his 1850 *Economic Harmonies*, Frédéric Bastiat asks his reader to contemplate solving a problem so complex and daunting that it seems impossible: feeding Paris. Paris has so many people, each with different tastes and interests and preferences. How could we possibly even know, let alone accommodate, such variety? As Bastiat describes with some detail the mind-boggling number of possibilities and variables we would have to address and reckon to accomplish this task, we quickly realize the point: namely, we could not, in fact, do it. But then Bastiat reminds us that this impossible task is already accomplished, every day. The problem for us is that we conceive of this as a single gargantuan problem that requires a

---

[5] This information is provided by the U.S. Census Bureau; 2008 is the most recent year for which data is available. See http://www.census.gov/compendia/statab/cats/business_enterprise.html.

[6] I say "imagine" it, but I think it is actually impossible to imagine—like asking a person to imagine a googolplex.

single near-omniscient problem solver when, in fact, it is thousands, even millions, of small problems that are solved by thousands, even millions, of discrete problem solvers. Paris does not need to be fed. Instead, this Parisian, and this one, and this one need to be fed. Each will be fed through the cooperation of all the thousands, even millions, of other people—all acting on their own and without any single over-arching superintendence—to serve their mutual ends. The mistake, then, is to conceive of the separate tasks and challenges people face as if they were just one amalgamated problem, perhaps because we categorize the separate problems under a single topic heading. We might call this the *totalizing fallacy*, and it recurs again and again in discussions of political economy.

Every autumn, leaves fall off the trees across North America. Imagine if someone asked you how you would propose removing all those leaves. How would you gather them? How would you transport them? Where would you take them? Whom would you employ? How would you coordinate all the people required to accomplish the task? And how much would it cost? One would rapidly realize that this problem is so impossibly complex that *no one* could solve it. Fortunately, no one has to solve it because the problem is already solved by all the millions of people who individually, in cooperation with others, break the problem into millions of constituent parts and handle them locally and individually. And they do it every year. They do not do it perfectly, of course, and after the fact one might be able to imagine a more efficient system of removal. But it is already handled ably, reflecting the needs and preferences and wherewithal of relevant individuals, responding to their changing localized decisions over time. Similarly, I argue, with many of the problems that we routinely assume require centralized solutions.

Consider health care, for example. We tend to think that some central solution or some centrally coordinated set of solutions must address the real needs of people. But why? Indeed, solving "the nation's health care problem" would be far more difficult than removing the nation's autumn leaves or even feeding the nation since the needs are so much more dependent on the changing localized realities that each and every individual faces. It is merely an assumption that there must be some single, centralized solution to a problem such as this, and the assumption is highly suspect given how unique each individual's situation is.

Consider how many hundreds of thousands of people in America will
need haircuts, condoms, or erectile-dysfunction pills today; how many
will need massages; how many will need smart phones or wireless
internet access; how many will eat doughnuts or apples; how many
will dip into their retirement savings to pay for reconstructive sur-
gery on their dog's knee; and on and on, almost literally without end.
These examples are not arbitrary: each of them has been suggested as
properly falling within the purview of a federal agency charged with
addressing health care and thus requiring centralized superintendence.
In each case, however, and in countless others like them, we assume
that these are really just one big problem—when in fact they are countless, distinct smaller problems—and we thereby create for ourselves a
problem we almost certainly cannot solve.

There will be cases—some kinds of pollution, for example—where
centralized, and even globalized, solutions are required, but cases
like these are the exception. Even here, however, decentralized solutions are to be preferred, all else being equal, to centralized solutions,
owing to the enormous variety of challenges that individuals and their
communities face and the enormous variety of resources, preferences,
tradeoffs, and opportunities available to them.

From Millions to One. The extreme limitations on individual
knowledge is illustrated not just by considering how difficult—even
impossible—it would be for any individual to make all the decisions
required to run, say, an entire company, but also by considering the
knowledge that is required to run only one's own life. Suppose my
colleagues and I were to fancy ourselves some combination of smarter,
more expert, more objective, and more virtuous than you, from which
we conclude that we could run your life better on your behalf than
you could run it yourself, even if in only some areas. How would we
fare? Poorly—because we know virtually nothing about you. Nor do
we know anything about almost anyone else. Those are not flippant or
casual considerations. Would-be centralized decision makers may be
in possession of statistical generalities, and thus they may be in a position to make some general predictions about what populations characterized by some of your traits might do, but what they do not know
about you is what makes you *you*, as opposed to someone else. They

do not know your hopes and dreams, your purposes and goals, your skills and abilities; they do not know what opportunities are available to you; they do not know what your tastes and preferences are; they do not know the people with whom you associate, or might associate, or would not associate—and they do not know any of these things about any of those other people, either. Consequently, they can have no real idea what decisions you should make.

Should you go to college or trade school? Should you go to law school or work for a bank? Is it time, finally, to quit your lousy job or should you stick it out for another few months? Should you buy a new car or invest in an evening MBA program? Should you move to the city or stay in the suburbs? Should you rekindle that friendship or let it die? Should you take the risk of working for an exciting start-up with great potential but no guarantees, or should you take the job at the more stable firm that offers less potential down the road? Where should you grab lunch today—or should you skip it altogether to continue working on that project (or check your e-mails or Facebook)? Think for a moment about all the decisions you make for your own life every single day. They concern matters big and small, light and weighty. All of them, however, involve tradeoffs: if you do *this,* it means you cannot do *that.* All of them, moreover, involve costs. The costs may be monetary, of course, but they are just as often other things that are equally or even more significant. Consider time: your time on earth is absolutely limited and is thus a truly scarce resource. If you devote one year, one month, one week, or even one hour to one project, that is time you cannot ever spend on any other projects. Time once spent is gone forever.

Consider also the cost of forgone opportunities. Suppose you decided to go to graduate school in philosophy instead of law school. Your decision to study philosophy presumably resulted in both benefits and liabilities (one hopes more of the former than the latter!). If you wished now to conduct a full evaluation of your decision, however, you would need to consider not only the benefits and liabilities associated with your chosen field, but also those of the forgone opportunities. What would the likely costs and benefits have been if you had decided instead to go to law school? These are much harder to estimate since they did not, in fact, happen and are thus unseen. But that makes them no less real.[7] You forsook that opportunity, as well as numberless further opportunities associated with it, so those are real losses. If that life would have been miserable for you, then you lost a largely negative life, meaning your decision was a good one. If the calculation goes the other way, well, you know what that means. Now, the fact that calculations like these involve difficult-to-assess possibilities is only one part of the point I wish to make here. It is also the case that they are real, and that hence a full and honest accounting of one's life decisions requires a reckoning of them.

Now consider a case in which some choice you faced was decided not by you but by someone else. Take a relatively innocuous example: suppose you decided not to go a particular deli for lunch because the mayor of the city where you live banned soft drinks over sixteen ounces, and you like a big soda with your hero.[8] Suppose you were not dead-set on going to this deli anyway, so something as seemingly trivial as this was enough to tip you in a different direction. What was the result? You did not get your super-sized drink and sandwich for lunch, and that deli did not get your business. That is probably not a disaster for you or the deli. But consider two further points.

First, it cannot be known by the mayor of your city whether you were better off going somewhere else because of that large soda ban. You *might* be better off, even if only marginally, but *possible* does not mean *probable*. If we wished to justify such a ban on the grounds that it would benefit people, we would have to demonstrate that it would benefit people—or at least that it is likely to benefit people. But this cannot be shown for you—or, probably, for any other single person. Perhaps the result in your case is that instead of walking to that deli . nearby, you chose to drive your car to a restaurant a few miles away.

---

[7] See Bastiat's 1848 *What Is Seen and What Is Not Seen*. When I was early in my graduate career at the University of Chicago, Richard Epstein, a professor in its law school, took me aside and told me to leave philosophy immediately and go to law school instead. "Law professors make twice as much and have half the workload," he said. A full judgment about whether my decision not to take his advice was correct would have to include such forgone benefits.

[8] Former New York City Mayor Michael Bloomberg recently proposed the banning the sale of sodas larger than sixteen ounces in restaurants purportedly to help combat the growing incidence of obesity. See http://www.huffingtonpost.com/2012/09/13/new-york-approves-soda-ban-big-sugary-drinks_n_1880868.html. A court recently overturned Bloomberg's ban; he has appealed, and as of this writing the matter is pending.

But driving a car is statistically far more dangerous than walking; thus, holding other things equal, this would have slightly increased the possibility that something bad would happen to you.[9] People change their behavior in response to changing circumstances; unfortunately (or fortunately, depending on your perspective), people—unlike inanimate objects and nonrational animals—often change their behavior in unpredictable ways. That is part of what is unknown to the would-be central planner, thus part of what cannot be accounted for in advance, and thus what cannot be the basis for either the construction or defense of a policy restriction or redirection of people's behavior.

Second, individual decisions at the margins can accumulate, leading to big changes down the road—and these cannot be predicted either. What effects will the soda ban come to have on that deli? Who can tell? Remember, too, that the deli is itself but one node in a profoundly ramified web of interdependence, so changes that affect it also affect other people, businesses, industries—even municipalities—in numberless and unpredictable ways. This holds true, of course, not only for the soda ban and the deli, but also for all similar impositions, restrictions, and redirections. They alter people's incentive structures, payoffs, preferences, costs and benefits, and so on in ways that can neither be known nor predicted. Some of these alterations may be good; some of them may be bad. Are they *on balance,* or *all things considered,* good (or bad)? It is impossible to know because such calculations depend on details of individuals' situations that are unknown to any single person, or any group of persons, attempting to make such a reckoning.

I argue that the difficulties involved in knowing what would result from such centralized decision making shift the burden of proof to the person proposing the policies. Because we are contemplating redirecting the behavior of actual human beings, a higher standard of proof is warranted than what might be required by, say, a zookeeper or

---

[9] According to the Centers for Disease Control, in 2009 (the most recent year for which data is available), there were 34,485 deaths as a result of motor vehicle accidents in the United States, compared to 1,110 pedestrian deaths. The former accounted for 29.2% of all deaths caused by injury, making it the eleventh overall leading cause of death; the latter accounted for 0.9% of all deaths caused by injury, which is not enough to place it among the top fifty leading causes of death in the United States. See http://www.cdc.gov/nchs/data/dvs/deaths_2009_release.pdf.

entomologist. The person who claims that an imposition, restriction, or redirection of human beings' decisions would benefit them must show, not that it is *possible,* but that it is *probable* that the proposed policy will have the intended effect. That means that such a person will have a lot of work to do beyond merely articulating general goals or general requirements of justice.

Perhaps one might reject my argument on the grounds that it sets too high a standard: Why would we need to know exactly, or with full certainty, what the effects of such a policy would be before we implement it? Why are reasonable guesses not sufficient? The answer is: reasonable guesses *are* sufficient. Unfortunately, not even *that* is present in such a case, or in most others like it. Unless we can show—indeed, unless we have shown—that the reasonable guesses are actually likely outcomes, then they are merely *guesses* without the *reasonable.* Without knowledge of individuals' purposes, values, preferences, opportunities, tradeoffs, and so on—knowledge often captured in prices and communicated by people's localized decisions in light of them—one cannot know whether this or any other similar policy is likely to achieve its desired results. That means that it fails to justify a policy based on the probable achievement of its desired goal.

What is difficult, perhaps impossible, to do on the individual level becomes yet more difficult when one contemplates orchestrating the decisions of more than one person. As one builds up from individuals to groups (including firms or industries or even an entire economy), it is not only the scale that increases the magnitude of the knowledge one must possess. One must also account for the fact that people respond to each other dynamically. When people cooperate, interact, associate, or exchange, they make real-time, on-the-spot adjustments to their behaviors based on what others around them are doing. From the way they speak, the jokes they tell, and the clothes they wear to the books they read, the music they listen to, and the food they eat: all of these decisions—and innumerable others—are affected, continuously and every day, by the decisions made by others around them and their decisions are affected by yet others' decisions, and so on. There are here so many variables, so many margins, so many possibilities that it, as Smith puts it, "exceeds all computation."

Yet the situation for the centralized decision maker is still worse: much of the knowledge one would need to organize people's behavior does not actually *exist*—at least not in advance, when it would be needed for policy making. Many of the preferences people have are not known even to them until they face situations that elicit them. You may believe you know exactly what you will have for breakfast tomorrow, but what if your friend calls you unexpectedly and asks you to join her at a bagel shop—and you like your friend but not bagels? What will you do? If it is almost impossible for *you* to answer this question in advance (so much more would need to be known: which friend, which shop, when, and so on), then how likely is it that I, or any other person who does not know you, could guess correctly? Even if almost everything about you until now were known—suppose scientists had been monitoring your every move for the past month—still they could not know (1) that your other friend would call you or (2) what you would decide to do if she did.

That is a small example. But the point is that this uncertainty characterizes nearly everything in each individual's life and can be managed only on the basis of the intense personal familiarity each person has with her own situation. The more distant from you would-be planners for your life are, the more about you do they not know; and if we begin to multiply the number of people's lives under their putative superintendence, it quickly becomes obvious—indeed, all too obvious—not only how little they can know, but also how small the chance is they can direct your life for you better than you can. That chance is effectively zero.

That does not prevent people from believing they can do it nevertheless. Much political economy is concerned with trying to figure out how to get people to do what we want them to do as opposed to what they themselves want to do. If you start looking for all the ways we try to coerce or nudge each other, you might be surprised, even shocked, at just how much of our personal and public behavior has some aspect of this to it. There seems to be a robust prejudicial faith in our own judgment, as well as suspicion of that of others, in human social relations—and probably neither is justifiable.

The Great Mind Fallacy

But let us not make a philosophical point on the basis of armchair psychologizing. Instead, let me elevate the discussion with an actual argument concerning what I call the Great Mind Fallacy.[10] One of the more famous passages in Smith's writings is his discussion of the "man of system" in *The Theory of Moral Sentiments* (TMS). Smith there criticizes the legislator who believes he can arrange human beings "with as much ease as the hand arranges the different pieces upon a chess-board" (TMS, 234). The "man of system," according to Smith, understands that "the pieces upon the chess-board have no other principle of motion besides that which the hand impresses upon them; but [fails to realize] that, in the great chess-board of human society, every single piece has a principle of motion of its own, altogether different from that which the legislature might chuse to impress upon it" (ibid.). We might call this the Herding Cats Problem of centralized policy making: because human beings have their own ideas about what to do, a central planner wishing for them to conform to his plan, however beautiful and attractive it might be to him, is bound to be frustrated. Human beings upset patterns, and they do so in numerous and unpredictable ways.[11] Hence, the central planner is faced with either giving up on (some parts of) his beautiful plan or attempting to impose it—the former being abhorrent to the planner, the latter abhorrent to everyone else.

The Herding Cats Problem constitutes an argument about the relative difficulty of certain kinds of state action and centralized organization, but it does not by itself establish that we should not make an attempt. Perhaps, after all, despite the difficulty, cats still need to be herded—for the common good or for their own good. But what if it is not simply difficult to herd cats, but impossible?

Smith's case proceeds on the basis of three connected arguments. First is his Local Knowledge Argument (LKA): given that everyone has unique knowledge of her own "local" situation—including her goals, desires, and available opportunities—each individual is therefore the person best positioned to make decisions about what courses of action she should be taken to achieve her goals. The argument in Smith's words: "What is the species of domestick industry which his capital can employ, and of which the produce is likely to be of the greatest value, every individual, it is evident, can, in his local situation, judge much

---

[10] See Otteson 2010.
[11] See Nozick 1974: 160–4.

better than any statesman or lawgiver can do for him" (WN, 456).[12] That does not mean that people are infallible in judging their own situations. Indeed, as numerous commentators today emphasize, we know that people are far from perfectly rational. As Robert Frank reports, "a large body of research has demonstrated that people are not attentive to costs and benefits in the manner required by traditional theories of rational consumer behavior" (2011: 23). Yet this does not constitute an objection to Smith's Local Knowledge Argument. The LKA does not assume that people are perfectly rational; it assumes only that they are *relatively better positioned than others* to make decisions about their own lives, for two important reasons: (1) they possess relevant localized knowledge others do not and (2) it is they, not centralized authorities, who will most acutely feel the consequences of those decisions, so they have more incentive to get them right and to adapt to feedback appropriately. Thus, individuals have a better chance of knowing how best to use their own resources (starting with themselves) and what courses of actions to take to achieve their own goals than do third parties, and they are more likely to take appropriate actions and learn from experience—even if it is true that we all make mistakes, suffer from various biases and prejudices and failings, and so on.

The second point above leads to Smith's second argument, which I call his Economizer Argument (EA). It holds that because each of us continuously seeks to better his own condition (however each of us understands that), each of us is therefore led to seek out efficient uses of his resources and labor, given his peculiar and unique circumstances, to maximize their productive output and return on his investment. This argument in Smith's words: "The uniform, constant, and uninterrupted effort of every man to better his condition, the principle from which publick and national, as well as private opulence is originally derived, is frequently powerful enough to maintain the natural progress of things toward improvement, in spite both of the extravagance of government, and of the greatest errors of administration" (WN, 343).[13]

[12] Other statements of the Local Knowledge Argument can be found throughout WN. See, for example, WN, 20, 530–1, 534, and 687.

[13] Smith continues: "But though the profusion of government must, undoubtedly, have retarded the natural progress of England towards wealth and improvement, it has not been able to stop it. The annual produce of its land and labour is, undoubtedly,

We wish to satisfy our own purposes, whatever they are, but as economizers we tend to try to expend the least amount of our own energy possible while at the same time trying to get the largest, richest, or most extensive achievement of our goals as possible. We seek, as it were, the best possible return on our investment of our energies.[14]

Smith's third argument is his famous Invisible Hand Argument (IHA), which holds that as each of us strives to better her own condition as provided for in the Economizer Argument, each of us thereby also, if unintentionally, tends to better the condition of others. Smith's claim is not that people do not act intentionally; rather, it is that they typically act with only their own local purposes in mind, and they are typically unconcerned with—even unaware of—whatever larger effects their behavior might have on unknown others. Now their "local" purposes are not necessarily related exclusively to themselves; they regularly include concerns about family and friends and groups with which they are affiliated. Our concern for others fades, Smith thinks, the farther away from us—and thus more unknown to us— they are, but Smith thinks our concern for others closer to ourselves is real and undeniable. According to the IHA, the search for efficient use of our energies tends to benefit not only ourselves and those close to us about whom we care (the direct objects of our concern), but even others totally unknown to us. This happens because when we specialize or concentrate our efforts on some small range of tasks or talents, we usually produce more of it than we can ourselves consume

---

much greater at present than it was either at the restoration or at the revolution. The capital, therefore, annually employed in cultivating this land, and in maintaining this labour, must likewise be much greater. In the midst of all the exactions of government, this capital has been silently and gradually accumulated by *the private frugality and good conduct of individuals, by their universal, continual, and uninterrupted effort to better their own condition.* It is this effort, protected by law and allowed by liberty to exert itself in the manner that is most advantageous, which has maintained the progress of England towards opulence and improvement in almost all former times, and which, it is to be hoped, will do so in all future times" (WN, 345; emphasis added). This argument, too, can be found throughout the *Wealth of Nations*. See, for example, WN, 99, 139, 285, 341, 342–3, 374–5, 405, 454, 455, 540, 674, and 718. See also Smith's *Lectures on Jurisprudence*, 384.

[14] The Economizer Argument does not hold that people always seek to *minimize* the effort they expend: there are many cases of people deliberately taking difficult paths in life. The argument's claim is, rather, that people's decisions about how much energy to expend, and on what to expend it, are (1) indexed to their local schedules of value, and (2) informed by a general preference of expending as little as possible given that schedule.

or use, which means we create a surplus that we can sell, trade, or give away—which in turn means that the overall stock of goods and services increases, and thus their prices decrease, for everyone. Moreover, as we seek out behaviors, exchanges, forms of contract and association, and so on that serve our local interests, others may learn from us and imitate our successes and avoid our failures, thereby saving themselves time and energy, enabling them to go marginally further in securing their—and thus, indirectly, everyone else's—ends. There is thus a multiplier effect implied by Smith's argument. Here is Smith's famous phrasing of this argument:

As every individual, therefore, endeavours as much as he can [...] to direct [his] industry that its produce may be of the greatest value; every individual necessarily labours to render the annual revenue of the society as great as he can. He generally, indeed, neither intends to promote the public interest, nor knows how much he is promoting it. [...] [H]e intends only his own security; and by directing that industry in such a manner as its produce may be of the greatest value, he intends only his own gain, and he is in this, as in many other cases, led by an invisible hand to promote an end which was no part of his intention. (WN, 456)[15]

It is this that, according to Smith, effects the "universal opulence which extends itself to the lowest ranks of the people" (WN, 22) that is for him the primary goal of political economy.

The Invisible Hand Argument does not imply that the unintended social orders produced by this invisible hand mechanism *guarantee* beneficial results. People can make unwise, imprudent, even immoral choices and those choices can lead to behaviors and habits that are not, in fact, conducive to everyone's benefit. We are fallible creatures, after all, as Smith is well aware. But *because* we are fallible, Smith's argument focuses not on what is ideally best but rather on what is *relatively better* among options that are actually possible—what, in other words, is relatively likelier to lead to improved conditions.[16] Smith claims that

---

[15] Smith continues: "Nor is it always the worse for the society that it was no part of it [that is, his intention]. By pursuing his own interest he frequently promotes that of the society much more effectually than when he really intends to promote it. I have never known much good done by those who affected to trade for the publick good" (ibid., p. 456). Smith repeats variants of this argument throughout WN as well. See, for example, WN, 11, 277, 347, 454, 533, and 630.

[16] David Sloan Wilson claims that the Smithian argument assumes that people's individual activities *always* benefit others (Wilson 2011: chap. 20). It does not assume that. The argument is instead about overall tendencies.

the best way to make such discoveries is by allowing the invisible-hand mechanism to work itself out and by granting the results of this trial-and-error process presumptive, though not absolute, authority. What Smith describes as "the obvious and simple system of natural liberty" is large-scale allowance of the invisible-hand mechanism to operate. Here is how he concludes the argument:

All systems either of preference or of restraint, therefore, being thus completely taken away, the obvious and simple system of natural liberty establishes itself of its own accord. Every man, as long as he does not violate the laws of justice, is left perfectly free to pursue his own interest his own way, and to bring both his industry and capital into competition with those of any other man, or order of men. The sovereign is completely discharged from a duty, in the attempting to perform which he must always be exposed to innumerable delusions, and for the proper performance of which no human wisdom or knowledge could ever be sufficient; the duty of superintending the industry of private people, and of directing it towards the employments most suitable to the interest of the society. (WN, 687)

What I call the Great Mind Fallacy is summed up in the following passage, which appears directly after Smith's "invisible hand" passage: "The statesman, who should attempt to direct private people in what manner they ought to employ their capitals, would not only load himself with a most unnecessary attention, but assume an authority which could safely be trusted, not only to no single person, but to no council or senate whatever, and which would nowhere be so dangerous as in the hands of a man who had folly and presumption enough to fancy himself fit to exercise it" (WN, 456). The statesman's attention is "unnecessary" because, according to the LKA, the EA, and the IHA, people's decentralized and uncoordinated strivings to better their conditions are far more likely to succeed than centralized and coordinated attempts would be; thus, what the statesman would (or should) wish to achieve—namely, bettering people's conditions—is more likely to happen if he does little beyond establishing a "tolerable administration of justice." The "folly and presumption" of the statesman is manifested in his perhaps tacit belief that he can overcome both the Herding Cats Problem and the knowledge problem as indicated in the Local Knowledge Argument. Such a mistaken belief is "dangerous" because, Smith suggests, it often leads the statesman to impose, or attempt to impose, his plan for society—which

Smith believes must necessarily be inferior to a decentralized and spontaneously created order.[17]

Conclusion

Effective planning requires knowledge that is based not only people's localized situations but is also sensitive to their changing circumstances. Prices can reflect this information, but only if they arise in a decentralized way. Centralized planners are unable to exploit this localized knowledge, and, to the extent that they attempt to channel or restrict people's economic activity centrally, they attenuate the functioning of prices and thus compromise their own ability to plan effectively. By contrast, decentralized political-economic decision making, within the context of "tolerable administration of justice," allows people to exploit their localized knowledge and thus generate benefit both directly to them and indirectly to others.

---

[17] More generally, and more technically, the fallacious argument takes the following form: (1) I know that good thing x should be promoted or bad thing y should be discouraged; (2) since the state is justified in promoting good things and discouraging bad things, it should therefore be empowered to promote x or discourage y; (3) because it is known how to encourage or discourage specific human behavior, (4) once so empowered the state will take proper actions to increase the incidence of x or decrease the incidence of y; therefore, (5) there will be more x or less y, and (6) people will therefore be better off. The knowledge problem challenges the reliability of assertions like those in premise (1), and the Herding Cats Problem challenges premise (3). The Smithian argument is that (5) and (6) follow only if one presumes the existence of a Great Mind able to (a) verify the claim in premise (1), (b) discover what premise (3) assumes, and (c) ensure that premise (4) is faithfully executed. Because (alas!) there is no such Great Mind, however, the argument fails. For paradigmatic commissions of this fallacy, see Sunstein 1997 and 2013.

3

Knowledge: Value, Equality, and Experts

Introduction

An attempt to plan people's economic activities centrally can utilize only a fraction of the knowledge that individuals themselves possess, from which it follows that centralized attempts will be less likely to succeed than allowing decentralized decision making. The error we often make is overestimating what we do or can know.[1] This error manifests itself in numerous ways. How often, for example, do we assume that our own schedule of value is not only correct for us but should be adopted by others as well? That others should value, and sacrifice scarce resources for, what we value and to the same extent that we value it? That they should be willing to make the same tradeoffs, tolerate only the same risks, and associate with only the same people as we would, and under only those arrangements that we ourselves would accept? Much political philosophy includes criticism of others' judgments and values for their failure to comport with the critics' judgments and values. If the Local Knowledge Argument, as well as the Great Mind Fallacy, holds, however, then such criticism rests on a weaker foundation than is often supposed.

Individual Value

Robert Skidelsky and Edward Skidelsky idealize a society characterized by the "sculptor engrossed in cutting marble, the teacher intent

---

[1] See Hayek 1988.

on imparting a difficult idea, the musician struggling with a score, a scientist exploring the mysteries of space and time" (2012: 9). Karl Marx, for his part, imagines a society in which

Nobody has an exclusive area of activity and each can train himself in any branch he wishes, society regulates the production, making it possible for me to do one thing today and another tomorrow, to hunt in the morning, fish in the afternoon, breed cattle in the evening, criticize after dinner, just as I like, without ever becoming a hunter, a fisherman, a herdsman, or a critic. (1994: 119)

Leon Trotsky imagines a society in which people "will rise to the heights of an Aristotle, a Goethe, or a Marx. And above this ridge new peaks will arise."[2] Similarly, today one might imagine a society in which more, or fewer, people live on family farms or work with their hands[3]; or in which more, or fewer, people live in cities[4]; in which more, or fewer, people go to college[5]; in which more, or fewer, people are actively involved in politics[6]; and so on across all the hundreds of variables that people integrate into their individual lives. Theorists' imagined societies entail not only people living their lives and conducting their personal affairs in some fairly specific ways, but they also entail people cooperating with each other, and not cooperating with each other, in numerous fairly specific ways and according to fairly specific patterns. Put aside whether any of these visions of society are attractive or not; indeed, grant that all of them have something important going for them. The point, rather, is that the theorist who imaginatively constructs these patterns of social cooperation assumes more knowledge than she in fact possesses. The theorist cannot be sure—cannot even begin to be sure—of two crucial matters: (1) whether any particular policy change she might recommend would actually result in behavioral patterns along the lines she wishes, and (2) whether the patterns of human behavior she champions would actually serve the affected persons well.

Too often, then, the theorist is in the unenviable position of the person Adam Smith calls the "man of system," who, as we saw in Chapter 2,

[2] Quoted in Robert Skidelsky and Edward Skidelsky 2012: 63.
[3] See, for example, Strange 2009 and Crawford 2011.
[4] See, for example, Glaeser 2011.
[5] See, for example, Murray 2009 and Bennett and Wilezol 2013.
[6] See, for example, Brennan 2011.

seems to imagine that he can arrange the different members of a great society with as much ease as the hand arranges the different pieces upon a chess-board. He does not consider that the pieces upon the chess-board have no other principle of motion besides that which the hand impresses upon them; but that, in the great chess-board of human society, every single piece has a principle of motion of its own, altogether different from that which the legislature might chuse to impress upon it. (TMS, 234)

Smith's man of system is not an immoral person; indeed, he might have the highest motives and the best intentions. In addition to over-estimating what he knows, however (which is, after all, a common, even natural, mistake), he also forgets that, as moral agents, others make decisions of their own and that as rational (if flawed) beings possessing both local knowledge about their own situations and natural motivations to get things right, their own decisions are likelier to lead in generally good directions. The latter facts suggest that we should give individuals the benefit of the doubt, establishing as a baseline default the presumption that people have reasons for what they do and that they should be respected in those reasons. The former fact implies that the prospect of devising institutions with the purpose of alter-ing people's behaviors in specific directions is far more difficult than one might suppose. If what is desired is improving people's decisions and conduct, then our intentions to do so are not enough. The results matter. Thus, we must evaluate policies on the basis of their actual or probable consequences, not on the supposed or inherent desirability of imagined consequences. The difficulties involved with the former are so formidable that we might indeed never get to the latter.

   This argument applies specifically to what we can know, and there-fore judge, about people's schedules of value. Should A spend that much money on that car? Should B spend that much on that house? Should C value whatever enjoyment she receives from smoking a cig-arette more than the risks she is running with her health? Should D value whatever enjoyment he receives from eating doughnuts more than the risks he is running with his health? Should E accept that job for that pay? Should F sell her kidney and run the attendant risks for that price? The answers to these questions depend on facts about the individual agents involved. Because the relevant details of these agents' situations are unique to them, no single answer can apply. Does that mean that for some people under some circumstances the additional cigarette or doughnut might be exactly what they should choose? Yes, it does.

Consider obesity, for example. Much contemporary socialist-inclined theory and policy is motivated by a desire to combat obesity, which is growing in incidence and in the risks it poses to individuals' health. Yet consider: Is it possible for a person to be *rationally morbidly obese?* Imagine a highly intelligent person with a high level of education—a PhD in philosophy, say—who makes this claim: "I am fully aware of the medical, social, and financial risks involved with morbid obesity. Indeed, I have studied them carefully. Yet I am also fully aware of the delights and pleasures that I receive from eating what I like to eat, as well as the displeasure I receive from exercising. After careful deliberation, I have decided that the pleasures are worth the risks to me. I do not say my conclusion applies to everyone, or even to anyone, other than me." Such a person might be making a fully rational decision. The fact that you or I might not make the same decision is, while perhaps true, nevertheless irrelevant. All that would mean is that *we* do not value the pleasures more than the risks; the point is that *he* does. Other than the prejudice that our own schedule of value is better than his, on what reasonable grounds can we justify forbidding him from acting on his judgment?

The fact that many of us agree, or claim we agree, on how much people should value particular activities should not cloud the fact that we cannot know from a distance whether those particular activities are appropriate for any given single person. Almost everyone will agree that, *ceteris paribus,* obesity is bad. But that "ceteris paribus"—"other things equal"—gives the game away. In real life, other things are almost never equal. The question, "Is this doughnut worth it?" is, despite its seeming simplicity, unable to be answered as stated because it assumes a context with details that the question neither supplies nor possesses. Worth what? To whom? When? At what cost? To arrive at a judgment of whether a doughnut is worth it, we have to answer these questions; otherwise, we are engaging in idle speculation. As Robert Frank pointedly asks, "Would any sane person really want to stand before an informed audience to defend the assertion that context doesn't matter?" (2011: 28).

A similar argument applies to any number of risks people take. Would you drive a motorcycle? Would you go skydiving? Would you try cocaine? Would you volunteer in a third-world country to combat poverty or agree to serve as an embedded journalist during live military action? Would you give (or sell) your kidney to another person? And on and on: people have not only different tolerances of risk but also different tradeoff points as determined by their respective unique schedules of value. Maybe you would do some but not others of these things; maybe you would have done some at one time in your life but not now, and you might again later. I used to drive motorcycles; when my first son got old enough to notice and become intrigued by my motorcycle, I got rid of it. I once jumped from a high cliff into a frigid Aegean Sea; I would not even consider doing that again. And so on. You will have similar examples from your life, as everyone else will have from his. The point is that whether these or any other activities are rational—or, loosening the definitional strictures a bit, reasonable, wise, or prudent—depends on details about you that no central planner can possibly possess. If the central planner crafted laws or regulations in order to prevent, steer, or nudge you in one direction or another, she has almost no chance of getting it right for you. Even if somehow she did, it might apply only to the Today You, not to the Tomorrow You—let alone Next Year You—because your schedule of value changes, along with many other things about you. And yet the policy, once erected into law or regulation, would remain.

The claim that value is individualized and indexed to particular valuing agents does not entail that any course of action is equally viable, wise, or prudent with any other. It may well be that for any given agent in any particular set of circumstances there is but one thing she should do. The LKA takes no position on which values all of us, or any of us, should ultimately pursue. Its claim instead is that the decisions we make are themselves reasonable (wise, prudent, etc.) only in light of the values they serve. Consider that all of us value justice, security, freedom, equality, individuality, diversity, excitement, tranquility, love, friendship, compassion, respect, honor, pleasure, education, experience, health, and so on[7]: the length, and even mutual incompatibility, of the items on the list do not mean that we do not value them all, but they do demonstrate that we cannot organize our lives and make decisions about what to do except by attempting to integrate all of these in some

---

[7] See Kekes 2010.

way, balancing the relevant tradeoffs in the continuous reassessments that characterize human reasoning, decision making, and acting. This, or any other, list of values might command general assent in the abstract, and we might even be able, at least in principle, to argue, discuss, or persuade our way to a consensus regarding their relative rankings. I have my doubts about that,[8] but even if we could do so, it would still not give us any way of knowing how, concretely, any given individual should organize her daily life in the service of those values.

The freedom to make these decisions for oneself regardless is also important—indeed, I believe it is an integral part of what it means to be a full moral agent with dignity. But I make that case in Part II.

Equality

Perhaps the single strongest motivation driving the socialist inclination is a desire for equality, and the concomitant aversion to inequality. One might expect our discussion of equality to appear in Part II, where the focus is on more properly "moral" issues, since equality is clearly a moral concern. And equality is discussed later. But there is an important cluster of issues concerning equality that arise as practical problems, antecedent to any ostensibly moral concerns.

G. A. Cohen argues that the "socialist equality" he endorses "seeks to correct for all unchosen disadvantages, disadvantages, that is, for which the agent cannot herself be held responsible, whether they be disadvantages that reflect social misfortune or disadvantages that reflect natural misfortune." He continues: "When socialist equality of opportunity prevails, differences of outcome reflect nothing but difference of taste and choice, not differences in natural and social capacities and powers" (2009: 18). Cohen's argument reflects a position held by many others. John Rawls, for example, argued that "the initial endowment of natural assets and the contingencies of their growth and nurture in early life are arbitrary from a moral point of view," and that "no one deserves his place in the distribution of natural assets any more than he deserves his initial starting place in society" (1971: 311–12). Rawls takes the claims that (1) one's natural assets are morally arbitrary and (2) one does not morally deserve them to support

[8] See Gaus 2010.

his argument that the principles of justice do not need to respect them. Rawls:

> Imagine, then, a hypothetical initial arrangement in which all the social primary goods are equally distributed: everyone has similar rights and duties, and income and wealth are evenly shared. This state of affairs provides a benchmark for judging improvements. If certain inequalities of wealth and organizational powers would make everyone better off than in this hypothetical starting situation, then they accord with the general conception [of justice]. (1971: 62)

Cohen, for his part, does not elaborate on the specific institutions that would be required to instantiate, or even to make headway toward, the socialist equality he recommends; nor does he investigate what the costs associated with attempting to instantiate it would be. Hence Cohen's position is difficult to assess. With no concrete idea of what it would entail in practice, it is hard to view his recommendation as much more than a Nice-If Claim: Wouldn't it be *nice if* such-and-such were the case? We can grant the claim—yes, it would be nice—without granting it any political-economic purchase, because without a reckoning of the potential costs involved, a Nice-If Claim does not rise to the level of an argument admitting of assessment and therefore can warrant no definitive assent.

Rawls, by contrast, does suggest some of the practical implications of his position. If we are to begin with equality—not only political equality before the law, or *formal equality*, but also a *substantive equality* in "income and wealth" as the benchmark, with any deviation from that requiring specific justification showing that it benefits everyone, or at a minimum that it primarily benefits our least advantaged—then this will require state institutions to effectuate the desired results. Specifically, Rawls suggests five branches of government: (1) an *allocation branch*, which will "keep the price system workably competitive"[9]; (2) a *stabilization branch*, which will "bring about reasonably full employment"; (3) a *transfer branch*, whose responsibility is the "social minimum," which means it will "take needs into account and assign them an appropriate weight"; (4) a *distribution branch*, which will "preserve an approximate justice in distributive shares by means

---

[9] I note that Rawls does not address the calculation problem regarding centralized setting of prices, discussed in Chapter 2.

of taxation and the necessary adjustments in the rights of property";
and (5) an *exchange branch,* "which consists of a special representative
body taking note of the various social interests and their preferences
for public goods" (1971: 275–82). It is a formidable, although at least
initially plausible, list. But will these branches of government suffice?
Will they achieve what is desired? For example, how exactly will the
Stabilization Branch bring about "reasonably full employment"? Not
all of the ways it might undertake to accomplish that end are morally
appropriate, of course. Slavery might work, but that is ruled out by
Rawls's first principle of justice. What means, then, do not violate this
principle, yet are available and likely to achieve the goal?

If what is required to justify these policy recommendations is not
that they *could* suffice or achieve what is desired but that they are
likely to do so, then, even as initially plausible as Rawls's suggestions
might seem, we need much more than he gives us. This point is especially acute for Rawls, since he argues that "[e]ach person possesses an
inviolability founded on justice that even the welfare of society as a
whole cannot override" (1971: 3). This claim implies a higher burden
of proof that must be met before the government agencies can be justified in their described redistributive and regulatory tasks. If Rawls's
claim about individual inviolability is to have practical import, it must
require that any proposed imposition on some for the benefit of others
be shown to be at least likely—if not guaranteed—to actually benefit
those others. If Rawls has not done so, then it will have to be done
before his branches of government are established. But what if he cannot do so?

Rousseau's Great Mind. To illustrate the difficulty, consider Jean-
Jacques Rousseau's reliance in his *Social Contract* on the personage
he calls the "legislator." "Discovering the rules of society best suited to
nations would require," Rousseau tells us,

a superior intelligence that beheld all the passions of men without feeling
any of them; who had no affinity with our nature, yet knew it through and
through; whose happiness was independent of us, yet who nevertheless was
willing to concern itself with ours; finally, who, in the passage of time, pro-
cures for himself a distant glory, being able to labor in one age and find enjoyment in another.[10]

[10] *Social Contract,* 162–3.

Lest one think this might be a *reductio ad absurdum* refutation of such an idea, Rousseau takes the time to describe both what this legislator must do and what kind of person he is:

> He who dares to undertake the establishment of a people should feel that he is, so to speak, in a position to change human nature, to transform each individual (who by himself is a perfect and solitary whole), into part of a larger whole from which this individual receives, in a sense, his life and his being; to alter man's constitution in order to strengthen it. [...]
>
> The legislator is in every respect an extraordinary man in the state. If he ought to be so by his genius, he is no less so by his office, which is neither magistracy nor sovereignty. This office, which constitutes the republic, does not enter into its constitution. It is a particular and superior function [...]. (1988b: 163)

Rousseau's discussion seems to anticipate mine about the Great Mind. In fact, his description of the kinds of superhuman knowledge and abilities his legislator must possess lays bare, better perhaps than I did, why exactly such a person is not likely to be forthcoming. No actual human being could fulfill the role Rousseau describes, quasi-mythical stories of Lycurgus, Solon, and so on to the contrary notwithstanding. Many contemporary theorists' depictions of necessary and proper duties of government seem to require similar mythical personages to succeed. More importantly, socialist-inclined policy seems to *depend* on them. Because no such people exist, however, the tasks they would need to execute remain unfulfilled—or only partly, and imperfectly, fulfilled—which may help explain why experiments in socialism fail.

Rousseau's discussion illustrates the cognitive skills, as well as the scope of knowledge, that are required to organize and manage a society. Even if one argues that establishing a small pocket of decision-making superiority is worth the material equality it might bring about for the rest of us,[11] it turns out they will not be able to accomplish the goal in any case because they will lack the knowledge required to achieve it.

Luck Egalitarianism. Yet consider a related recent discussion in political philosophy regarding luck. The proponents of what is called "luck egalitarianism" argue that the moral imperative of equality should be

---

[11] As both Cohen and Wilson suggest; see Cohen 2000: 178–9 and Wilson: "We must learn to become wise managers of evolutionary processes" (2011: 11).

understood as a mandate to equalize those parts of a person's life—including native endowments and external circumstances—for which one cannot personally claim responsibility.[12] Some people are luckier than others: they are born with better genes, or into better families, or in better neighborhoods; they have better schooling and nutrition; they have good accidents of fortune happen to them. These things can confer benefits—and, of course, liabilities—for which the individual herself can be neither praised nor blamed, and for which she can therefore take no credit. A just political system, argues the luck egalitarian, is one that attempts to equalize these undeserved inequalities. Because, however, luck egalitarianism recognizes that people are responsible for at least some of what they do and at least some of the successes and failures in their lives, it does not attempt to eliminate all inequalities. It argues instead for eliminating, to the extent possible, only the undeserved, "lucky" factors in people's successes and failures.

The luck egalitarian position begins on solid ground. It is hard to deny that at least some portion of each person's life is explained by factors outside his control. People might reasonably disagree about the exact proportions of within-one's-control vs. outside-one's-control, but clearly at least some part of each person's life falls into each category. The second step in the luck egalitarian's argument is also plausible: if the only grounds on which one can claim to deserve something are that it is a result of factors within one's control, then one cannot claim to deserve every success or failure one has (or at least not all of each success or failure). The next step in the luck egalitarian's argument is less obvious: the state is therefore not debarred, at least not on grounds of injustice, from taking some proportion of the successful person's achievements and redistributing it to people who are less successful through no fault of their own. Let us accept the luck egalitarian's claims about justice and moral desert, however, and grant that even the third step in the luck egalitarian's argument is justified on moral grounds. The question is where we go from there. As becomes readily apparent, the implementation of the luck egalitarian program faces formidable obstacles. The position also involves difficult moral

[12] There is a large literature here. Some of the discussions I have found instructive are Anderson 1999; Arneson 1989, 2000, and 2004; Cohen 1989; Dworkin 2003; Scheffler 2003 and 2005; and Vallentyne 2002.

questions, which I discuss in Part II, but there are two important
practical reasons to be concerned about this line of argument.

The first practical problem is that the central authority making these
decisions does not possess the knowledge necessary to have a justified belief that the policies he imposes and the allocations he makes
will actually conduce to the end they are supposed to serve. Will, for
example, a steep progressive taxation on income lead to less material
inequality? Will a luxury tax? Will a flat tax but with its proceeds
directed toward K–12 education? It is problematic to maintain that
policies like these would lead to the desired results, in part because
each has already been tried at local, state, and federal levels in the
United States, and it is not clear that inequality has decreased.[13] It is
unfortunately also true that there might be hundreds of other possible policies one might contemplate, and there seems no clear way
ex ante to distinguish the promising candidates from the unpromising. Some evidence exists, indeed, that capitalist-inclined institutions
are correlated with reductions in inequality, whereas socialist-inclined
institutions are correlated with increased inequality.[14] This renders
insufficient the simple Rawlsian-style argument that (1) (certain kinds
of) inequality are undesirable; (2) state institutions x, y, and z could
conceivably reduce inequality; (3) therefore, we should pursue x, y,
and z. We can accept premise (1); it is premise (2) that is undersubstan-
tiated, and thus where all the work remains to be done.

One way to respond to my claim is to draw a distinction between,
on the one hand, what justice (say) requires and, on the other hand,
what mechanisms are required to implement justice in practice. If justice requires end result x, then saying that we do not know how to
achieve, or even promote, x in practice might simply mean that we
need to try something; perhaps some empirical experimentation is in
order. But that would not by itself entail that one's conception of justice is wrong or that one is wrong in holding justice to entail x. My
response to this line of reasoning is to concede it all. In Part II of this
book, I explore the moral implications of competing conceptions of
justice. Here I restrict my argument to the political-economic claim

---

[13] Indeed, Joseph Stiglitz has recently argued that policies like these have had precisely
the opposite effect—namely, increasing inequality in the United States; see Stiglitz
2012: esp. chap. 1.
[14] See Lawson et al. 2013.

that granting that certain kinds of inequality are undesirable tells us nothing about what, if anything, we can or should in practice do about it—and thus, it does not move the political-economic discussion forward.

Cohen argues that socialism serves two main goals: community and equality. The equality Cohen focuses on is "unchosen" inequalities—those that might be the result of luck or accident. There seems something intuitively right about this: Why should one person prosper, and another not, based on features about them that neither chose, and thus for which neither can be held morally responsible or claim to have deserved? The real objection, however, is not to success or failure that is due to unchosen luck, but rather to *only that part* of success or failure that is due to unchosen luck.[15] At least some of our success and failure are due to our own choices, so even on a Cohen-esque argument we deserve that and are hence entitled to its consequences. The problem, then, is how to disentangle what we are responsible for from what we are not responsible for—the results of what we chose and what we did not. That would be difficult to sort out.

But the reality is actually worse, because there are significant costs associated with the attempt to disaggregate and then redistribute based on our findings. There are, first of all, two kinds of costs associated with *monitoring:* not only selecting, training, and then monitoring the people who will do the assessing, disaggregating, and redistributing; but also monitoring the changes generated by people's subsequent activities—and then reassessing, re-disaggregating, and re-redistributing. Moreover, there are costs associated with mistakes (both honest and dishonest), with the attempts to rectify the mistakes, and with the monitoring required to keep track of all of it. These costs, alas, would be substantial, and they would, again alas, have to be borne by someone.

There is, however, yet another cost involved with the directive to correct "unchosen disadvantages," namely the disincentive this creates to engaging in wealth-producing labor, and the resulting risk of lowered standard of living. In the first Jamestown Colony of 1607, most of the original 104 settlers starved to death, despite the existence

---

[15] I note that Cohen distinguishes between "regrettable choice" inequality and "option luck" inequality (26ff.). The distinction does not directly affect my argument here, so I pass over it without comment.

of flourishing sea life, abundant flora and fauna, and rich soil. After reinforcements arrived from the Old Country, the winter of 1609 cut the numbers from 500 to 60. Why? The colony was organized on a principle of equal distribution and communal ownership: everyone was obliged to work to whatever extent was possible, but then everyone got an equal share of the total production (modified by central judgments about need) regardless of how much each person individually produced. It turned out that some settlers preferred to starve, even to death, rather than work if they thought that someone else would get what they produced.[16] This is an important aspect of human psychology. If people come to believe that their productive activity will be monitored by third parties with an eye toward determining how much they may keep according to the third parties' assessment of their relative "chosen" contribution, a resentment can build that inclines them to produce less—for some of them, all the way to zero. There is no way for a person to know what proportion of the fruits of her activities the Disaggregation and Redistribution Board will deem to have been the result of her own choices and thus deserved by her; that means the disposition of any gains she herself achieved would be quite uncertain. Moreover, one might reasonably conclude that injuries, psychological disabilities (including laziness[17]), and other obstacles could easily count as 'not having been chosen' and would therefore allow one to receive a portion of the overall produce without having to contribute to it. The logic of the commons—concentrated benefits, dispersed costs—would then generate its familiar "tragic" dynamic.[18] Finally, resentment at the thought of others living, even lounging, off one's labor can grow strong enough to incline some to be willing to remain idle rather than work for others one perceives as undeserving.

But there is yet a further problem. The main kinds of "unchosen" disadvantages or advantages discussed are family, natural endowments, and luck.[19] Consider family. Some people are born into much better

---

[16] See Schmidtz 2008: 204–7.
[17] This is an implication of the claim that people's propensity toward industriousness and hard work is also unchosen—that it is a product of their genes, their upbringing, or both. Rawls: "[I]t seems clear that the effort a person is willing to make is influenced by his natural abilities and skills" (1971: 312).
[18] See Hardin 1968.
[19] See Rawls 1975: 96. For discussion, see Olsaretti 2003 and 2004.

family environments than others, and, since no one chooses the family into which she is born, no one should be held responsible for the advantage or disadvantage her family conferred. But here is the problem: for any given individual, we have very little idea what an "advantageous" family is. No one really knows what constitutes a good parent for any particular child, what the right parenting techniques are for any child, or what the right, best, or properly stimulative environment is for any child. We may know the general correlations over populations, but we cannot conclude therefrom anything about any particular member of the relevant population. Would it be best for a given child to have, for example, one sibling? Many? None? Authoritative parenting? Lax? Bryan Caplan produces evidence suggesting, in fact, that none of this makes much difference in the long run, which means that one's upbringing and family life may turn out to be relatively unimportant in determining what kind of person one ultimately becomes.[20] Indeed, some argue that evidence exists supporting the counterintuitive claim that having a relatively *difficult* life is actually advantageous: witness the relatively higher rates of success of orphans.[21]

Judith Rich Harris argues that peers matter far more than anything parents do (other than in contributing their genes).[22] Should we conclude, then, that we should strive to equalize the peer groups of youngsters? If equalizing luck is morally required, then arguably we should. Suppose we do; what would be involved? What sorts of monitoring devices, groups, people? What coercive measures, what incentive structures? And what would all of this cost—not only directly, but also indirectly in the loss of productivity that people would otherwise have been engaged in were they not spending their time observing and manipulating children's social groups? We all want children to have good childhoods. But the difficulties arise when we try to implement policies aiming to accomplish that good end without drawing on the particularized knowledge necessary to give our policies a chance to succeed. Because they do not possess that requisite knowledge, attempts

---

[20] See Caplan 2011. Caplan argues that this research should help parents relax and enjoy their parenting more. It can also make them feel pointless and superfluous.

[21] See, e.g., Eisenstadt et al. 1989. For classic treatments, see Samuel Smiles's 1859 *Self-Help* and Andrew Carnegie's 1889 "The Gospel of Wealth."

[22] See Harris 2006.

by third parties to secure good family lives might well be exercises in futility—and expensive ones at that.

Similar (indeed, potentially worse) difficulties face two of the other main categories of "unchosen" advantages/disadvantages, namely natural endowments and luck. The dangers involved with attempting to correct for unchosen lucky genes are not only chilling to consider, but have actually been exhibited in numerous grisly experiments in the twentieth century. These experiments highlight not only how little, in fact, we know about the biological and psychological factors that go into constituting any particular individual's personality, but also the unpleasant motivations that a directive to "correct" people on such fundamental and deep levels of their existence can unleash.[23] Few today advocate human genetic correction of any kind, even if our increasing technological prowess is raising the issue again. Given the risks and our history, caution seems in order—*particularly* if it involves one group proposing to make centralized decisions for others. Even among those who recognize the relatively intractable nature of our genes, however, there are those who nonetheless advocate coercive psychological manipulation to achieve the changes in people's behavior they desire.[24] Again, humanity's sordid past experience with such matters would seem to counsel against such lines of thought. But my argument does not require setting any particular limits or even entering into the discussion of, say, how much government funding should be available, which initiatives should be supported, and so on because my argument holds that the only hope people have of making good decisions about such matters is when they *both* (1) have intimate knowledge of the details of any particular case *and* (2) face properly aligned

---

[23] If you have the stomach for it, see Baumslag 2005.

[24] Consider this example from philosopher Garrett Cullity. Cullity believes we should be more "self-sacrificing." He then argues: "How could you go about making yourself more self-sacrificing? A more and a less radical option will be open to you. The less radical option is to achieve progressively greater levels of self-sacrifice through a gradual process of habituation. After you get used to a new, lower level of spending on yourself, it is likely that there will be scope for reducing it further without impairing your own productivity. And if this does not work, there is the more radical option: *externally imposed mental conditioning*. There is evidence that for almost all of us, there are *techniques of psychological manipulation* which could be employed to *weaken our personal attachments* and make us more impartial, inducing the political or religious convert's conviction that 'service is perfect freedom'" (2004: 81–2; emphases added).

incentives so that the decision makers themselves face responsibility for the decisions they make.[25] This effectively rules out policies drawn up by centralized planners.

One aspect of luck that concerns many is education. Long-running and continuing attempts to structure educational environments in order to raise achievement levels of disadvantaged populations have, however, proved remarkably resistant to our intentions. For example, as educational per-pupil spending in the United States increased during the twentieth century, academic achievement nevertheless remained disappointingly flat.[26] The educational pessimists claim that there is little long-run effect that policy or institutions can have on any given child's academic performance. Charles Murray claims, for example, that false beliefs to the contrary have imposed severe psychological costs on students, which would compound the losses from the hundreds of billions of dollars spent as well as the indirect losses of whatever better or more productive uses to which that might have been put.[27] I offer no proposal about how that money might have been better spent, but neither I nor any other third party is in a good position to know. That reality is reflected in the numerous educational programs, initiatives, regulations, standards, and on and on that have been attempted and implemented by governments in the United States, with depressingly little to show for them (except frustration and cost).[28] But what does follow from my position is that if we had left at least some of that money in the hands of the people with both the relevant local knowledge and proper incentives—people like parents, for example—then it is likely that it would have been more effectively spent.

The point in mentioning human experimentation and difficulties with educational policy is to highlight once again how little we actually know about such issues. Even with the best of intentions, and with

[25] I have more to say on incentives later in this chapter.
[26] Hanuschek and Rivken 1997 claim that in the 100-year period from 1890 to 1990, total per-pupil educational spending in the United States (in constant 1990 dollars) went from $164 to $4,622, a nearly 30-fold increase; yet during that time U.S. students' academic performance remained relatively unchanged.
[27] See Murray 2009.
[28] One particularly spectacular failed attempt to improve the educational achievement of disadvantaged children was the 1985–1997 Kansas City, Missouri experiment under the supervision of the well-intentioned but deeply misguided Judge Russell G. Clark. For discussion, see Otteson 2006: 230–1.

enormous sums of wealth at their disposal—and the legal authority to use it—still the results from centrally planned undertakings range approximately from disappointing to ghastly. Success is very hard to find, and when it is, it is almost always both short-lived and local, not to mention unduly costly—exactly as the argument would predict. The desire to reduce inequality, then, regardless of its merits in itself, is fraught with systematic difficulties and costs that make it much more difficult to effectuate than one might initially expect.

Equality and Diversity. Two final points regarding the difficulties associated with attempting to redistribute to achieve equality. The limits of centralized authorities' knowledge discussed earlier entail that they would make decisions based on factors other than concrete knowledge of people's actual situations. Under such circumstances, individual citizens will not be able to predict what decisions the centralized authorities will make. The further removed from personal familiarity with those individual citizens the decision-making authorities are, the less likely will their decisions reflect the actual situation of the individual citizen, and the less connected it will be to the citizen's lived reality. As Armen Alchien has demonstrated, however, the uncertainty this generates has the perhaps surprising effect of making it actually *more* likely that either corruption or luck will account for people's success and failure in life (Alchien 1950). The people who will succeed in such cases will not be those who most efficiently exploit their local circumstances productively or generate value to others, but instead those who (1) have ingratiated themselves in the political favor of those making the centralized decisions (and can thus get decisions, regulations, restrictions, and so on made that benefit them particularly), or (2) simply take wild risks that happen, by sheer chance, to pay off. The introduction and deployment of centralized authorities in an effort to diminish the effects of luck (or crony-capitalist corruption) in human affairs ends up, then, exacerbating exactly the problems it was intended to mitigate.

Second, there is reason to believe that the more diverse a community is, the less effective redistribution or regulation in the service of equalization will be. When human communities have been able to achieve fairly flat levels of equality, it has historically happened within small groups that were relatively united in their schedule of value and hierarchy of purpose—for example, monasteries, kibbutzim, and other small religious communities. They have typically also been poor, although that tradeoff is usually accepted by the community's members. The communities also tended to be short-lived (something the members did not want, at least initially) or sustained by wealth generated in market-based societies outside them, or both. Regardless, as such communities grow in numbers, or as they grow in the diversity of ideas, schedules of value, judgments of appropriate tradeoffs, and so on, it becomes far more difficult not just to organize them centrally in general, but specifically to centrally redistribute their wealth to maintain or approximate equality. People's differing schedules of value decreases the chances of agreement about what to redistribute, from whom, and to whom; it compromises the elders' judgments about what people are able to sacrifice and what people actually need; and it introduces the various opportunisms familiar to students of modern politics: rent-seeking, free-riding, logrolling, and so on. If diversity is a community's strength, it is only when the central organization of the community superintends as little of people's lives as possible—only then can people realize the considerable gains from cooperation, exchange, and association, and only then do they come to see other people as opportunities instead of threats.[29]

Expert Knowledge

One might argue, however, that the Local Knowledge Argument as I have presented it implies that *no* one—including individuals in their own cases—can be trusted to know what to do with his time, talent, and treasure since uncertainties are apparently shot through everything we do. If we cannot trust centralized authorities' judgments about how people's behavior should be corrected or redirected in order to serve desirable ends, why should we trust individuals to do any better? There is indeed much that we do not know, not only about how the world, the nation, or the economy works, but even about how things will work out in our own individual lives. Yet there are people who are experts in various aspects of human behavior and who therefore might seem appropriately positioned to make informed judgments about human behavior. The medical doctor, the psychologist,

---

[29] For discussions on various aspects of this argument, see Lockwood and Weinzierl 2012; Pipes 1999; Putnam 2000 and 2007; Rose 2012; and Seabright 2010.

the neuroscientist, the economist—perhaps even the philosopher!—all have real, and increasing, knowledge about how human beings operate and about how they can prosper. Does the LKA lead, then, to the implausible conclusion that we should never listen to such experts? If so, this would seem a significant problem for the argument.

General Knowledge. There are two things to say in response. The first is that although expert knowledge is certainly real knowledge, it is nevertheless general, not specific, and thus does not constitute the kind of knowledge required for crafting policy that would serve the ends desired. This is an important point, so please allow me a moment to flesh it out. I do so by first looking at a handful of recent theorists who enumerate the kinds of decisions they believe government experts can, and should, make.

Begin with Cass Sunstein, who argues that legislators or governmental experts should engage in "the inculcation [in citizens] of critical and disparate attitudes toward prevailing conceptions of the good"; pursue "aggressive initiatives with respect to the arts and broadcasting" including "subsidizing public broadcasting, ensuring a range of disparate programming, or calling for high-quality programming"; investigate and educate people about the correct "risks of hazardous activity"; and not only enforce nondiscrimination policies, but also investigate and educate people regarding "the beliefs of both beneficiaries and victims of existing injustice [that] are affected by dissonance-reducing strategies," such as "blaming the victim."[30] Sunstein continues:

[G]overnmentally required disclosure of risks in the workplace is a highly laudable strategy [to "provide information and to increase opportunities"]. In a few cases, however, these milder initiatives are inadequate, and other measures are necessary. A moderately intrusive strategy could involve economic incentives, which might take the form of tax advantages or cash payments. For example, the government might give financial inducements to day-care centers as a way of relieving child-care burdens. Such a system might well be preferable to direct transfers of money to families, a policy that will predictably lead many more women to stay at home. In view of the sources of and consequences of the differential distribution of child-care burdens, it is fully legitimate for the government to take steps in the direction of equalization.[31]

---

[30] All these quotations come from Sunstein 1997: 26–9.
[31] Ibid. Sunstein continues: "The American government should compile and distribute an annual 'quality of life' report, including, among other things, per capita income,

More recently, Sunstein, with Richard H. Thaler, has argued that the government should pursue a course of "libertarian paternalism"—a position they argue is not contradictory because although it endorses framing the presentation of options, arranging incentives, and deliberately creating psychological impressions that encourage people to make good decisions (the paternalistic part), it nevertheless still allows people the option to choose otherwise (the libertarian part).[32] They explore various subtle and not-so-subtle ways that people might be, as they put it, "nudged" to make decisions that are good ones, or at least relatively better ones, without overtly coercing people and indeed often without people realizing they were nudged in the first place. Examples they cite are the deliberate arrangement of foods in a cafeteria to increase the amount of fruits and vegetables people select, the purposefully designed signature of default settings in investment and retirement plans to increase rates of certain kinds of investment, and the reframing of the discussions of teen drinking and smoking to create the impression that only fringe and uncool minorities engage in those unhealthful activities.[33] Thaler and Sunstein emphasize the importance of allowing free choice, but they nevertheless recommend nudging people in directions reflecting what is truly good for people. They argue that their goal is not to rob people of their freedom to choose, but rather to help individuals make choices that the individuals themselves *would* have made *if* these individuals were perfect reasoners—that is, if they "had paid full attention and possessed complete information, unlimited cognitive abilities, and complete self-control" (*Nudge,* p. 5).

Unfortunately, because people's decisions are influenced also by their unique schedules of value, Thaler and Sunstein cannot know what any individual would choose even under such idealized circumstances. Thus their actual policy recommendations end up reflecting

poverty, housing, unemployment, average weekly earnings, inflation, child mortality, longevity, subjective to violent crime, literacy, and educational attainment. The report should also specify minimum standards for such things as income, education, health, and housing and allow for comparison across regions, between men and women, and among different racial and ethnic groups" (123).

[32] The possession of the authority to say "no" is indeed a crucial aspect of equal moral agency. I discuss this further in Part II.

[33] See Thaler and Sunstein 2009: 1–6, 103–31, and 67–8, respectively. Further references to this book are on the page given in parentheses.

guesses as to what mechanisms would induce people to choose what Thaler and Sunstein wish more people would choose. So what begins with the goal of neutrally helping people choose what they themselves would ideally want turns out to be nudging others to adopt Sunstein and Thaler's schedule of value. This becomes evident when one looks at their list of goals that governmental "nudges" might be designed to encourage: climb Mount Kilimanjaro, travel to Mongolia, learn to juggle seven oranges and a watermelon, run a marathon, save more money, use less gas and electricity, quit smoking, stop gambling, and so on (231–3). This list is quite idiosyncratic, to say the least—which pellucidly illustrates the problem. Although those may be Thaler and Sunstein's goals, they are certainly not the goals of all others, and because Thaler and Sunstein do not know what the goals of everyone in society are, what their relative schedules and rankings of values are, what the opportunities and resources available to them are, and so on, they cannot claim to have any way of knowing whether these are good goals for any individual.[34]

Consider next Liam Murphy and Thomas Nagel, who write, "In addition to public goods in the strict sense,"

> there are other institutions that clearly confer a public benefit, so that their provision by the state is supported by the motive of collective self-interest. Roads, air traffic control, a postal system, some regulation of airwaves depending on the technological situation, education that ensures near-universal literacy, the maintenance of public health, a reliable system of civil law—all these are plausible candidates for systemic conditions that have benefits for everyone in the society through their large effects on safety, the economy, and the smooth functioning of social conditions.[35]

Yet the "large effects on [...] social conditions" of such state-enforced policies is part of the worry about whether the legislator is justified in

---

[34] Interestingly, Thaler and Sunstein recognize this problem during their discussion of a particular case—that of "nudging" people to invest their money. They write, "we do not have any way of knowing the preferences of individual participants [in retirement plans], and we also do not know what assets they may be holding outside the social security system, so it is not possible for us to say anything definitive about how good a job they did picking a portfolio [of investments]" (149). Quite right, but this problem is an instance of a systematic lack of information regarding other areas of other people's lives.

[35] Murphy and Nagel 2002: 46–7. Further references to this book are on the page given in parentheses.

believing he can anticipate and effectuate them properly with central policy making. Murphy and Nagel continue:

Included prominently in this category [that is, "the large one of state action that aims to benefit individuals"] are social services such as unemployment compensation, disability benefits, retirement pensions, child care support, health care, aid to dependent children, food stamps, free school lunches, and so forth. Also included are many kinds of educational support, including public universities, subsidized student loans, publicly financed scholarships, and financial support, direct and indirect (through tax deductions, for example), to private institutions. (48)[36]

Samuel Fleischacker argues that to allow for "the judgment that we need for truly free choices," the government must do all of the following[37]: (1) provide "good information about the [employment] options among which one is choosing"; (2) provide "a thorough education in the skills of interpretation and the assessment of evidence," including education in "the skills of aesthetic interpretation" and in applying "those skills to the decisions [people] need to make about running their own lives"; (3) provide "access to rich, clear, and clearly organized facts about products and jobs"; and (4) provide "centralized computer services open to everyone" where such information will be available at no cost to the user. Moreover, to alleviate some of the problems to which Fleischacker believes free markets give rise, the state must also ensure (5) that all citizens are raised "from childhood on with adequate nutrition, shelter, and health care"; (6) that citizens know "they would receive considerable aid in unemployment"; (7) that they know they "could take any job in the country because funds [are] available to transport them there"; (8) that they are "well trained in evaluating evidence and [have] easy access to a large amount of information about their opportunities"; and (9) that they have "sufficient leisure to reflect on their lives and alter them if necessary," on the

---

[36] Murphy and Nagel go on to claim many more authorities on behalf of the state: "The government must operate more like a price-discriminating monopoly. It must figure out how much the public good is worth to each individual and charge each of them accordingly, financing the total cost of the good out of the sum of the unequal assessments and setting the level of provision at a point where for each person the assessment is less than or equal to that person's reserve price for that level" (2002: 83). For other tasks they believe the legislature can and should oversee, see also pp. 91, 181–2, and 184.

[37] Fleischacker 1999: 238–9.

order of "six weeks a year, or a several-month sabbatical every few years."[38]

Or consider the notion of "basic needs" or "basic goods" that many claim should be provided or guaranteed centrally. Here is David Copp's list:

> Any credible analysis of the concept of a basic need would imply that all or most of the following are either basic needs or forms of provision for a basic need: the need for nutritious food and water; the need to excrete; the need otherwise to preserve the body intact; the need for periodic rest and relaxation, which I presume to include periodic sleep and some form of recreation; the need for companionship; the need for education; the need for social acceptance and recognition; the need for self-respect and self-esteem; the need to be free from harassment.[39]

Copp adds, however, that his list "is perhaps not complete," and he claims that although the state cannot directly provide citizens with several of these things (like self-respect and companionship), its duty nevertheless is to enable citizens to meet these basic needs, meaning that the state is morally required, and therefore should be empowered, to pursue means necessary to these ends—whatever the centralized experts determine those are (1988: 124). Martha Nussbaum, for her part, gives the following list of "basic capabilities" that political action should create or aim to foster: "comprehensive health care; healthy air and water; arrangements for the security of life and property; protection of the autonomous choices of citizens with respect to crucial aspects of their medical treatment." She continues that state provision of "basic capabilities" "requires sufficient nutrition and adequate

---

[38] Duties (1) and (3) require not only that the state provide information, but also that it procure or generate it; duties (4), (6), and (7) require not just that the state notify citizens of services, but also that it either provide or pay for the services. That suggests that Fleischacker's full list is perhaps longer. See also pp. 18–19.

[39] Copp 1988: 124. Cf. the Universal Declaration of Human Rights adopted by the United Nations General Assembly in 1948, which—in addition to the standard life, liberty, and property—includes among everyone's "universal rights" such things as "a right to social security" (Article 22), "the right to [...] periodic holidays with pay" (Article 24), and "the right to a standard of living adequate for the health and well-being of himself and his family" (Article 25). It also asserts that "[e]veryone has the right to education. Education shall be free, at least in the elementary and fundamental stages" (Article 26). The document asserts several other "fundamental human rights" as well, although it does not discuss costs or other difficulties associated with their universal provision.

housing; and these are to be arranged so as to promote the choices of citizens to regulate their nutrition and their shelter by their own practical reason. [...] It requires protection to regulate their own sexual activity [...;] institutions promoting a humanistic form of education [...] support for rich social relations with others [...]."[40] And so on: her list continues.

Working out the range of information required to successfully implement these lists of putative state duties or responsibilities exposes a dependence on a surprisingly large body of required knowledge. Consider Fleischacker's claim that the state should provide all citizens with six-weeks' leisure time per year or a several-month sabbatical every few years. Put aside the unaddressed issues of how to afford or account for the loss in productivity from such a policy; even if we all agree that leisure is good—even necessary—to live a happy life, there is no way to know whether that is the right amount of leisure time for any single person. Perhaps, given my personality, six weeks of enforced leisure per year would make me miserable; perhaps your religious values require you to work six days every week. And so on. Or, to Copp: Who knows exactly how to procure and provide people with proper "social recognition," whatever that turns out to be—not just in the abstract, but for specific persons? To Nussbaum: even if we agree in general that people should have "rich social relations with others," what this constitutes for particular persons, and how third parties could support it for particular persons, is unable to be known by centralized authorities. To Sunstein and Thaler: suppose that I would welcome a nudge in the direction of climbing Mt. Kilimanjaro, but I am a paraplegic; suppose further that the technology exists to take me to the top of the mountain nonetheless, but that it requires resources that would, at the margins, preclude another person from receiving job training she needs. As Sunstein well understands, government agencies regularly make decisions like these about tradeoffs.[41] So whose interests should the centralized planners decide to serve, and whose should be sacrificed? Given the limitations in knowledge they face, there can be little doubt that the relevant decisions they will make will reflect

[40] Nussbaum 1998, 152–3; see also Nussbaum 2006 and 2011.
[41] Sunstein discusses these kinds of tradeoffs in, for example, 1997: chaps. 2 and 3 and 2002.

their own schedules of value—which may have little coincidence with yours, mine, or those of anyone else their policies affect.

And how can we be sure that the decisions the centralized authorities make will actually effectuate the ends they deem appropriate? Suppose that the 100 residents of my neighborhood are, on average, 20 pounds overweight, and we all agree that, again *ceteris paribus,* that is probably not a good thing. What should a central-planning-inclined person recommend? There are indefinitely many possibilities. Perhaps that no one be allowed to eat more than one doughnut per day, or that no one drink "sugary sodas" bigger than sixteen ounces at a time? The problems are apparent. To begin, what is true of the population—on average twenty pounds overweight—is not necessarily true of every individual; indeed, it is not necessarily true of *any* individual. Moreover, what might help one person achieve his desired weight (say, eating fewer doughnuts) will not necessarily help any other individual—and it might not help any single individual in this population. Finally, there will inevitably be new tradeoffs and thus unintended consequences to a ban like this, since, as Adam Smith put it, people, unlike chess pieces, have a "principle of motion all their own." Because we cannot know in advance what exactly those unintended consequences might be, we cannot know that they do not cancel whatever benefit the central planner might have hoped to achieve. Although the recommendations the central planner makes might apply to the population as a whole, the policy does not affect "the population as a whole": it affects individuals separately. Thus any policy that would be appropriate to a population of discrete individuals is one that would take their respective peculiar situations into account, which the centrally proposed policies cannot do.

The first reason, therefore, why the default should be to leave people unmolested in the decisions they make based on their own assessments of their schedules of value and the opportunities available to them is that however expert the central planners might be in their particular fields—economics, psychology, medicine, ecology, nutrition, and so on—the knowledge they have is general and abstract, not tied to particular individuals.

Incentives and Getting Things Right. The second reason that we should prefer individuals' judgments about how to arrange their own time, talent, and treasure over the judgments of third parties, however expert, is because of the incentives involved. If I follow your proposed policy and it does not benefit me, or perhaps even harms me, on whom do the negative consequences fall? It is not on you; it is on me. But because you did not get that feedback, it may not incline you to correct, or even respond to, this consequence of your policy. I, on the other hand, who did suffer the negative consequence, would presumably respond to it, but since I am not making the decisions about the policy, my response has muted effectiveness. Suppose you worry about people's salt intake because you believe it is connected with heart disease, and so you move to restrict the salt that restaurants can supply in your city; it turns out, however, that my heart condition actually requires elevated amounts of salt.[42] Your policy might thus affect me negatively rather than positively, even if it is true, or at least might be true, that statistically such a policy should have positive effects on more people than those on whom it has negative effects. Now, if I am the one making the decisions about how much salt I ingest, I will probably respond relatively quickly to the effects of those decisions. I am not infallible, of course, so my responses will not be perfect. But you are not infallible either, and I, unlike you, have the considerable benefit of directly receiving the feedback from my actions. Hence I am better positioned to make good decisions about my situation than you are, even given my fallibility. Because I actually experience the consequences, I have strong incentives to get decisions right; the more important the decision—meaning the more consequential and weighty the potential effects on my life or on the lives of those I care about—the stronger the incentive I face to get things right. You, by contrast, face no such incentives, which means you are in a far worse position from which to hope to make good decisions. This is not an indictment of your character, just as it is no encomium to mine; it is merely a consequence of the knowledge you do not have—namely, knowledge about me—and the disciplining feedback you do not receive.

---

[42] Neither of these is hypothetical. In 2009, New York Mayor Michael Bloomberg launched what he called the "National Salt Reduction Initiative"; see here: http://www.nyc.gov/html/doh/html/cardio/cardio-salt-initiative.shtml. And I do have a congenital heart condition requiring me to consume higher levels of salt.

The Nirvana Fallacy. A third and final reason we should be skeptical of third parties' judgments of how we should expend our time, talent, and treasure is captured by three related fallacies articulated by Harold Demsetz as constituting what Demsetz calls "the nirvana approach" to public policy: the "grass is always greener fallacy," the "fallacy of the free lunch," and the "people could be different fallacy" (Demsetz 1969).

The grass is always greener fallacy occurs when one compares an actually existent situation against an ideal but unrealized situation: inevitably the former is found lacking, from which the conclusion is to adopt the latter. But that does not follow, since the latter—the unrealized ideal situation—is typically not itself subject to the same searching analysis to which the actually existing situation was. Pointing out that problems exist under current policy does not by itself mean that another policy is therefore to be preferred. It is possible, after all, that current policy is handling the problems as well as they can be, or at least better than the proposed alternative. Thus identifying problems to which allowing people to make their own decisions about their lives and preferences might lead does not by itself entail that they should not be allowed to do so, much less that someone else should make those decisions for them. Until a comparison is made among actually available alternatives that subjects them to similar analysis, we are in no position to judge whether the current set of institutions should be changed, whatever its faults. The grass is not always greener.

Avoiding a "nirvana approach" thus requires a full, good-faith estimate of the costs involved with changing institutions or policies from what they currently are. As I have argued, these costs can be surprisingly extensive—in part because many of them are "unseen." No change in policy is costless, however, so the costs must be anticipated and estimated to the extent possible if we are to entertain any proposed alternative as a serious and viable option. There is no free lunch.

Finally, if a proposed alternative set of institutions assumes in its idealized form that people's attitudes, motivations, or personalities undergo significant change—they become less self-interested, for example, or more risk averse, less religious, less partial to their own family and friends, and so on—then the idealized proposal is incomplete, and therefore not dispositive, until it can be demonstrated that this change from the way people are now is not only possible but likely. That people *could* be different does not mean they *will* be.

Conclusion

The legislator or theorist can have little hope of making good decisions about how individuals should organize their lives because she cannot begin take into account the indefinitely large number of peculiar and unique variations in time, talent, and treasure, in schedules of value, and in opportunities in individuals' lives. As James Buchanan has written, "[t]he economy allegedly organized on the command-control principles of managerial socialism simply cannot, and demonstrably could not, deliver the goods in any manner even remotely comparable to those economies organized under the principles derivative from Adam Smith's system of natural liberty" (2005: 21). A legislator or theorist's presumption that she can nevertheless somehow do so is what Adam Smith calls the "conceit" of the "man of system," and to act on that "conceit" is to commit the Great Mind Fallacy.

4

Knowledge and Community

Introduction

One reason G. A. Cohen endorses progressive taxation, even aggressively progressive taxation, in the service of socialist equality is because he believes that great inequality imperils genuine community. Cohen asks us to imagine a wealthy and privileged person, and a poor and unprivileged person. Both of them enjoy the "negative" freedom accorded by Adam Smithian "justice," which Smith defined as comprising only three things: integrity of one's person, integrity of one's property, and integrity of one's voluntary promises and contracts. Because the Smithian government's primary responsibility is to protect this conception of justice, its main duties are hence the protection of life, property, and contract. Smith called these duties "negative" because, as he vividly put it, one could "fulfil all the rules of justice by sitting still and doing nothing" (TMS, 82). Justice for Smith thus contrasted with other, "positive" virtues, which required taking positive action to fulfill, and included things like friendship, loyalty, charity, hospitality—all the virtues that fall under Smith's general heading of "beneficence." Suppose, then, both Cohen's wealthy person and his poor person are enjoying protection of this minimalist Smithian justice, and hence the Smithian state owes neither of them anything more. Yet the vastly different experiences each of them would have had over the courses of their lifetimes would make them, Cohen argues, vastly different people. They would have different home lives, different schooling and education, different vocations and job training; they would likely not eat in the same restaurants, take their children to the same parks, shop in the same stores, read the same books, watch the same television shows, vacation in the same places. They would, in short, live in virtually separate worlds, even if physically proximate: if they happened to ride the same bus one day, they would hardly recognize each other as fellow citizens and would scarcely have anything even to talk about. Cohen concludes that they can therefore share no real community (2009: 36).[1] He further concludes that the large inequalities in wealth that capitalism allows, including when innocent under the Smithian minimalist definition, nevertheless have significant costs in community. Unless one argues, then, that the only thing that matters in public policy is protection of "negative" justice—a position Cohen regards as implausibly extreme—then one ought to entertain the possibility of allowing the state to take affirmative actions that would enhance community, even if it means going beyond the narrow strictures of the Smithian state.

Justice vs. Beneficence

Smith, for his part, did not believe that protecting his conception of justice was all that mattered in public policy. In particular, he believed the state should also entertain the provision of limited public works.[2] But he did argue that his conception of justice was the first thing to which the state should attend. Justice was, he argued, the pillar that supported the edifice of society, whereas the beneficent virtues were the embellishments that made it inviting. He used a striking analogy to flesh out his position:

The rules of justice may be compared to the rules of grammar; the rules of the other virtues, to the rules which critics lay down for the attainment of what is sublime and elegant in composition. The one, are precise, accurate, and

---

[1] Charles Murray 2012 makes a similar argument.

[2] Smith argues that there are three proper duties of government: (1) defending the nation from foreign invasion, (2) defending the members of the society from assault or injustice from one another, and (3) "erecting and maintaining certain publick works" (WN, 687–8). Smith suggests, however, that to qualify for government provision, a "publick works" proposal must meet both of two criteria: first, it must benefit the entire nation, not simply one group at the expense of another; second, it must be unable to be provided by private-sector initiative (see WN, 688 and 723). It would seem that few putative public works would satisfy both those criteria.

indispensable. The other, are loose, vague, and indeterminate, and present us rather with a general idea of the perfection we ought to aim at, than afford us any certain and infallible directions for acquiring it. A man may learn to write grammatically by rule, with the most absolute infallibility; and so, perhaps, he may be taught to act justly. But there are no rules whose observance will infallibly lead us to the attainment of elegance or sublimity in writing; though there are some which may help us, in some measure, to correct and ascertain the vague ideas which we might otherwise have entertained of those perfections. And there are no rules by the knowledge of which we can infallibly be taught to act upon all occasions with prudence, with just magnanimity, or proper beneficence: though there are some which may enable us to correct and ascertain, in several respects, the imperfect ideas which we might otherwise have entertained of those virtues. (TMS, 175–6)

This fundamental difference between the rules of "negative" justice and the rules of the other, "positive"[3] virtues entailed for Smith that the latter, unlike the former, could not be articulated or known from afar. We could know, for example, what "just magnanimity" requires of a person only when we know the details of her particular situation: the who, what, when, where, and why. Without those details, any rules of "just magnanimity"—like the rules of all the positive virtues of beneficence—would be either so vague as to provide little or no concrete direction, or, if rendered specific, would be inapplicable in numerous actual relevant instances. Suppose, for example, your proposed rule is "give to a friend in need." That sounds plausible, but it gives you little to go on in actual cases. Is this person a (sufficient) friend? Does he really need it? Am I required to give him everything he needs? Does his need outweigh my other obligations? If one attempts to avoid problems like these by making the rule more specific—perhaps "if one of your good friends needs up to $100, then you should give it"—difficulties still remain. What if I do not have $100 right now? What if this is the seventh time this month she has asked me for money? What if she is an addict who earlier, in a sober moment, made me promise not to give her any money in the future? And so on.

The conclusion Smith reaches is that because the rules of justice are "precise, accurate, and indispensable," they are fit, and proper, objects of the state's attention. By contrast, because the rules of beneficence

---

[3] Smith himself uses both the terms "negative" and "positive." See, for example, TMS, 78–82.

are "loose, vague, and indeterminate," they are instead fit, and proper, objects of individuals' localized attention and judgment.

Knowledge and Community

That might be the Smithian answer to Cohen, but Cohen's concern here is for human community, not just state provision of "positive" benefits. Smith, who argued in his first book, *The Theory of Moral Sentiments,* not only (1) that human beings are naturally social but (2) that their moral sensibilities develop only in communities and (3) they can be happy only in association with others, could hardly agree more on the importance of community. The difference, however, is that, for Smith, proper community must be organic—that is, it must arise "naturally" as a result of human beings associating, and dissociating, with one another according to their own lights. If one attempts to engineer communities from the top, or even if one attempts merely to encourage some kinds of community and discourage other kinds by restrictions or artificial inducements, one will be unable to exploit the local knowledge required to understand what kinds of community are actually beneficial for any given individuals. We simply cannot know with anything like the required level of specificity what kinds of community other people need. Consider: Should you get married? To whom? Should you go to church? Which one, and how often? Should you join this club or that group? Should you make friends with this person, or this one, or this one? Would you be better off leaving this community and joining that one? You will often find it difficult to make these determinations for yourself. You will often have recourse to the advice of your family or friends, but the level of confidence you invest in their advice is in no small part a function of their level of familiarity with you and your situation. How much confidence, then, should you invest in the opinion of someone who knows nothing of you? However smart that person might be, without detailed and intimate knowledge of you, his advice can be nothing but generalities. The hard part is knowing whether, and if so when and exactly how, any given generality applies to your life, and this requires not only intelligence but also informed judgment—informed, that is, by the relevant details of your life and circumstances.

In her book *Women and Human Development,* Martha Nussbaum offers a list of ten "central capabilities" that she argues should be incorporated into the conception of "justice" that she calls on governments to achieve in each of their citizens.[4] Not all of Nussbaum's list includes or directly affects community, but at least three do: (1) "bodily integrity," which includes, *inter alia,* "having opportunities for sexual satisfaction"; (2) "affiliation," which includes (2a) "[b]eing able to live with and toward others, to recognize and show concern for other humans, to engage in various forms of social interaction; to be able to imagine the situation of another" and (2b) "[h]aving the social bases of self-respect and non-humiliation; being able to be treated as a dignified being whose worth is equal to that of others" (78–90). Suppose we agree that these are important parts of a full or complete or properly human life; in fact, I suspect we do agree. What would rescue Nussbaum's position from being merely an aspirational Nice-If Claim is if there accompanied it several further discussions: (i) a fairly specific list of the agencies that would be required to provide or encourage these goods, along with an estimate of their full costs; (ii) reasons why these costs are worth the necessary tradeoffs against other goods or services that might otherwise have been pursued with those resources; (iii) reasons why we should expect the relevant required agencies to succeed despite the difficulties that all large-scale, centrally managed public operations face, along with (iv) specific and credible criteria for determining success and failure and credible procedures for acting on success and failure.

Unfortunately, Nussbaum provides no discussion of any of these matters. Consider, as one telling example, how Nussbaum could overcome the formidable principal–agent problem—that is, the problem of getting one's agents to actually do whatever it is the principal wants them to do. The principal in this case is Nussbaum, who has specific ideas about what the government or regulatory agencies should do; but the agents who would carry out her directives have interests and purposes of their own, and she cannot always be there to make sure they are doing what she wishes. The principal–agent problem

---

[4] She claims that this list does not exhaust her conception of justice, but is, rather, the "decent social minimum," adding that the list is "open-ended and humble." See Nussbaum 2001: 75–80.

dogs agencies, bureaucracies, and firms, and much time, money, and research have been spent in ongoing efforts to address it. Given the quite personal nature of some of the things Nussbaum is calling on governments to provide or ensure, it would seem especially incumbent on her to explain how her ends would actually be served, or at least might likely be served, by the mechanisms available to government agencies. Yet she does not do so, perhaps because it is not clear how she could plausibly overcome the difficulty.

Returning to Cohen, his concern for community, while widely shared (including by me),[5] is unfortunately not dispositive. Like Nussbaum's list of central capabilities, it is unclear what specific policies it proposes or what the state should do to achieve community. Regarding his example of the alleged lack of community between the rich and the poor person, the Smithian would caution that Cohen knows less than he thinks. Is he sure they have nothing to talk about or cannot be friends? How can he know whether they should be friends in the first place? Even if he could answer both of those questions, what can he—or any other third party—really know about how in practice to encourage community between them? Imagine a Cohenite suggesting (steep) progressive taxation as a remedy: there is a very long way between that and proper community between these two imagined bus riders. There is also a very long way between the imagined bus riders and any two actual persons, and we must use extreme caution in applying a lesson derived from the one (real or imagined) case to another (real or imagined) case. As David Hume argued in another context:

But observe, I entreat you, with what extreme caution all just reasoners proceed in the transferring of experiments to similar cases. Unless the cases be exactly similar, they repose no perfect confidence in applying their past observation to any particular phenomenon. Every alteration of circumstances occasions a doubt concerning the event; and it requires new experiments to prove certainly that the new circumstances are of no moment or importance. [...] And unless the objects be quite familiar to us, it is the highest temerity to expect with assurance, after any of these changes, an event similar to that which before fell under our observation. (1988: 18–19)

---

[5] See Otteson 2006. For a compelling investigation of the need for community especially within the context of a market order, see Röpke 1998; for an excellent contemporary discussion from a somewhat different perspective, see Rose 2011.

Conclusion

If the limits of human knowledge we have explored are correct, then we can have less confidence in centralized attempts to create proper or beneficial communities than in decentralized and organic attempts. That is not to say that communities created by decentralized individual decisions are perfect, or could not be improved, or even are the best that can be hoped for: none of those claims is licensed by the argument based on limited human knowledge. What does follow is that the communities formed by decentralized and uncoordinated decisions, as flawed and mixed and uneven as they might be, are nevertheless far more likely to conduce to people's actual benefit than anything centrally conceived and administratively imposed.

5

The Day Two Problem

Introduction

The other main category of practical obstacles that socialist-inclined policy faces is encompassed by what I call the Day Two Problem. Having now discussed the problems associated with our lack of knowledge, the Day Two Problem requires much less space to explain. It has two principal parts: the first dealing with production, the second with redistribution.

Discussion of socialist-inclined policy is notably thin on the topic of production.[1] This is especially odd since advocates of socialist-inclined policy, like Peter Singer for example,[2] frame their positions as being motivated at least in part by the desire to alleviate poverty and its attendant miseries. But the solution to material poverty and deprivation is material wealth and abundance, and the only field of human activity known to generate material wealth and abundance is business:

---

[1] Some examples: Cohen does not discuss it in *Why Not Socialism?* (more on this in a moment) or in *Self-Ownership, Freedom, and Equality*. Cohen does discuss it in his *Rescuing Justice and Equality*, chap. 5, but his discussion there relies on the supposition of fundamental changes in human nature and in natural human motivation to maintain production in the face of socialist policy. Rawls does not discuss production in *A Theory of Justice*, Sandel does not discuss it in *What Money Can't Buy*, Satz does not discuss it in *Why Some Things Should Not Be for Sale*, Singer does not discuss it in *Practical Ethics*, the Skidelskys do not discuss it in *How Much Is Enough?* and Thaler and Sunstein do not discuss it in *Nudge*. Eagleton broaches the topic in his *Why Marx Was Right* (see chap. 2, for example), only to provide no actual discussion.

[2] See Singer 2009 or 2011b, for example.

creation, commerce, exchange, cooperation, entrepreneurship—in other words, everything captured by the term *production*.

Yet consider, for example, the way G. A. Cohen's argument proceeds in his *Why Not Socialism?* Cohen begins by describing an imaginary camping trip attended by several different families, and he argues that the trip exhibits principles that capture his socialist vision of a just society. Cohen's description of this camping trip is therefore quite important for his overall argument. Here is how Cohen begins his description of the trip:

> You and I and a whole bunch of other people go on a camping trip. There is no hierarchy among us; our common aim is that each of us should have a good time, doing, so far as possible, the things that he or she likes best (some of those things we do together; others we do separately). We have facilities with which to carry out our enterprise: we have, for example, pots and pans, oil, coffee, fishing rods, canoes, a soccer ball, decks of cards, and so forth. And, as is usual on camping trips, we avail ourselves of those facilities collectively: even if they are privately owned things, they are under collective control for the duration of the trip, and we have shared understandings about who is going to use them when, and under what circumstances, and why. (2009: 3–4)

This is an unpromising start to Cohen's argument. Why, for example, is there no hierarchy among us? No one knows the area better than others or has more camping experience than others, and thus has opinions that should be granted more weight? Moreover, why would we assume that our "common aim" is that "each of us should have a good time"? We might all care about that to some extent, but presumably each of us would have other aims as well, including aims that are more important to us individually or within our own families than that "common aim." I want to teach my children to fish; you want to be left alone to read; another wants to hike and explore; and so on. Any of these aims, none of which are jointly shared, might be more important to us than making sure others are having a good time.

Finally, however, and most to the point here: Where did those "facilities with which to carry out our enterprise" come from? Where did we get the pots and pans, canoes, soccer balls, oil, coffee, "and so forth"? Cohen does not tell us. Indeed, Cohen nowhere discusses production: not how the socialist proposes to continue production of the goods and services he intends to redistribute, not what effect socialist-inclined policies might have on production of those goods and services.[3] At times the socialist presumption seems, as in Cohen's argument, to be that wealth is like a naturally occurring phenomenon that will continue to exist, possibly even grow, regardless of what policies are implemented—that is why the socialist does not need to address it. But goods do not appear out of nowhere: every particle of them is produced by human labor and thus costs scarce resources that might otherwise have been expended elsewhere.

At other times the assumption is that the effects of centralized redistribution, progressive taxation, or regulation are likely to be only relatively benign relocation of some units of wealth, which might be a bargain worth making. What is typically not contemplated or examined is that socialist-inclined policies might substantially affect the production of goods and services, potentially leading to declines in standards of living. Singer, for example, asserts that taking even one-third of the income of the "superrich" "would be unlikely to reduce their standard of living to any significant degree," and hence would not lead them to alter their economic behaviors in any significant degree. He makes a similar claim for those who are less wealthy than the "superrich": "If your income doesn't put you in the top 10 percent, you still almost certainly have income that you can spare."[4] One can infer similar sentiments from others who advocate socialist-inclined policy but do not discuss its effect on production of wealth, since if they thought it would have a significant effect on wealth production, they would discuss it. A utilitarian—like Singer, for example—would weigh the likely costs against the likely benefits and then judge accordingly. The absence of discussion of production implies, then, an assumption that socialist-inclined policy will have only a negligible effect on production, and for

[3] Later, Cohen begins an argument by offering this hypothetical example: "A table is before us, laden with apples and oranges. Each of us is entitled to take six pieces of fruit, with apples and oranges appearing in any combination to make up that six" (2009: 19). Cohen goes on to discuss how we might allow the fruit to be distributed such that it can satisfy people's preferences while simultaneously forestalling any resentment or jealousy. But look again at how his scenario begins. Where did those apples and oranges come from? Who put them there? Why is each of us "entitled" to take six pieces? Failing to address those questions is not simply an omission: it effectively brackets out many of the issues—like private property and voluntary contracts and agreements that can give rise to entitlements—that capitalist-inclined policy deems not only relevant, but also potentially dispositive. Cohen's omission thus prejudices the discussion from the outset.

[4] Singer 2009: 162 and 166, respectively.

that reason the matter is inconsequential. That assumption, however, is false. The Day Two Problem explains why.

The Day Two Problem, Part I

The first part of the Day Two Problem is that once we have both determined what the proper distribution of wealth should be and we have effectuated the proper redistribution (assuming for the moment that we can overcome the Great Mind Fallacy, the knowledge problem, and so on), by the next day things would no longer conform to the pattern we wanted.[5] Because human beings have principles of motion all their own, they will move and behave and decide in ways we cannot predict, and there is no reason to believe that they will do so in ways consistent with the goals or aims that motivated the centralized plan. Indeed, there is good reason to believe they will *not* behave in the ways our plans would envision—because they are in possession of unique local knowledge that they can incorporate into their decision-making calculations. Whatever mismatches or misallocations might arise between what the centralized decision makers want and desire, and what other people want or desire, will thus be present at the outset of the second iteration. We know this because there will not have been time, before the next redistributive iteration would need to commence, (1) to survey all the actual reallocations of yesterday, (2) determine whether and to what extent the reallocators matched the planner's mandates (the principal–agent problem applies here again), (3) determine whether and to what extent people behaved in accordance with expectations, and (4) what would be required to remedy failures in (2) and (3). Because neither time nor people stand still, the central planners would therefore have to issue a second round of redistribution and allocation mandates before errors in the first round were corrected. But the second round would face the same difficulties that dogged round one, thereby entailing at least as much mismatch and misallocation as the first round. At the end of round two, then, there would remain the first

---

[5] My discussion here bears some resemblance to Nozick's Wilt Chamberlain example (1974: 160–4). One important difference is that I do not assume the justice of property relations, of private property itself, and so on. My argument here addresses a logistical challenge involved with redistribution regardless of the ultimate justice of property relations.

round's mismatches and misallocations, now compounded by those of the second round. But time constraints would mean that the second round's could not be addressed and alleviated before the third round must commence. And so on.

Adam Smith's Economizer Argument—which holds that people economize on their energies by seeking out the biggest or richest return on their investments of energy—suggests that if there exists an apparatus that centrally gathers wealth in order to redistribute it, some people will be inclined to seize on this opportunity to take a portion of that wealth to enrich themselves. This is the problem economists now call rent-seeking.[6] The creation of a redistributive agency simultaneously also creates special-interest groups who now have a vested interest in the continuance and expansion of the agency, regardless of whether the agency serves or completes its initial stated aim. This is an instance of the principal–agent problem because the principal, who in this case might be the citizens, has some goal or goals he wishes to accomplish with the creation of the agency, while the agent, who in this case is the congress that created or the people staffing the agency, has her own goals that may or may not coincide with those of the principal. It is important to see that we do not have to assume bad faith on anyone's part. As Smith's Economizer Argument assumes, people respond to incentives; when they can serve their ends by rent-seeking, they, or at least some of them, will do so. The benefits to them are manifest because they are concentrated, while the costs to citizens are hidden because they are dispersed.

The costs involved here can be especially hard to detect when they are initiated by *inaction:* a congressman or regulator might tell an industry that he is thinking about imposing a costly new regulatory rule on it. To prevent that from happening, some firms might offer campaign contributions, contracts to favored suppliers, junkets, and other forms of recompense in exchange for the congressman or regulator refraining from imposing the new regulation.[7] Dynamics like these not only

---

[6] See Tullock 2005.

[7] See McChesney 1987, Stigler 1971, and Tullock 2005. In order to reduce the competition they face, entrenched firms will sometimes actively seek out centrally mandated regulations that impose costs that newer or smaller competitors are less able to weather. This is easier to detect, however, since it includes positive regulatory findings or rules.

increase the cost of such attempted redistribution or regulation, but they inevitably come at the expense of the overall economy—which inevitably means that the poorest tend to be hurt *most*. The Smithian solution to such problems is to not create centralized apparatuses that can be put to such opportunistic use in the first place. If the number of such apparatuses is low, or if the amount of centralized gathering and then distribution is relatively small, then whatever inefficiencies they generate might be borne without much overall negative effect. As their number or the proportion of wealth they redistribute increases, however, the opportunities for rent-seeking and other extractive behavior increase as well. What cannot be known in advance is exactly how many rent seekers will arise, how much extractive behavior this will encourage, or how much otherwise productive activity will thereby have been prevented.[8] What can be known in advance is that all these negative consequences will in fact transpire. Their increasing negative effects will have to be reckoned into any analysis of proposed redistribution mechanisms.

Each iteration would therefore lead to marginally larger misallocations and mismatches, constituting correspondingly larger costs and thus greater burdens on production. Although the government's agencies can transfer wealth from one group to another, what actually gets transferred is less than what was initially taken and what one wanted transferred. Arthur Okun said this is because the government's transfer apparatuses are a "leaky bucket" (Okun 1975). I would say that they are more like giant milkshakes into which lots of people put their straws as they travel from the soda counter to the customer. Either way, what we would expect to see as redistribution and reallocation begin is that wealth production will first begin to increase at a decreasing rate; then, if the course is not changed, production will begin to stagnate; eventually, if central redistributions and reallocations continue or grow, production will decline, potentially all the way to collapse.

---

[8] One often unappreciated effect of such dynamics is the discouragement it provides to entrepreneurs to innovate. Armen Alchian argues that as centralization proceeds, uncertainty increases—with this perhaps surprising conclusion: "the greater the uncertainties of the world, the greater is the possibility that profits would go to venturesome and lucky rather than to logical, careful, fact-gathering individuals" (1950: 213).

A Few Real-World Examples. In real life, things are much more complicated than this. As Adam Smith said, there is a "great deal of ruin in a nation"[9]—meaning that a nation, especially a large and thriving one, can weather quite a bit before stagnation, let alone collapse. Nevertheless, the dynamic of centralized redistribution and reallocation of resources, and the centralized restriction of voluntary cooperation and exchange, entail the accumulating costs of mismatch and misallocation described earlier. Although those costs can sometimes be absorbed—even, depending on their scale, without much noticeable difference—their tendency is to move exactly, and inexorably, in this direction.

That, I submit, goes some substantial way toward explaining why the Soviet Union's economic experiment failed the way it did. It is why Cuba's economy has stagnated and declined, why North Korea's has as of this writing all but collapsed, and why China's stagnated for centuries before only in the last few decades beginning to show signs of life—when market reforms were introduced and decentralized economic decision making was allowed.[10] It helps explain, moreover, why the United States created more wealth than any other nation in the history of humankind, as well as why its rate of wealth production has begun to slow; and it helps explain why Western Europe's formerly formidable economic production has been ebbing for some time.

It also helps explain the remarkable arc of Sweden's economy over the last 130 years. Because many supporters of socialist-inclined policy hold Sweden out as a model, its case is worth a few more words. Free-market reforms in the 1860s allowed Sweden to begin enjoying the gains in productivity happening elsewhere during the Industrial Revolution. These reforms led to spectacular innovation and entrepreneurship, including the founding of iconic Swedish companies like IKEA, Volvo, and Ericsson. In the late 1930s, Sweden decided it could sustain its robust growth while at the same time creating a welfare state that included modest worker and retirement benefits, unemployment protections, and so on. Its previous economic engine enabled it to continue growing into the 1950s, when Sweden decided to dramatically expand its centralizing efforts: government spending of its gross

---

[9] See *Correspondence of Adam Smith*, 1987: 262 n3.
[10] See Coase and Way 2013.

domestic product went from averaging less than 10 percent in the period of 1870–1938, to approximately 20 percent in 1950, and then to fully 50 percent in 1975. Despite its small and homogenous population, and despite its cultural consensus in favor of both equality and hard work, this level of government centralization proved too much for Sweden to sustain. A series of economic shocks ensued, which led, over the next two decades, to currency devaluations, inflation, rising unemployment, stagnating production, and anemic growth. Matters came to a head when its fixed exchange-rate policy collapsed in 1992. This led Sweden to rethink its priorities: it began privatizing state-owned companies, deregulating parts of the economy, and scaling back its welfare state. This re-transition to its previous free-market success has been bumpy and difficult, but Sweden's economy is finally showing signs of returning to some growth and vitality. Sweden eliminated its inheritance tax in 2005, its wealth tax in 2007, and its taxes on residential property in 2008; it cut taxes on labor and disallowed union membership dues from qualifying for tax relief; it installed a competitive voucher system for education and allowed a growing private health care system; and it has made all its welfare benefits less generous. As *The Economist* reports, these reforms have led to a mild increase in material inequality in this country that formerly led the world in its material equality, but the tradeoff has been that now more people work, its economy is growing, and the country is reducing its debt, thereby making it, according to *The Economist,* once again a model for other countries—but this time for the reversal of stagnation and return to prosperity that market-based reforms can enable (2012).

The lesson: the relative degree to which economic decision making in all these countries was undertaken centrally, as opposed to being uncoordinated and decentralized, not only correlates with relative economic success, but also, as the previous argument demonstrates, helps explain it. And the available evidence now covers a large breadth of countries, times, cultures, and places.[11]

---

[11] For evidence of the historical correlation between policy and prosperity, see, for example, Acemoglu and Robinson 2012, Maddison 2007, McCloskey 2006 and 2010, and Tomasi 2013.

The Day Two Problem, Part II

After our initial redistribution of wealth and reallocation of resources, we would then—on Day Two, as it were[12]—be faced with determining and then effectuating yet another redistribution; and so on indefinitely. The argument so far has focused on the mismatches that are attendant on centralized economic decision making. But things are actually worse than this. With each iteration of the process there would be *successively less* to redistribute, owing to a number of factors: first, there are the losses constituted by the wealth going to the redistributors, who are not themselves engaged in wealth-producing activity; second, there is the disincentive such policy provides for others to continue producing wealth; and third, there is a tragedy-of-the-commons dynamic initiated by converting wealth production from a positive-sum enterprise into a zero-sum bounty or prize. The reasons for these costs were explored in Chapters 2 and 3. I wish to argue now that a policy of centralized redistribution, reallocation, and regulation entails the impoverishment of its people as its ultimate, if not its proximate, end. How long it can survive before reaching that end, and what digressions or unexpected turns it might take on the way, are impossible to predict, but they will depend in large part on the extent of the centralized decision making. Hence, even if, in a particular instance, the people in a country following socialist-inclined economic policy do not become impoverished, it follows at a minimum that they will be less wealthy than they otherwise would have been.[13] It is also surely the case that there is some tipping point—some threshold beyond which we cannot stop the Day Two problematic, but before which interventions and redistributions *can* be absorbed with marginal but not fatal loss. But no one knows where that tipping point is.

---

[12] I use the terms "day," "yesterday," and so on metaphorically: it is not necessarily twenty-four hours ago; it might be a week, a month, a year. Although it might seem that allowing for more time would help central planners, in fact it makes things more difficult for them because longer time means people stray further from the plan they had on Day One.

[13] Dawson and Seater 2013 estimate that federal regulations in the United States have prevented its gross domestic product, which is currently approximately $16 trillion, from being approximately $54 trillion (in constant dollars). That means the median household income in the United States could have been, instead of its actual $53,000, an incredible $330,000 (again, in constant dollars).

The costs of these losses and forgone gains fall particularly on the poorest members of the community. The more wealth one has, the better able one is to insulate oneself from the effects of declining over-all standards of living. The poorer one is, the less able one is to do this, and thus the more vulnerable one is to even relatively minor overall slowdowns or regressions. These effects of socialist-inclined policies therefore disproportionately affect precisely those in whose name they are often proposed and undertaken.

Still, might that tradeoff be worth it? Might, perhaps, certain moral goals be important enough to warrant sacrificing some of our wealth, even a great deal of our wealth, in their pursuit? Or are perhaps some moral evils bad enough to justify forsaking some wealth and prosperity in the hopes of avoiding them? We will take up these questions next. But before we can have an informed discussion of them, it is requisite to know, and be fully aware of, the costs involved in the tradeoffs we are contemplating.

Conclusion

The main worry G. A. Cohen, and many others, have had about socialism—its "infeasibility"—is indeed a serious and substantial problem. Human knowledge is unfortunately too limited for us to have confidence in central planners' abilities to make good decisions about how firms should allocate their resources, how you or I should work or associate or exchange or cooperate, how to effectuate equal-ity, or how to encourage or create community. Moreover, even if these problems could somehow be overcome, socialist-inclined redistri-bution and reallocation of resources will lead to steadily less being available for redistribution and thus for consumption. I believe these are grave problems, made all the worse because, in many cases around the world, actual lives are at stake. People live and die because of economic policy decisions governments make. That means that "prac-tical" problems with socialist-inclined policy, in fact, have not merely an economic, but also a moral dimension. That brings us to Part II.

PART II

SOCIALISM'S PROBLEMS IN PRINCIPLE

The two sets of obstacles political economists must overcome in order to justify their preferred system are the practical and the principled. The former include all those difficulties attendant on implementing the system. Many a slip 'twixt the cup and the lip, as they say: there is a long and often painful path between one's preferred system as it is conceived in theory, constructed though it may be with careful thought and due deliberation, and what happens when that system is applied to the "crooked timber of humanity," as Immanuel Kant put it, out of which "nothing straight can be made" (1992: 46–7). In Part I, we investigated several of the obstacles facing socialism that together, I argued, bring the feasibility of any socialist-inclined program of centralized political-economic decision making into serious doubt. Yet one might think that practical objections should be explored only after the system itself—in its ideal form, as it were—is articulated and justified. One might believe, that is, that the moral or principled arguments should be brought forth and examined first, perhaps on the grounds that practical issues are relevant only if the principled have already been shown to be compelling. If so, this Part of the book should have come before the previous one.

I argue that the reverse is the case. One important principle of moral philosophy is *"ought" implies "can"*: if there is something that I or we *ought* to do, it must be something that I or we *can* do. If we cannot do it—if it is beyond our capabilities or asks too much of us— then it is not actually binding on us. If my moral system held it as a duty that, say, everyone ought to bench press 500 pounds, the fact that almost no one can actually do that should constitute an objection to its being a real duty. But the ought-implies-can principle is not absolute. Sometimes we cannot perfectly or fully satisfy our moral ideals; perhaps we can never do so. Indeed, most ideals are not fully attainable. Their function is instead twofold: one, to serve as targets or goals that we strive to accomplish ever more closely, even while knowing that perfection is impossible; and two, as yardsticks against which we measure how closely we are approximating the ideal in our lives. Thus the fact that an ideal is not fully attainable does not by itself disqualify it as a moral ideal.[1] There are other things that do disqualify moral ideals, however, which we will explore later. For now it is sufficient to understand the ought-implies-can principle as a tocsin: if a moral system requires us to do things that seem impossible, then that raises a red flag; the putative duty then needs special justification showing why we should retain it nonetheless.

Thus in our evaluation of socialist-inclined political economy, after initially articulating its main features, the first task was to determine whether its "oughts" fall reasonably within our "can." Our previous discussion has shown that the requirements of socialist-inclined political economy are significantly more difficult and costly than one might have expected, and more than most people making socialist-inclined arguments seem to presume. I suggested that those difficulties and costs might, in fact, be fatal to the position, in no small part because its costs fall disproportionately on those least able to bear them—namely, the poorer among us. Supposing we disagree about just how insurmountable the obstacles and prohibitive the costs are, however, then the next step would be to bring forth and evaluate the arguments—the "moral" or "principled" considerations—that would justify making the attempt despite the obstacles and costs.

What, then, are the moral reasons for thinking that socialist-inclined political economy is worth the costs? What are the moral considerations suggesting that the ideal that socialism proposes is superior in itself to the ideals of other systems, including that of capitalism? Indeed, do the moral arguments on which socialism draws involve ends so weighty that they should be pursued *regardless* of the costs? That is the subject of this Part.

[1] For discussion of ideal and nonideal theory, see Schmidtz 2011 and Simmons 2010.

6

Economics and Morality

Introduction

In Part I, I argued that economic costs were, in fact, moral costs. We are often inclined to dismiss or depreciate economic considerations as being merely about money, as appealing only to lower, even sordid, aspects of our psychology, or as misunderstanding what really matters in life. Yet economics concerns itself with human behavior in a world of scarce resources: with imperfect human beings trying to make their way in a world that offers them less than what they would like. Those two factors mean that conflict is almost inevitable, and conflict, which is sometimes violent, has real costs in human life. Indeed, throughout human history conflict has been one of the main causes of human misery. If economics—or, more properly now, political economy—can figure out a way to mitigate the conflicts, that can be a great good for humanity. One way it might be able to mitigate those conflicts, and thus elevate the quality of life, is to figure out what the institutions are that allow and encourage cooperation instead of conflict. Another would be if it can discover the institutions that allow people, as Adam Smith put it, to better their conditions. So far we have not invoked any theory of justice or fairness; we have talked only about raising humanity out of the grinding poverty and misery that has marked almost all of its existence. That is the real goal of political economy. And it is a moral one.

In *The Wealth of Nations,* Smith repeatedly expresses his concern for raising the estate of the "common man," of the lowly "day labourer," of the devastatingly poor Scotch Highlanders, of the "people," and so on. If the wealth that rich people enjoy enables them to take relatively better care of themselves whatever system of political economy we have, it is instead poor people, who are relatively less able to bear the burdens of bad systems of political economy, about whom Smith worried. It was they who most stood to benefit or suffer from well or badly conceived systems of political economy. It was their condition that prompted Smith's investigation, and it was the hopes of improving their lot that animated Smith's recommendations.[1] Some scholars have mistakenly suggested that Smith's concern for the poor means he must have been on the political left. That is to misunderstand his project—and, I would argue, the project of economics generally, including the project of this book. Smith's goal—like that of economics, and of my own work—is first to understand how human social institutions work, and then to make recommendations accordingly in the hopes of helping to reduce human misery and to promote human prosperity. That is not a partisan project; it is not an ideological project; it is not even overtly a political project. It is a humane project. And, again, certainly a moral one.

Amoral Economics?

Robert Skidelsky and Edward Skidelsky take a different view of economics. They quote Lionel Robbins's famous definition of economics—"the science that studies human behaviour as a relationship between ends and scarce means which have alternative uses" (Robbins 2000 [1932]: 16)—and then claim: "Robbins's definition both puts scarcity at the center of economics and brackets out judgments of value" (Skidelsky and Skidelsky 2012: 12–13). Take each of these claims in turn.

It is indeed hard to imagine a discipline like economics without scarcity. Adam Smith's contemporary and friend David Hume

---

[1] Smith vividly announced what was at stake already in the "Introduction and Plan of the Work": pre-commercial "nations, however, are so miserably poor, that, from mere want, they are frequently reduced, or, at least, think themselves reduced, to the necessity sometimes of directly destroying, and sometimes of abandoning their infants, their old people, and those afflicted with lingering diseases, to perish with hunger, or to be devoured by wild beasts" (WN, 10).

claimed that the "scanty provision nature has made" for mankind is a necessary factor in the development of the rules of justice (2000: 318); he argued that if, by contrast, "nature supply'd abundantly all our wants and desires," then "the jealousy of interest, which justice supposes, cou'd no longer have place" (2000: 317). Hume's claim is that if people either already had, or could easily acquire, everything they wanted regardless of whatever others had or acquired, then the rules of justice would be pointless—and indeed, would not have arisen. The notions of "mine" and "thine," as he puts it, have place only when people have conflicting desires for the same objects or possessions. Claims to ownership, limits of property, and rules about trade, exchange, and so on are required only in, and precisely because of, a world of scarcity relative to our desires. That is already on the way to developing the characteristically economic way of viewing the world. Contemporary economist Thomas Sowell repeats and extends the insight: "The Garden of Eden was a system for the production and distribution of goods and services, but it was not an economy, because everything was available in unlimited abundance. Without scarcity, there is no need to economize—and therefore no economics" (Sowell 2007b: 2).[2]

The other claim the Skidelskys make, however—that Robbins's definition of economics "brackets out judgments of value"—could not be further from the truth, and indeed it is false in an importantly instructive way. Like many others, the Skidelskys apparently envision economic calculations as cold, lifeless, and inhumane, the amoral search for efficient use of resources without recognition that those resources depend on and affect actual live human beings. When we hear Hume, Robbins, Sowell, or any other economist speaking of investigating ways to allocate scarce resources and then recommending patterns of efficient allocation, we must remember not only that the decisions about how to allocate these resources are made by human beings but also that the resources themselves are the product of human action. They are not made mechanically or by robots, and they do not simply appear like manna from heaven. They are instead created by people on the basis of their own schedules of value, given the opportunities and resources available to them. Those decisions, in other words, reflect the values

---

[2] See also Boettke 2012: chap. 1.

of the decision makers, and those resources result from human labor. When you decide to spend an hour at the gym rather than at the office, you have made an allocation of scarce resources (your time, for example) based on your schedule of value; when you decide to become a philosophy professor instead of working at your father's bowling alley, you have made an allocation of scarce resources (time again; also perhaps money) based on your schedule of value. Not only is it *not* the case that judgments of value are bracketed out, then, but those decisions could not be made without your schedule of values. This aspect of the discipline of economics—namely, its dependence on values— is implicated in the last part of Robbins's definition: "scarce means *which have alternative uses.*" Your resources—your time, talent, and treasure—might be put to any number of uses, or expended in any number of ways; many of those various uses and ways, however, are mutually incompatible, meaning that you cannot exercise them all at the same time. Decisions must be made: How are you—how are any of us—to make them? On the basis of our (respective) schedules of value.

These decisions are not made in a vacuum, however. They are a function not only of one's own values, but also of the opportunities available to one. Perhaps there is some price at which the would-be philosophy professor would decide to work at the bowling alley. If the demand for bowling alley workers increased, the price paid for them would also increase, and there is probably some threshold at which he would decide to change his mind. But these decisions cannot be made except as informed by the values and preferences of the people involved. "The people involved": the other central part of economics concerns what Smith referred to as humanity's natural "propensity to truck, barter, and exchange" (WN, 25). Humans are, as Smith goes on to describe, naturally social animals and, when allowed, they will exchange: truck, barter, cooperate, associate, negotiate, discuss, and on and on. Thus the other central part of economics addresses the "market," which, as James Buchanan put it, is just "the institutional embodiment of the voluntary exchange processes that are entered into by individuals in their several capacities" (1999 [1964]: 38). Because these associations are made on the basis of values we hold, including, in particular, moral values, economics again depends crucially on— and could not proceed without—human morality.

Autonomy and Judgment

What is the conception of human morality that Adam Smith, political economy classically understood, and capitalist-inclined policy assume? It is one that conceives of human beings as moral agents with two principal and defining features: *autonomy* and *independent judgment*.

To be human is, first of all, to possess the power of choosing otherwise. What did you wear today? What did you eat? To whose e-mails did you respond, and to whose did you not respond? What car did you buy? Where did you decide to live? Where did you decide to work? In all these cases, and countless others, you could have chosen otherwise. That does not mean that there would not have been costs or difficulties involved. Perhaps you felt pressured by your parents or your friends or your conscience or a pushy salesman. Autonomy does not require that there were no influences on you, or that there were no external circumstances to which you responded or that you took into consideration. What it requires instead is that you could have chosen otherwise—and in all those cases, you could have.

What exactly constitutes autonomy, and what the circumstances and conditions are that characterize it, is, however, much more complicated than this. Consider, for example, the continuum ranging from, say, (1) disinterestedly providing information to (2) recommending to (3) exhorting to (4) pressuring to (5) threatening to (6) coercing. This is a spectrum, and both external and internal circumstances will fall along it; at some point—perhaps between exhorting and pressuring—we cross the line from acceptable influence into unacceptable. Merely providing information, making recommendations, even trying hard to talk someone into something are all acceptable because they accept and even rely on the fundamental principle that the decision about what to do ultimately lies with the decider. When by contrast I pressure, threaten, or coerce you, I operate on the assumption that my will should supplant and substitute for yours. You become in that case an instrument or vehicle of my will, with my actions aiming only at making sure your actions comply with my will. But that fails to respect that you have an autonomous will of your own, which, unless you have given me specific permission otherwise, entails that I may not replace your will as the deciding factor in your actions with mine. The difference, then, between acceptable and unacceptable influence rests on the sometimes subtle yet nevertheless crucial difference between whether the decider is the agent herself.

That simple principle properly adjudicates the vast majority of human behavior, telling us when the influence was acceptable and when it was not. There will remain hard cases about which people of good faith will disagree, but unfortunately there is no rule or set of rules that will mechanically determine for each such case whether it was acceptable. In the hard or marginal cases, we will have to rely on detailed knowledge of the particulars involved—who, what, when, where, why—and then exercise judgment. Yet even then disagreements will remain. Consider just a few of the variables that can make a crucial difference: Is the person a child or an adult? Of sound mind and body, or infirm? Under compulsion or duress? *Believed* she was under compulsion or duress? Such questions reflect, not this principle in particular, but rather the nature of imperfect creatures in an unpredictable world. All general principles of human action require judgment in application to particular circumstances.[3] Although we tend to focus our thinking on the hard cases—they are, after all, the most intellectually stimulating and challenging—still, they are the anomalies. The disproportionate attention they receive can lead us to believe they are more common than they in fact are and can blind us to the large majority of cases in which it is clear whether the influence was acceptable or not, whether the decision was the agent's own or not.[4]

The capacity to choose otherwise, what I am calling "autonomy," is what gives human beings *dignity*. It is what elevates their status above that of nonhuman animals and inanimate objects. By making choices, one takes ownership of one's life, and one comes therefore to take responsibility for it. When one makes poor choices, one is then properly held accountable for them, just as one is properly rewarded for making wise choices. This is easier to see when one contrasts human responsibility with the lack of it possessed by other creatures. We do not curse or blame the table leg on which we stubbed our toe, and when a bear attacks a human being we do not pass moral judgment on its violent act, even if in both cases we regret or lament what

---

[3] For a demonstration of this claim, see Fleischacker 1999: chaps. 2–4.

[4] I have obviously not resolved all difficulties regarding the nature and extent of human autonomy. I explore the notion more carefully in Otteson 2006: chap. 1. See also Sunstein 1997: chaps. 1 and 2, and Taylor 2005.

happened. We do not blame the weather when it does not fit our plans; we do not blame the door we accidentally close on our fingers; we do not blame the snake that bites its owner. Even for the so-called higher nonhuman animals, we are loath to place moral praise or blame on what they do. An example: in 2009, Charla Nash was attacked by her friend's chimpanzee; she suffered horrific injuries, including having her face completely torn off, and she very nearly died.[5] In the many stories and editorials written about that incident, one can find much laying of blame—on Nash's friend, on the treatment of the chimpanzee, on the very notion of private "ownership" of chimpanzees, even on Nash herself. Yet one does not find any that blame the chimpanzee for what it did. Why not? If it had been Nash's friend who attacked her so viciously instead of the friend's chimpanzee, we certainly would have blamed her. The reason we do not blame the chimpanzee is that we do not consider it a moral agent that could have chosen otherwise. The chimpanzee is sentient, capable of feeling pain, intelligent, even lovable (well, perhaps not this one, but others might be), but it is not a moral agent. Thus it cannot be held morally responsible for its actions, and thus it does not possess the moral dignity arising from autonomy. Human beings do.[6]

The ability to choose otherwise logically implies the ability to say "no" to any proposal, and saying "no" is indeed perhaps the most exemplary act through which human beings can demonstrate their moral agency. Others may have power over one, through superior force or threats of force, but when one can say "no" one demonstrates

---

[5] A recent story outlining the event and Nash's many reconstructive surgeries is available at: http://today.msnbc.msn.com/id/45380267/ns/today-today_health/t/chimp-attack-victim-speaks-about-new-face-new-hopes/.

[6] This has to be qualified, of course. There are some human beings who, for a variety of reasons, are incapable of choosing otherwise; do they therefore not have dignity? I suggest in such cases it is appropriate to apply the *dignity halo effect:* if we are dealing with a person who did at one time possess autonomy, or with a person who will or might in the future possess autonomy, then that fact produces a "halo" of dignity that reaches in time beyond the limit of its actual possession. Moreover, even in those exceedingly rare cases involving a human being who never had and we are sure never will possess moral autonomy, the halo effect extends from those autonomous moral agents who love and care for the person in question. That does not mean that we should hold such persons responsible as moral agents; it means instead that they deserve a high level of humane treatment—high enough that we imagine that if they were to become autonomous moral agents they would approve.

one's moral equality to those who would command, direct, even nudge. When by contrast I do not allow you to say "no" to my proposal; when I do not allow you to decline to be directed or regulated or restricted; when I do not allow you to disobey my command, my nudge, my request for information about you, my tracking of your movements, my listening to your phone calls and reading your emails, my search of your person or property: in all these cases my disallowance of your ability to say "no" compromises your moral authority. It makes your moral agency less efficacious than mine, and indeed it subordinates it to mine. It creates a relationship resembling that of master and servant, not of peer and peer. But that is unbefitting a free person, and it is thus disallowed by a principle of equal moral agency.

The fact that human beings are autonomous entails that they are the authors and owners of their own lives, that they are thus responsible for their lives, and therefore that they possess a uniquely human dignity. In my book *Actual Ethics* I argued that the most compelling picture of human agency is one that draws on Immanuel Kant and Aristotle to see human beings as, on the one hand, free and responsible individual centers of moral agency (the Kantian part), and, on the other hand, possessors of the skill of *phronesis* or practical judgment that must be used to develop properly (the Aristotelian part). These two aspects of humanity complement one another. To develop one's judgment properly, one first needs the freedom to make decisions for oneself, because judgment, like other skills, must be practiced to develop. But one must also be held responsible for one's decisions, because it is through feedback—negative and positive, as the case may be—that one learns to correct, hone, and develop one's judgment. This two-fold policy of allowing freedom to decide and holding responsible for decisions is appropriate only to those beings who are properly understood as possessing the capacities to decide, to respond to feedback and develop independent judgment, and to give an account of their reasons for deciding the way they did. That is human beings. Indeed, I claim that that is the *essence* of humanity. Thus human dignity derives from its exercise, and we show proper respect for that dignity by *both* granting people scope to exercise their judgment *and* holding them responsible for the judgments they make.

So human beings are *autonomous moral agents*. But when we choose, the faculty we employ is the other main distinctive feature of human moral agency, namely, *independent judgment.* Judgment is the faculty or power we have to know what the right thing to do is. Everything from morality to etiquette to social interaction to eating— from large matters to small—requires people to exercise their judgment. Should you give more money to Catholic Charities or use that money to send your child to a private school? How long should you hold the door open for a person coming behind you? You thought that joke was funny, but is it appropriate to laugh at it now? Should you be frank and honest now or protect your friend's feelings? Is this investment too risky? Is this an appropriate activity for a person like me? And on and on. We make judgments about what we should do, we pass judgment on others' behavior and activities, we pass judgment on ourselves—all day, every day.

But we do not only judge; we are also *accountable.* Good judgment develops not from merely making decisions, but also from experiencing the relevant feedback from one's decisions. In fact, without the experiencing of feedback, judgment cannot properly develop. Suppose you decide to learn to play the piano. At your first lesson, your teacher outfits you with a set of headphones that prevents you from hearing any sound you make on the piano, and she does not tell you whether you hit a correct or incorrect note, whether you played well or badly. The reason your teacher gives you for this unorthodox teaching method is that she does not want you to feel bad if you do not play well. It is a generous sentiment, perhaps, but a misguided one since it will prevent you from achieving your goal of learning to play the piano. Piano playing is a complex and difficult task; as anyone who can do it will tell you, it can be accomplished only by (lots and lots of) practice, under correction. You need both. Even if you have great natural potential, without proper feedback you will not develop that ability properly; similarly, if you get feedback, even the very best feedback, but have no opportunity to practice, again you will be unable to learn well. The same is true with any other skill one wishes to develop: riding a bicycle, driving a car in traffic, ballet dancing, speaking a new language, dressing appropriately, telling and laughing at jokes appropriately, learning to write well. These are not like learning the multiplication tables or memorizing when Caesar crossed the Rubicon—cases in which once one knows, one is done. Developing skills requires concerted effort with feedback, and as soon as one stops either practicing or experiencing feedback, one's ability begins to wane.

An especially important aspect of our independent judgment relates to the authority to say "no" that we discussed a moment ago. Saying "no" is often quite difficult. Others can be persuasive, as anyone who has encountered pushy salesmen, authoritarian officers of the public, bullies, or any other of many human types who use intimidation to get others to do what they want. But saying "no" is also a skill, and thus it, too, must be practiced to be vigorous. Because saying "no" is so crucial to establishing the boundaries of our selves, and to maintaining the integrity of our moral agency, it is especially important in this case to remind ourselves and others that we do, in fact, possess this skill, and that we should exercise it liberally. The proper response to bullies or others attempting to intimidate us is often not to call on others to intervene: it is simply to say, in an unequivocal and decisive way, "no." No, you may not do that; no, I will not go with you; no, I will not accept those terms; no, I will not answer your questions; no, I will not accept your offer. Few acts more clearly, and beautifully, demonstrate the power of human moral agency than standing up and saying "no."

This leads to another important moral category in which moral agency issues, namely *respect*. Being a moral agent means being autonomous, as well as possessing and using judgment. If we do not allow people to make choices, or if we do not allow people's independent judgment to determine their actions, or both, then we limit the extent to which they can be full moral agents. That means we depreciate their *dignity*. In addition, if we do not allow people to receive the proper feedback from their decisions, then we do not *respect* their independent judgment. By "proper feedback" here I do not mean a moral category. I mean instead the feedback that is fitting or appropriate given the actual consequences of their decisions. If I go outside in the cold without proper clothing, I may get frostbite, which is the "proper" feedback from the actual consequences of my behavior. If you tell an inappropriate joke, you might not get invited to the dinner party next time; that is again the "proper" feedback from the actual consequences—in this case, the real disapproval people felt—of your behavior. By contrast, if I tell my student that her paper is brilliant when in fact it is not, then that is "improper" feedback because it does not reflect reality, namely, the negative judgment I actually formed. If a dictator commands an audience to applaud his son's piano recital regardless of his actual performance, then the feedback the son receives does not reflect reality and is hence "improper." When we allow the actual consequences to be brought to bear, either "naturally" or through human agency, on the person whose decisions or actions gave rise to the consequences, then, whatever else we are doing, we are aiding in the proper development of that person's judgment and we *respect* their moral agency. When we do not, we do not.

These two features of our moral personalities—autonomy and judgment—thus go together, and they are united by the notions of dignity and hence respect. Possession of autonomous moral agency grants one a moral dignity, and possession and use of judgment lead to decisions that others are morally bound to respect. Recognizing people as moral agents, therefore, means *both* allowing them the freedom to make decisions for themselves *and* allowing them to experience the consequences, good or bad, of those decisions. It presumes that people are accountable and thus have reasons for doing what they do, even if those reasons are unknown or unpersuasive to us. The requirement is not that they do what we would have done, but, rather, that we presume they are capable of giving reasons for what they did, of giving an account of themselves that both they and we would understand as being reasons that support or inform their actions.[7] By contrast, if we were instead to intervene, whether to stop them from acting or to insulate them from the consequences of their actions, then we treat them as if they were not full moral agents. The injunction not to intervene is not absolute, since there are cases in which good judgment of local facts might justify intervening after all. The principle is rather a default from which departures must be specially justified, and a general guide to orient our thinking about future cases.

But what about cases when I take reasonable precautions, but because of bad luck I suffer from negative consequences nonetheless? As Elizabeth Anderson argues, being told that experiencing the consequences of one's choices is a requirement of one's moral agency

---

[7] See Darwall 2009: esp. chaps. 4–6.

"is small comfort to the person who led a cautious and prudent life, but still fell victim to extremely bad option luck" (1999: 299).[8] Fair enough. But two considerations soften the edge of her objection. First, the scenario Anderson has in mind can be identified as such only locally. As Anderson recognizes, it is not the case that all people who have their plans go awry could not, or should not, have anticipated the likely results. The fact that a person's plans went awry does not by itself suffice to tell us whether she should have acted otherwise; thus it does not tell us whether she bears some responsibility for what transpired (or how much responsibility she bears), and thus it does not tell us whether we or anyone else owe her any help. Second, even conceding the problems we have discussed with obtainment of the relevant knowledge about any particular case, it is still true that sometimes people simply need our help. In those cases, we should give our help—period. It may be that no particular political-economic policy is indicated, but that does absolve us from the duty to use our judgment to assess the situation ourselves and lend what help we reasonably can. The only way to determine what any of us is required to do is to deploy competent judgment on our local knowledge of the peculiar facts of the specific case. That is not an infallible prescription, but for all the reasons we have discussed it stands a better chance of achieving what needs to be done than would asking a distant and unfamiliar third party to do its best.

Human Dignity and Preciousness

I believe this to be the most compelling conception of human moral agency for several reasons: it gives us a way to understand the specialness, even preciousness, of each human being; it gives us reason to respect each human being, along with the decisions, valuations, and actions each makes or undertakes; it gives us reason to resist conferring any special privileged status on one group of people while denying it to another; and it gives clear parameters and lines of direction for helping others when we should. The equal mutual respect this

---

[8] The terminology "option luck" refers to those cases in which I experience consequences that are a result of a choice I freely made (they were my "option") but whose result was not what I anticipated owing to factors outside my control ("luck").

conception of moral agency demands also gives us reason to *trust* one another, as Adam Smith saw:

Frankness and openness conciliate confidence. We trust the man who seems willing to trust us. We see clearly, we think, the road by which he means to conduct us, and we abandon ourselves with pleasure to his guidance and direction. Reserve and concealment, on the contrary, call forth diffidence. We are afraid to follow the man who is going we do not know where. The great pleasure of conversation and society, besides, arises from a certain correspondence of sentiments and opinions, from a certain harmony of minds, which like so many musical instruments coincide and keep time with one another. But this most delightful harmony cannot be obtained unless there is a free communication of sentiments and opinions. (TMS, 337)

The mutual respect this conception of equal moral agency requires does not mean that we must all agree with one another, much less that we refrain from judging one another. Indeed, as Smith argued, it is the precisely the process of mutual judging, along with sharing of our judgments—this is the action/feedback dynamic—that allows us to develop moral sensibilities at all. To take a favorite example of Smith's: How could we possibly know what an appropriate or inappropriate joke to tell is, without having experience with joke telling and its feedback?[9] There is no a priori way to know whether a joke is appropriate, whether others will laugh at a joke, or how long one should laugh at another's joke without having had previous experience on which to draw. Similarly for most, perhaps even all, other rules of social interaction.

Social "harmony," writes Smith, is produced by "free communication of sentiments and opinions" because that allows standards to emerge from the patterns of approval and disapproval we observe both in our own and in others' conduct and judging. The rules of acceptable, or "proper," behavior are a result, then, of human interaction—but, on Smith's account, not just any human interaction. It must, in fact, have two characteristics: it must be "free," and it must include the expression of "opinion" or judgment. In other words, it must respect individual human autonomy and it must also hold people accountable. Smith's argument in *The Theory of Moral Sentiments* is that the process

[9] Smith mentions the example some five times in the first ten pages of his *Theory of Moral Sentiments*.

he describes by which people (1) develop moral sentiments at all, when they had none as infants, and (2) come to share these moral sentiments with others can be understood on the model of a *market*.[10] Similar to prices in economic markets, the sentiments in moral markets arise from human interaction, they are sensitive to local knowledge, and they arise largely unintentionally as people look for ways to achieve their goals in cooperation with one another. Because of the way free economic markets work, we can predict that they will tend to lead to increasingly efficient allocations of scarce resources, thus to increasing production of goods and services, and thus to increasing standards of living.[11] Analogously, we can expect that free *moral* markets will lead to standards of morality and etiquette that will tend to serve people's needs for peaceful and productive cooperation with one another. The fit will not be perfect, of course—no human institution or set of human institutions ever is—but because of its relative ability to exploit local knowledge and its dependence on people's actual desires and values, we can expect it to be better than ahistorical a priori models, especially at adapting to changing circumstances.

The key to whatever success it can achieve, however, is captured in that final sentence: "But this most delightful harmony cannot be obtained unless there is a free communication of sentiments and opinions." "Free" here means no third-party interpositions. No one outside of the people communicating their sentiments prevents them from doing so; or, at least, such interposition is minimized to the extent possible. Moreover, there must be consequences. No special privileges or protections can be allowed: to the extent that we allow such privileges or protections, we compromise the efficiency and integrity of the process. If you behave well, you receive approval; if you behave badly, you receive disapproval. Because, as Smith believes, we all deeply desire what he calls "mutual sympathy of sentiments"—that is, seeing our own sentiments approved in others—we are greatly pleased when we receive approval and greatly displeased when we become conscious of disapproval. Our principles of morality, then, according to Smith, arise on the basis of the interactions we have with one another and the judgments we give and receive of our own and others' conduct. If we wish

---

[10] I elaborate on this process in Otteson 2002.
[11] See McCloskey 2007: esp. "Apology."

those principles to be good ones—that is, conducive to people's actual goals—then this process must be undertaken *freely*, with as few third-party restrictions on what people may judge, how they may judge it, and how they may communicate their judgments, as possible; and they must face the judgment they cause, whether positive or negative.

Smith's explanation of human moral judgment making is thus consistent with the general conception of human moral agency I have urged. Its two parts of freedom and feedback parallel the twin aspects of the moral agency I described: autonomy and judgment. In both cases, recognizing others as equal moral agents requires granting them the same freedom we ourselves wish to enjoy to judge, decide, and behave according to our own lights. At the same time, however, it requires that we hold others, and we allow others to hold us, accountable and therefore responsible for our judgments, decisions, and behaviors. When we do so, a spontaneous system of moral sentiments arises that reflects the operation of equal human agency within a context of mutual respect.

Justice

For Smith, justice is "a negative virtue," meaning that it is comprised of *don'ts*, not *dos*. Specifically, it requires not molesting others, not stealing or trespassing on others' property, and not violating the agreements one has made voluntarily. In Smith's words:

The most sacred laws of justice, therefore, those whose violation seems to call loudest for vengeance and punishment, are the laws which guard the life and person of our neighbor; the next are those which guard his property and possessions; and the last of all come those which guard what are called his personal rights, or what is due to him from the promises of others. (TMS, 84)

Because justice is "negative," Smith argues, "[w]e may often fulfil all the rules of justice by sitting still and doing nothing" (TMS, 82). This is in contrast to all the "beneficent" virtues, which require positive action to fulfil. How can we tell the difference between the two? Smith suggests that "the violation of justice is *injury*: it does *real and positive hurt* to some particular persons, from motives which are naturally disapproved of" (TMS, 79; my emphases); by contrast, "the mere want of beneficence tends to do no real positive evil" (TMS, 78). If I commit an injustice toward you, then I have done you "real positive evil," which means I have made you worse off than you were before; that justifies punishment after the fact, and also institutions to prevent before the fact. On the other hand, if I fail to act with proper beneficence toward you, then I may have disappointed you if you were expecting me to do something I did not, but I have not left you worse off than you were before. Although disappointment is regrettable, it nevertheless does not rise to the level of *injury*. If you thought I was going to hire you, and then I did not, you may well be disappointed; unless I had made you some kind of promise, however, or was otherwise positively obligated toward you, you had no right to that job, and so your disappointment does not constitute an injury and thus does not rise to the level of injustice. If you did me a favor, you may reasonably expect that I will return the favor when the proper opportunity arises; if I do not, you may be disappointed, and disinterested observers might also disapprove of my ingratitude. But if we had no contract or other positive agreement, you are not *entitled* to a favor from me, even if your expectation was reasonable.

As we saw in Chapter 3, Smith argues that these rules of justice are relatively few, easy to comprehend, and universally applicable; the rules of beneficence so conceived are, by contrast, open-ended, indefinite, and context specific. Moreover, while no society—not even a society of "robbers and murderers" (TMS, 86)—could survive without respecting the rules of justice with each other, a society could survive if its members respected the rules of justice but ignored the virtues of beneficence: "Beneficence, therefore, is less essential to the existence of society than justice. Society may subsist, though not in the most comfortable state, without beneficence; but the prevalence of injustice must utterly destroy it" (TMS, 86). This means that justice has priority over beneficence, and it also means for Smith that the state is authorized to protect justice. Indeed, protecting this conception of justice becomes for Smith the central purpose of the state, and for two main reasons. First, no one, regardless of what her individual schedule of value is or what her goals and aspirations in life are, can hope for success in life unless she lives in a society in which these simple rules of justice are protected and respected.[12] Second, because the rules of justice are both simple and few, protecting them is something the state can do—whereas, by contrast, owing to the open-endedness and the

[12] For a more recent statement of a similar argument, see Epstein 1995.

context specificity of proper beneficence, the state is incompetent to enforce it. Centralized third parties are not in a position to acquire the relevant local knowledge required to know whether any given person is acting with proper generosity or charity toward another, and any list of rules they might devise would be insensitive to precisely the local details that determine proper behavior in such cases.

The Smithian government, then, is not laissez-faire: it is, in fact, robust in its protection of justice. On the other hand, the scope of its legitimate authority is limited to protecting justice.[13] In this it is respecting the conception of moral agency we have described. No one can exercise his moral agency if he does not live in a society in which justice is protected; justice is "the foundation which supports the building" of society, "the main pillar that upholds the whole edifice" without which society "must in a moment crumble into atoms" (TMS, 86). Respecting the autonomy of moral agency therefore authorizes society to require, even coercively, its citizens to respect the rules of justice. But a society of moral equals must also respect its citizens' independent judgment, which they employ in determining and acting on their obligations of beneficence. If society were to undertake to coerce its citizens to fulfill these positive obligations, it could do so only by robbing people of the opportunity to judge what their own and others' proper obligations are and to provide the relevant appropriate feedback both to their own and to others' behaviors. The government that respects both autonomy and independent judgment, then, is the one that protects Smithian justice and simultaneously refrains from taking any coercive or restrictive or corrective measures regarding beneficence.

That, I suggest, is the decentralist, or capitalist, government. Its features include institutions required for, as Smith puts it, "an exact administration of justice" (TMS, 217), which will include a military to defend against foreign aggression, police to protect against domestic aggression, and an impartial court system to adjudicate disputes. Its features do not include institutions for administering friendship,

---

[13] Smith allows for the possibility that the government should also provide "certain publick works" (WN, 687–8). But his prerequisites for what would qualify—(1) that it would benefit everyone *and* (2) that it is unable to be provided by private enterprise—would seem to limit significantly the possible candidates for governmental provision. For discussion, see Fleischacker (Princeton, NJ: Princeton University Press, forthcoming in 2015) and Otteson (Princeton, NJ: Princeton University Press, forthcoming in 2015).

generosity, magnanimity, or charity, for changing or altering people's schedules of values, or for inducing people to behave with their time, talent, and treasure in ways that others prefer. As long as one does not violate justice, the state leaves one free to lead one's life as one sees fit, to discover ways to cooperate with others for mutual advantage, and to own and author the course of one's life with the dignity and responsibility that human moral agency requires.

Capitalist Justice and Social(ist) Justice

This is a rather thin conception of justice: do not kill, steal from, or defraud others. Smith's position is that beneficence is indeed frequently morally required, but since it is positive, not negative, it is not part of *justice* and not justifiable for state or other third-party coercion. The Smithian government instead places positive obligations toward others on the relevant individuals themselves, and it leaves to those relevant individuals the responsibility of holding people accountable for their actions. The obligation to help others becomes your obligation and mine, and you and I are required to personally take action to fulfill those obligations. No state action, no corporate action, no collective action that distributes the costs of the relevant obligations across many people can discharge my obligation, because such communal activity transfers the burden of my obligation to others. Insofar as you or others bear the cost of my obligations, to that same extent I am not fulfilling them, and I can take no moral credit by having others fulfill my obligations. Indeed, if the government is undertaking to relieve me of my obligations of beneficence with my blessing, then I, in fact, deserve moral blame—because the only way the government can do so is by taking from others, at least some of whom must necessarily be unwilling (otherwise it would be voluntary charity). But that would be to violate the moral agency of those dissenting others, because it substitutes my will, or the will of the majority of us who win the political day, for theirs.

On this account, however, one might wonder what exactly the difference is between a government engaging in charitable activities on my behalf, on the one hand, and a private charitable organization engaging in similar activities on my behalf, on the other hand. Are they not both examples of others executing my obligation for me? The difference is that in the case of private charitable activity, my money (or my time, energies, and so on) are (1) voluntarily donated with (2) these specific purposes in mind. Governments, by contrast, engage in numerous activities—only a small proportion of them counting as charitable and of those, only a yet smaller proportion serving charitable purposes any one of us would voluntarily support. I cannot, in fact, have any idea what any of the money I myself pay to the government through taxes actually funds. Thus, my money supporting government activity fails criterion (2) above. More importantly, it also fails criterion (1): I must pay taxes whether I wish to or not, and any input I might fancy I have in the setting of tax rates or the spending of tax proceeds—say, because I vote for (or possibly against!) three of the 535 members of congress or for (or against) the president—is so far from having any dispositive effect that it cannot reasonably be said to be anything but nonvoluntary. And, of course, no one votes for (or against) any of the hundreds of thousands of federal agents who set, apply, or administer tax rules. I can say "no" to any private charity that solicits my donation, which means that my obligations to help others remain my obligations, and the responsibility for my helping or not when I should remains on me. I cannot say "no" to the Internal Revenue Service. Not even "no, thank you."

A Smithian conception of justice fails, however, to rectify, or even address, material inequality. It does presume a formal equality insofar as it holds all people equally subject to its conception of justice, but it would not deem material inequality per se as injustice. It would also run afoul a luck-egalitarian conception of justice that requires inequalities due to things other than deliberate choice (properly defined) to be reduced to the extent possible or feasible. A common objection to Smithian justice can be adapted from Peter Singer's argument that the existence of starving people in the world imposes obligations on those of us who are far from starving. According to Singer: (1) starvation is very bad; (2) if you can prevent something very bad from happening, without sacrificing anything nearly as important, you should do so; (3) by donating to hunger relief agencies, you prevent something very bad from happening without sacrificing anything nearly as important; therefore (4), you should donate to hunger relief agencies (Singer 2009). Singer's position presumes that a Smithian distinction between "negative" inaction and "positive" action does not hold, or at least is not decisive in determining moral culpability or obligation. For Singer, I am equally morally blameworthy whether I fail to help you when I could or deliberately make your situation worse. As he puts it, there is no moral difference between *killing* and *letting die*.

This has important policy implications. The Smithian maintains the distinction between justice and beneficence, and argues that the state can be plausibly charged with defending the former but not the latter. This leaves beneficence to private persons or groups, and absolves the state from responsibility for it. Singer denies such a distinction, believing instead that if it is wrong not to give money to hunger relief agencies, then there is no reason in principle why the state should not enact policy consistent with that moral obligation. Indeed, for Singer, justice *requires* state action when private initiative is not sufficiently forthcoming.

One might consider this objection to Smith's conception of justice under the heading of "social justice" because it relies on a conception of justice that requires us to take positive action to remedy at least some kinds of, as Singer puts it, things that are "very bad." Although "social justice" is defined differently by different people, one common feature is what I call the Incorporation Doctrine, or the incorporation into negative justice of at least some positive moral obligations—typically a positive requirement to help the poor, the hungry, the disenfranchised, the powerless, perhaps the undeservedly unlucky. The social justice argument suggests that the Smithian conception of justice, including the limitations it places on justified state action, is too narrow because it disallows too many important vehicles for the alleviation of misery and suffering, it fails to acknowledge any corporate obligation toward those less fortunate, and it seems unduly to privilege individual freedom over, for example, welfare or equality.

A Smithian would marshal three principal arguments in defense of this negative conception of justice.

First Argument: Knowledge. The first is based on Smith's Local Knowledge Argument (LKA): given that everyone has unique knowledge of her own "local" situation, including her goals, desires, and opportunities, each individual is typically therefore the person best positioned to make decisions about what courses of action she should take to achieve her goals. As we saw in Chapter 2, that does not mean that people are infallible in judging their own situations, but rather that individuals have a better chance of knowing how best to use their own resources and what courses of actions to take to achieve their own goals than do third parties because they are more likely to possess the knowledge (and motivation) required to make such determinations reliably.

The LKA applies here in the following way: because of the relative straightforwardness of "negative" justice, and the relative ease of discovering and punishing violations of it, the state's centralized apparatuses are competent to administrate it. By contrast, because of the open-endedness and local-context specificity of beneficence, the state's centralized apparatuses are incompetent to administrate it. Thus incorporating beneficence into justice overextends the state's competence and compromises what seems to be the only effective means there are to effect proper beneficence, namely localized and decentralized initiative.

Second Argument: Trust. Market-based societies generate a lot of material prosperity, yet they seem to require a background ethic that may not be produced by the market order itself. This ethic includes things like keeping one's word, honest dealing, industriousness, and so on—what Deirdre McCloskey calls the "bourgeois virtues" (McCloskey 2007). But there is another requirement that, while not a virtue, is still crucially important: trust.

Numerous studies have shown the high correlation between a country's prosperity and the relative level of background implicit trust its citizens have for one another: the higher their trust, the more prosperity; the lower the trust, the less prosperity.[14] One can see why: if people do not trust one another to keep their promises and not to steal even if confronted with what Robert Frank calls "golden opportunities" (Frank 1988: 73), then there is incentive not to enter into cooperative agreements—thereby negatively affecting the production of prosperity. The question is: How do we create, and then maintain, a high-trust society? I do not believe anyone has quite figured that out yet,[15] but

[14] See Rose (2011) for a compilation and discussion. I draw here on Rose's analysis.
[15] Deirdre McCloskey has told me that she believes she has figured it out and will explain it in forthcoming editions of her four-part series of books under the general title "The Bourgeois Era." See also Zak 2012.

what we can demonstrate is what one principal *threat* to trust is: the Incorporation Doctrine of Singerian "social" justice.

Singerian justice requires that we ask ourselves, when contemplating action, what the likely consequences might be, and then we act on whatever it seems would lead to the best overall consequences.[16] It requires us, that is, to incorporate some aspects of beneficence into our deliberations about justice, and doing so may lead us in specific situations to believe we should violate Smithian negative justice. The Singerian position implies that there are no specific actions or rules that must always be followed or avoided. Instead, we determine, on a case-by-case basis, what potential action we might take that we judge would lead to increasing utility (or perhaps to achieving social justice); that judgment then determines what we do. Thus in my associations with you, although my default might be to keep my promise to you, I nevertheless deliberate about what I should do *this* time, and I will do so every time I make a promise to you; similarly, I will deliberate about whether I should steal or not every time I am faced with an opportunity to do so; and so on. You will do the same.

A Golden Opportunity presents itself when one can benefit from violating one of the Smithian rules of justice but yet believes one will not get caught. But that is only half of the dynamic, namely, the part regarding one's own utility; the other half is that we can easily imagine scenarios where either there is no discernible victim (so no one whose interests we did not equally consider) or the harm is so small as to be effectively zero (so we cannot identify anyone who is injured). Suppose I have the opportunity to take a ream of paper from my company's supply closet and use it at home for personal use. I clearly benefit, but who is harmed? Consider: there is no identifiable victim (who would it be?), and the cost to the company is so small relative to its overall budget that it might literally be unable to reckon or even detect the loss. Or consider inflating the damage to one's car after an accident so that the insurance company pays for an unrelated repair as well: I benefit, and so does the auto body shop, but whom does that deception injure, and how could the company even detect my particular instance of such a small cost—$500, say—in its multibillion-dollar budget? Such

---

[16] We do not need to spend any time on defining "best": assume it means something uncontroversial, like reducing the most misery, or perhaps Rawls's maximin principle of redounding most to the benefit of the least advantaged in society.

Golden Opportunities confront us all the time. If we are Singerian utilitarians, then we should exploit them, meaning we should violate the relevant rule of Smithian justice because the correct rule will allow exceptions in cases when some clearly benefit (the auto body shop, say) but no one is clearly injured.[17]

Put aside for the moment whether the intent or the ultimate aim of the actions I take as a result of these deliberations is good or beneficial. Consider instead merely the effects of the *uncertainty* that is generated when you do not know whether I will follow the rules of Smithian justice no matter what. Perhaps you have run your own consequentialist calculation and determined that, all things considered, I should keep my word and not steal, and this initially inclines you to trust and hence cooperate with me. But then you realize that you cannot know whether my own calculations will run the same way—and nothing I can tell you will give you dispositive evidence one way or another, because my statements, too, will be subject to my calculations. Thus, you cannot confidently predict what I will do: you cannot know whether I will steal, defraud, or renege *this* time. But since you do know that theft, fraud, or default would leave you worse off, this uncertainty generates a disincentive for you to cooperate with me. Thus, whatever gains we might have achieved from our associations with one another are forgone. As this process is repeated across society—meaning, if more and more people employ a Singerian ethic to guide their actions—more and more potentially mutually beneficial gains are forgone, leading to real, if unseen, losses.[18]

By contrast, if the people in a society have a background ethic that includes following Smithian rules of justice no matter what, then cooperation is encouraged. Because Smithian justice rules out the main

---

[17] I think the reasoning here applies to the standard accounts of both rule- and act-utilitarianism, although making that case is beyond the scope of the argument here.

[18] Smith: "The moment he thinks of departing from the most staunch and positive adherence to what those inviolable precepts [of justice] prescribe to him, he is no longer to be trusted, and no man can say what degree of guilt he may not arrive at. The thief imagines he does no evil, when he steals from the rich, what he supposes they may easily want, and what possibly they may never know has been stolen from them. The adulterer imagines he does no evil, when he corrupts the wife of his friend, provided he covers his intrigue from the suspicion of the husband, and does not disturb the peace of his family. When once we begin to give way to such refinements, there is no enormity so gross of which we may not be capable" (TMS, 175).

threats to mutually beneficial cooperation—namely assault, theft, and fraud—it is relatively easy to predict what it will require and thus, relatively easy to rely on. It can thus conciliate the trust in society that is necessary for generating prosperous cooperation.

Third Argument: Failure to Launch. The final argument a Smithian would marshal in defense of Smith's thin conception of justice is this: being *undeservedly unlucky* and suffering *reasonable disappointment* do not, even when combined, necessarily justify rectification.

Suppose Jack and Jill have been dating for some time. They are in love, and Jack is preparing to ask Jill to marry him. His expectation is that she will say "yes," and Jill, for her part, not only expects Jack to ask but also plans on accepting. Right before Jack asks Jill to marry him, however, Jill meets Joe. Jill and Joe fall for one another instantly. Joe asks Jill to marry him—and she says "yes." They decide to elope. Jack, of course, is devastated. He has invested a lot of time, energy, and emotion into his relationship with Jill, and he developed reasonable expectations that their relationship would continue indefinitely into the future. His deep disappointment at this unforeseen, and obviously unlucky, change of fortune is both understandable and lamentable. We feel for Jack (no doubt Jill does, too). But: Should we do something about it? What would we do?—Prevent Jill from marrying Joe? Prevent people like Joe from meeting or proposing to people like Jill? Should we allow Jack to sue for damages or demand compensation? The answer to all these is no. Jack's disappointment at this undeserved bad luck is entirely reasonable. But he has no *right* to Jill. He has no right to Jill's affections or to her company. He also has no right to prevent Joe from associating with her if he and she so choose, and he has no right to punish either of them, or anyone else, if they choose differently from what he wishes they would. Thus neither *undeserved bad luck* nor *justified disappointment* by themselves—even both of them together—constitute injustice or warrant correction.

The same logic applies to firms that go out of business in commercial economies. Suppose I have been frequenting Coffee Shop A for some time, and the owner has come to expect that I will continue to do so; indeed, I expect I will continue to do so. Then I hear of Coffee Shop B, and I am surprised to discover that I like its offerings better.

I therefore stop going to Coffee Shop A. Does its owner have any cause against me, or against the owner of Coffee Shop B? No, and for the same reasons Jack has none against Jill or Joe. If enough people turn out to prefer Coffee Shop B so that Coffee Shop A can no longer remain in operation, then Coffee Shop A still has no claim to press: customers are entitled to patronize whatever coffee shop they wish, and because the owner of Coffee Shop A has no right to or justified claim on them, the owner also has no right to their money to support her business. The disappointment that the owner of Coffee Shop A suffers is real, but it generates no justifiable limitation on others' choices or on others' behaviors. We can lament the disappointment, we can provide our own help to Coffee Shop A's owner or employees, and we can try to convince people to patronize Coffee Shop A instead of Coffee Shop B. But we may not force people to patronize Coffee Shop A who do not wish to, and we have no more justification in imposing costs on people who choose not to patronize Coffee Shop A than Jack does in imposing costs on people who choose not to marry him.

Smithian justice denies that one may seek reparation or compensation unless one was done "real and positive hurt" in one's person, property, or expectations generated by voluntary promises; since none of those obtain in these cases, neither Jack nor the owner of Coffee Shop A can claim injustice and thus neither of them can justifiably call on state or other third-party coercive intervention. To claim otherwise would entail the disregarding, and disrespecting, of the equal moral agency of others, which would itself generate injustice and is thus morally disallowed. By contrast, the social justice position holds that justice can require compensation either because of (undeserved) bad luck or because your legitimate expectations were not fulfilled—and especially if both those obtain. But these examples indicate that the Smithian conception is more plausible. Bad luck and real disappointment are regrettable, and in specific circumstances they may require us to offer help, but they do not by themselves constitute injustice because we must respect other people's moral agency, too.

Conclusion

Despite the common opinion to the contrary, economic decisions are not amoral. On the contrary, they are made only in virtue of people's values, including their moral values. Allowing people to make their own economic decisions is reflective, and even constitutive, of the autonomy they possess as moral agents. Moreover, holding them responsible for the consequences of their decisions not only respects them as accountable beings, but it also gives them the feedback they need to develop their independent judgment. It is in respecting others' autonomy and judgment that we recognize their dignity as equal moral agents. Finally, the government limited to protecting "negative" justice is consistent with this conception of equal moral agency, as is leaving the positive obligations of beneficence to localized and decentralized individuals and voluntary associations.

7

Respect and Individuality

Introduction

In his recent book *What Money Can't Buy,* Michael Sandel offers a long series of things he believes should not be for sale—prison cell upgrades, access to the car pool lane during rush hour, foreign surrogate mothers to carry one's baby, the right to immigrate to the United States, so-called concierge medicine, holding one's place in line, and so on (2012: Introduction and passim). Another of the things he argues should not be for sale is attendance to papal masses. As he reports, when Pope Benedict XVI made his first visit to the United States in 2008, tickets to the limited-seating event were distributed for free by local dioceses and parishes. Because the demand was so high, however, scalping went on, with tickets selling for hundreds of dollars apiece (ibid.: 37). To justify his objection and motivate centralized restrictions on markets in some goods and services, Sandel makes his own use of the concept of "respect": "Treating religious rituals, or natural wonders, as marketable commodities is a failure of respect. Turning sacred goods into instruments of profit values them in the wrong way" (ibid.).

Socialist Respect

But Sandel has misplaced the proper object of respect. It is not the goods that deserve respect. It is the people. It is people who have dignity as moral agents, not the things that they create or exchange.

Material and inert things have no intrinsic value at all; they have only the value that moral agents grant them. Proper respect should begin, then, with respecting the agents who are making choices. If you ban some of their associations, or if your forbid them from engaging in activities or transactions with which you disagree, then, whatever your goals or intentions, you disrespect *them*.[1]

A similar misplacement of sacredness—and thus, respect—occurs in much socialist-inclined thought. One often finds veneration for abstractions, such as equality or "the poor" (not specific poor people), or for visions of community or human relations unlike what actually obtain. These abstractions can loom so powerfully in one's mind that they overshadow what should be our proper objects of veneration and respect—namely, individual persons. Now, it does not follow from my argument that every choice that people make should be approved or venerated. Quite the contrary: respecting others also entails—not just allows, but *entails*—that we address them as rational agents capable of giving and understanding reasons, of being held accountable for their decisions and behaviors, and as capable of deliberately changing or correcting their behavior as a result of changing their minds. Thus if I believe that tickets to attend a papal mass should not be sold for a profit, I should address my concerns to the people selling or buying them, and give them my reasons. Proposing to enact legal prohibitions from afar does not attempt to persuade people or change their minds,

---

[1] One might wonder about historical artifacts or irreplaceable works of art: Should we not protect the Pyramids, for example, even if the local people were to decide to tear them down? Perhaps. The difficulties here, however, go in both directions. On the one hand, if we start making centralized decisions about what things should be protected, even over private owners' or local residents' wishes, then that introduces all the dangers—with hidden costs borne by others, misaligned incentives, lack of local knowledge, and so on—that plague other kinds of centralized decision making. On the other hand, if we adopt a policy of never intervening in local decision making, then we might run the risk of temporary fashion or fads that can permanently destroy great or important works. Because moral agents value things differently, conflicting judgments are inevitable. If my argument here has a policy implication, it would be a default of avoiding taking action to save or protect the inanimate object at the expense of other agents' wishes—because the putative act of saving or protecting inanimate objects means, in fact, valuing some people's schedules of value over others—but allowing for the possibility of exceptions in extraordinary cases. What counts as "extraordinary cases" cannot, however, be determined a priori, and thus must be adjudicated on the basis of localized judgment. The burden of proof would fall on those arguing for third-party intervention. Of course, one way to safeguard the Pyramids is to buy them.

however: it coerces them. Instead of *engaging* their moral agency, that *disregards* it.

Engaging the moral agency of others is a difficult prospect, however, and it often, frustratingly, ends in failure. Respecting the agency of another requires that if we wish him to change his preferences, beliefs, or behaviors, we may attempt, as Mill put it, "remonstrating with him, or reasoning with him, or persuading him, or entreating him" (1997 [1859]: 9). Unfortunately, that is a costly, time-consuming process and its success is highly uncertain. But the ability to coerce does not imply the morality of coercion, and the fact that we find others' preferences to be incorrect or distasteful—even immoral—does not by itself justify coercing them, as long as they are moral agents and are not positively injuring another. We may override the distasteful preferences of our dog, or of our children, because they are not, or are not yet, moral agents. But other adults are moral agents. Hence, they deserve respect. Hence, their preferences, their choices, their behaviors—as well as the consequences of all three—deserve our respect as well.

Socialist Individuality

Socialism sees in capitalism class struggles and class interests, and it sees in its own fulfillment a resolution of those struggles by the elevating of the lower class and the lowering of the higher class so that substantially only one class remains—that of all human beings, united as, in Marx's term, "species beings." The solidarity socialism offers can be achieved when we cease to see ourselves as primarily individuals but rather primarily as members of communities. Only then will we truly incorporate ourselves into a joint project and find fulfillment in a joint destiny.

This is the ultimate promise of socialism—but also its fatal error. Human beings are members of social classes only metaphorically, not literally. Unlike the members of a football team, say, or the Elks Club, who deliberately join a designed organization for a specific and specified purpose, society consists of human beings who, qua human beings, are discrete moral agents with separate and discrete consciousnesses possessing unique reservoirs of knowledge and experience and unique schedules of preferences and values. There is no sense other than abstract and accidental that my interests are the same as those of other members of my socioeconomic class but distinct from those of members of other socioeconomic classes. We may all want more money, improved conditions, more success, higher status, and so on, but put that way, the alleged similarities are general and give no substantive guidance. What should I do to get more money? What should you do? What counts as bettering my condition? What counts as bettering yours? What counts for me as having higher status? What counts for you? And so on. These things, for better or worse, are unique to each of us as individuals, and, although conceiving of us as interchangeable members of various social classes makes it easier for us to comprehend a complex and diverse world, it remains a metaphorical or nominal categorization.

I argue that it has, in fact, been one of the great triumphs of human civilization to conceive of human beings not as members of classes but as individual and unique centers of moral agency. It is that which has enabled the moral principle that each of us possesses a unique dignity that demands respect. That single, simple insight—individual dignity demanding respect—is what has enabled us to condemn humanity's formerly ubiquitous slavery, to condemn genocide and ethnic cleansing, and to work out and endorse a notion of universal human rights. We should not underestimate the transformative and epochal significance of that, nor the dangers attendant on weakening our commitment to it.

An Inspiring Individual: John Lilburne

Consider as an example John Lilburne. Free-Born John, as he was called, was born in Greenwich, England in 1614 or 1615 to a family of low-level gentry, and he was an agitator and troublemaker almost from the beginning. In 1630 he began an apprenticeship to a Puritan cloth merchant in London, and shortly thereafter he joined the radical opposition to Charles I. In 1637, at the tender age of twenty-two, he smuggled from Holland outlawed copies John Bastwick's account of the punishments he had suffered for denouncing Catholicism. When one of Lilburne's accomplices betrayed him to the Archbishop's agents, Lilburne was arrested and tried before the ghastly Star Chamber, a body Lilburne detested and whose existence he protested. When Lilburne was brought to the bar before its judges, however, he *refused to bow.* He also refused to take the customary oath pledging to answer all interrogatories. Lilburne explained that as a free-born Englishman, he was, as he put it, the "peere and equall" of both the bishops and the Star Chamber's judges; there was therefore no reason for him to show the deference they demanded. For this shocking snub to the authority of the Chamber, he was fined, publicly whipped and pilloried, and finally imprisoned, receiving over time increasingly harsh punishment because he refused to stop denouncing the presumed authority of the bishops. Lilburne remained in prison until he was finally liberated by the Long Parliament in 1640 after a speech on his behalf by Cromwell (a man who himself would one day imprison Lilburne).

Thereafter, Lilburne became the most famous—or infamous—leader of the Levellers, a group of political agitators seeking extension of the franchise and other democratic rights. They were called "Levellers" not because they sought to level all property holdings—that was the position of a contemporaneous group called the Diggers. The Levellers were called "Levellers" instead because they sought to equalize the privileges and rights of citizens: no one was by nature or by God entitled to less authority over his own life than anyone else, and no one was justified in asserting authority over anyone else without the latter's willing consent.

Lilburne was tireless and fearless. Even as he was put in the stocks, he issued one pamphlet and speech after another denouncing the presumed authority of the bishops, of the Star Chamber, of Parliament, and then even of Cromwell. He was again arrested, and he spent most of August 1645–August 1647 in prison. But Lilburne was unbowed.

On May 1, 1649, while imprisoned yet again, he published a pamphlet arguing that people had a right to their private consciences by birth, not by pleasure of government; furthermore, that the authority of each individual's conscience for himself was equal to that of everyone else; that therefore a person's religious beliefs were only his own business; and that therefore no one was entitled to any answers about others' beliefs.

Lilburne's message and example resonated. On May 2, 1649, some of the troops under Cromwell refused to follow Cromwell's orders to march on the Levellers. This defiance inspired mutiny of further troops, until by May 14th, some 1,200 men stopped taking orders from Cromwell, demanding instead the release of Lilburne. This was the last straw for Cromwell. Just after midnight on May 14th, Cromwell and a contingent of men still loyal to him surprised and crushed what remained of the army sympathetic to the Levellers, effectively putting an end to the Levellers as an organized political movement.

Lilburne was then arrested and tried for treason. He defended himself and argued to the jury, in defiance of the explicit instructions of the judge, that, as the judge's peers and equals, the members of the jury were empowered to judge not only the facts but also the law itself. To Cromwell's consternation, he was acquitted—and promptly returned to denouncing Cromwell's increasing imperiousness. Cromwell was so infuriated that in 1653 he re-arrested him and had him tried for treason again. Again Lilburne defended himself, and again he was acquitted. This second acquittal even led to a large popular demonstration in support of Lilburne, symbolized by thousands of sympathizers wearing the Levellers' characteristic sea-green ribbons on hats and clothing. This sufficiently worried Cromwell that he decided to keep Lilburne in prison despite the acquittals. Lilburne remained in prison until 1655, when he converted to the Quaker faith and apparently, finally, foreswore his aggressive, confrontational ways. In 1657, with his health failing, he was granted parole to visit his wife, Elizabeth. Exhausted from years of imprisonment and torture, he died in her arms at the age of forty-three.

Lilburne was no philosopher, but his agitations formed a surprisingly coherent philosophy of individualism, from which he derived several specific political policies. These included the rights to be free of arbitrary seizures, to a trial by a jury of one's peers, and to face one's accusers in open court. He also called for the extension of the franchise to all the freeborn men of England; he advocated free trade and private property; and he called for an abolition of legal economic privileges like state-enforced monopolies. He denounced the Levant Company's chartered monopoly of trade with the Middle East, arguing that the right to trade with whomever one wished was one of mankind's natural rights. Thus Lilburne was one of the earliest advocates of what would come to be recognized as classical liberalism, defending private property some 50 years before John Locke and free markets almost 150 years before Adam Smith.

When Lilburne had been brought before the Star Chamber in 1637, he stood his ground, asserting his equal right as an individual to the freedoms anyone else enjoyed. In 1641, Lilburne saw the Star Chamber abolished. That was a great *moral* leap forward, elevating the individual—even the low, the mean, the disrespected individuals— to the status of a moral agent equal in dignity to those in the favored classes.

This conception of morality and human personhood spread and eventually gave rise to many of the institutions we today in the West often take for granted. If no one, regardless of class, family, or wealth, had any justified authority over anyone else, then individuals no longer needed to beg leave from their "superiors" to own property, to select lines of work, to trade or exchange or cooperate with others, to worship and associate and they judge fit. Each person's success or failure in life was fundamentally his own responsibility, even if, of course, it necessarily involved relying on willing others. Individuality, diversity, and various inequalities—*except* formal or legal inequality—arose, and with them the unprecedented growth in human accomplishment, material prosperity, longevity, health, and nutrition that we have seen occur in the world in the last two centuries.

Lilburne was obviously not solely responsible for this, but he inspired many others and was emblematic of a changing conception of morality and thus politics.[2] The lesson to draw from the example of Lilburne is that each individual is unique and precious, which issues in a moral imperative of equal respect. The Smithian government that promotes justice for all while at the same time respecting each person's dignity as an equal moral agent is consistent with, even an embodiment of, this moral imperative.

Respect for Persons

It is perhaps for this reason that Immanuel Kant called Smith his "favorite philosopher." Kant concluded that the peer-to-peer relationship Smith described as exemplified and fostered in market exchanges in fact reflects a mutual respecting of the categorical imperative Kant

---

[2] Lord Acton argued in the nineteenth century that this growing appreciation of the uniqueness, and hence preciousness, of each individual actually traces its roots to Judaism and then Christianity, which conceived of each human being, however low or mighty, as equally a child of God and equally responsible before God. See Acton 1985 (1877): 5–53.

argued should govern all our relationships. Kant offered several formulations of this categorical imperative, but the one he called the "practical imperative" is: "Act in such a way that you treat humanity, whether in your own person or in the person of another, always at the same time as an end and never simply as a means."[3] It is not wrong, according to Kant, to treat others as means to one's own ends. I treat the taxi driver as a means to my end of getting where I want to go; I treat the dentist as a means to my end of good dental hygiene; and so on. The way to treat others as ends in themselves, Kant argues, is thus not by refraining from relying on (willing) others, but by always respecting their right to say "no." The taxi driver, the dentist, and every other person from whom we get our goods and services and with whom we cooperate and exchange always retain the right to decline our offer, and we respect their moral agency as being equal to our own by respecting that right to decline. Aside, then, from whatever material benefits that markets can generate for those lucky enough to enjoy them, their demand that all exchanges be mutually voluntary therefore respects, as Kant saw, the dignity of humanity by satisfying the imperative to always treat others as ends in themselves and never merely as a means.

The Zookeeper Theory of Political Economy

I propose the aforementioned conception of human moral agency as a default, not as a categorical rule. There will be exceptions—cases in which we judge it right to prevent people from acting, or in which we judge it right to protect them from consequences. But those cases must be specially justified, on pain of disrespecting the dignity or the efficacy of moral agency. Mill articulated this position well: "Nobody denies that people should be so taught and trained in youth as to know and benefit by the ascertained results of human experience. But it is the privilege and proper condition of a human being, arrived at the

---

[3] Kant 1981 (1785): 36 (Ak. 429). Kant goes on to distinguish "persons," who have moral agency and must be treated as ends, from "things," which do not have moral agency and may thus be treated merely as means. He then argues that whereas the latter have prices, only the former have dignity. See Kant 1981 (1785): 35–44 (Ak. 428–40). For discussion, see Otteson 2009.

maturity of his faculties, to use and interpret experience in his own way" (1997 [1859]: 55).

The existence of exceptions (like children) or of hard marginal cases do not invalidate the principle. The contrasting position is illustrated by Rainer Maria Rilke's poem, "The Panther"[4]:

> His vision, from the constantly passing bars,
> has grown so weary that it cannot hold
> anything else. It seems to him there are
> a thousand bars; and behind the bars, no world.
>
> As he paces in cramped circles, over and over,
> the movement of his powerful soft strides
> is like a ritual dance around a center
> in which a mighty will stands paralyzed.
>
> Only at times, the curtain of the pupils
> lifts, quietly—. An image enters in,
> rushes down through the tensed, arrested muscles,
> plunges into the heart and is gone.

Rilke's powerful and beautiful panther, once free, now sees the world from behind bars, indeed behind "a thousand bars." As Rilke tells us, the great cat's beauty and power rapidly decline—not because she grows older, but because her spirit is caged and thus defeated. Sooner than one could expect the panther is, though alive, truly dead, because behind the bars she is no longer really a panther. Now the panther's well-intended zookeepers will say that in the wild her life is full of dangers. Nature can be parsimonious and unforgiving, whereas the zookeepers are benevolent and protective. So although behind the bars the panther is not free, she is at least safe and comfortable. They have a point. But the pampered and protected panther is still a *caged* panther—and so not really a panther at all.

Still, since the panther is not a full moral agent, perhaps you are not inclined to value its freedom very highly, and so you are inclined to think that a zookeeper morality is acceptable in this case. Fair enough. Human beings, however, *are* moral agents, and so the zookeeper morality is unacceptable for them. Living free is uncertain and sometimes dangerous, and it does involve both success and failure. But both

---

[4] Available at http://www.poemhunter.com/poem/the-panther/.

one's successes and one's failures are one's own. They belong to you and to me, and it is the true dignity of humanity to fully exercise all its abilities in striving and contending. As Calvin Coolidge said in 1923:

Unless [...] people struggle to help themselves, no one else will or can help them. It is out of such struggle that there comes the strongest evidence of their true independence and nobility, and there is struck off a rough and incomplete economic justice, and there develops a strong and rugged [...] character. It represents a spirit for which there could be no substitute. It justifies the claim that they are worthy to be free.

Human beings are capable of being worthy to be free. Human beings become noble, and, I would even suggest, beautiful, by the vigorous use of their faculties and they become dignified when their lives are their own—when all the forced care and protection of others is taken away—and the bars are thrown open.

This conception of moral agency allows one to be one's own person, and to stand, or fall, on one's own individual initiative, without having to beg for personal favors, without having to grovel at the knees of a king or flatter a lord or satisfy the pleasure of the Regulation Czar. It grants people the freedom to go where their own abilities and initiative—not someone else's mercy or condescension—can take them. Yet with that freedom comes responsibility for one's actions. If you succeed, then you reap the benefits—and no one begrudges you your success because it means you have done well both for yourself and for others. If you fail, however, then you pay the cost and (one hopes) you learn from the experience.

Let me emphasize that last point. Contrary to widespread opinion, failure is not something that public policy should attempt to eliminate. It follows from my argument that failure, and experiencing the bad consequences attendant on having made decisions that led to failure, is an indispensible part of moral agency. You are not fully human if you have never failed and borne the full brunt of the consequences of your failure. As I have argued, this is the only way that people can develop independent judgment: by experiencing the good results and positive feedback of choosing well, and by experiencing the bad results and negative feedback of choosing poorly. The alternative—preventing people from experiencing the consequences of their actions—may lead to less pain in the short run, but it purchases that at the price of robbing people of an integral aspect of their humanity. Developing and exercising judgment is something unique to human beings. If you prevent people from using their judgment by insulating them from the consequences of their decisions, then you degrade them to subhuman status. Like the caged panther, they may be alive, but they are not really living. As Russian writer Yevgeny Zamyatin wrote in 1923:

It is an error to divide people into the living and the dead: there are people who are dead-alive, and people who are alive-alive. The dead-alive also write, walk, speak, act. But they make no mistakes; only machines make no mistakes, and they produce only dead things. The alive-alive are constantly in error, in search, in questions, in torment. (1970 [1923]: 110)

Respect and False Consciousness

The presumption behind capitalist-inclined policy is that, unless there is clear evidence to the contrary, people are making decisions that are appropriate, or at least within the range of propriety, given their unique local knowledge and schedules of value. This assumption is consistent with, and even follows from, respecting people as moral agents possessing both autonomy and judgment. This conception of moral agency entails the noninterventionist policy that characterizes decentralized capitalist policy, quite apart from whatever strictly economic benefits might accrue from such a set of political-economic institutions.

Yet socialist-inclined policy is often justified by an appeal to freedom, on the grounds that people are not truly, genuinely, or authentically free unless they make their decisions from within specific contexts. Those contexts might include everything from having received the proper nutrition and education to being an active participant in the community's deliberations about the common good. By contrast with decisions made under those idealized conditions, the decisions people make in their actual situations often seem inauthentic, even if seemingly freely chosen. So, for example, the fact that women who live in a patriarchal society "freely choose" to occupy certain stereotypical roles does not mean that their choices are truly free: under other circumstances, they might well have chosen otherwise. Similarly, the fact that people who live in a capitalist society of private property "freely choose" to open businesses or compete or seek profit does not by itself prove that those are the choices they would make if they were authentically free—that is, free from the strictures of capitalism.[5] Instead, they might suffer from what some call "false consciousness," which Cressida Heyes defines as "the systematic mystification of the experience of the oppressed by the perspective of the dominant." Heyes continues that "despite the disagreements of many defenders of identity political claims with Marxism and other radical political models, they share the view that individuals' perceptions of their own interests may be systematically distorted and must be somehow freed of their misperceptions by group-based transformation."[6] In other words, what people think is in their interests might not, in fact, be in their interests, and yet, because they (falsely) believe it is, coercion might be required to break them out of their delusions.[7]

Virginia Woolf made a connected argument in her classic 1929 essay, *A Room of One's Own*. Woolf argued that the fact that there had been so few great female authors in the past did not imply that they were inferior to male authors, nor even that they simply preferred to spend their time otherwise. We could draw no such conclusions, she argued, because in the not-so-distant past women were not only banned from participating in many activities and from entering many establishments, but they could not even legally own property. Woolf asked: What would women do once they had these strictures lifted? What heights would female authors reach once they had the freedom to write, and to be writers? More than that, however, Woolf argued that they needed not just this formal freedom of having no artificial obstacles placed in their way, but they needed, in addition, to be free from financial dependencies. For a female author, Woolf wrote, "it is necessary to have five hundred [pounds] a year and a room with a lock on the door if you are to write fiction or poetry" (1929: 105).[8] Indeed, financial independence enabling one not to be beholden to a boss, or even to need a job at all, was so important that Woolf argued that if one had to choose between it and getting the vote: "Of the

[5] See Sunstein 1997: chaps. 1 and 2.
[6] See Heyes 2012.
[7] See Satz 2010, esp. chaps. 4–6 and 8.
[8] Five hundred British pounds in 1929 would be worth approximately £20,000 or $30,000 today. I note that Woolf's requirement of "a lock on the door" seems similar to my argument about the importance of having the authority to say "no."

two—the vote and the money—the money, I own, seemed infinitely more important" (37).

The general question Woolf's essay raises is: What might people have chosen to do if their circumstances had been significantly different? Further, what might people choose now, or in the future, if we altered their circumstances significantly? These questions are difficult to answer, and it must be conceded that the answers we give them are largely speculative. But the problem is that nothing follows from the fact that we would make different decisions under different circumstances. Of course we would: But does that mean that my actual decisions in my actual circumstances were inauthentic? Not necessarily. They might have been, but to know for sure would require intense localized knowledge about a particular case in question. It could not be known from afar. Moreover, even knowing that I might have preferred choices I would have made under other circumstances does not by itself mean I regret or have not genuinely benefitted from my current, actual life. Much more would need to be known about my circumstances before such a conclusion would be licensed.

Cass Sunstein argues that because *all* social institutions—political, economic, cultural—shape preferences in one way or another, the question of what people would choose in the absence of all such influence is a nonstarter. Instead, true "autonomy should refer," Sunstein argues, "to decisions reached with a full and vivid awareness of available opportunities, with reference to relevant information, and without illegitimate or excessive constraints on the process of preference formation" (1997: 19). Sunstein believes that experts, or well-informed and enlightened voters in a properly functioning democracy, thus "might override [people's] existing preferences in order to promote diverse experiences, with a view to providing broad opportunities for the formation of preferences and beliefs and for critical scrutiny of current desires" (ibid., 25–6). For Sunstein, although there is no such thing as utterly uninfluenced choice, nevertheless there is such a thing as (1) objectively better choice and (2) choice more in line with people's authentic preferences. The question whether to smoke—one of Sunstein's examples—is easy to judge on either criterion: objectively speaking, not smoking is better than smoking; assuming that people desire good health, the choice not to smoke is more consistent with that desire, even if in the moment the desire for a fleeting pleasure might override our calmer and cooler deliberation. Similarly with many other fleeting pleasures, including, according to Sunstein, not only eating unhealthy foods, but also listening to bad music, watching subpar television programming, not recycling, and so on (ibid., 30).

Like Woolf's argument, Sunstein's is motivated by the sound and humane intention of enlisting what collective powers we can to enable people to live better lives. By deploying enlightened "democratic controls" on the range of people's choices, by "enacting considered judgments into law," or by "counteracting, through the provision of opportunities and information, preferences and beliefs that have adjusted to an unjust status quo" (ibid., 30), Sunstein believes we can help people realize the selves they should be.

Sunstein does not call himself a socialist, and he would probably reject that label for his policy recommendations. He calls himself a progressive. But his position is socialist-inclined because it fits the criteria established in Chapter 1—in particular, its advocacy of making "progressively" more political-economic decisions centrally, thereby gradually restricting the range of decentralized decisions individuals may make for themselves. Such a policy often proceeds by identifying problems with capitalism or capitalist-inclined policy, including many that we have discussed: inequality, people acting out of vice instead of virtue, the failure to always compensate victims of bad luck, people developing preferences some of us dislike, the unwillingness of some people to remain in or form the kinds of communities we think best for them, the seeming inability to realize one's authentic self, and so on. These problems or failings are then compared against what we imagine might take place under a different comprehensive set of institutions, and then the failure of the former to live up to the hypothesized achievements of the latter is taken as reason to reform the former in light of the latter. We have discussed at length the numerous practical problems that beset proposals to move from capitalist-inclined policy to socialist-inclined policy, but we have not yet focused on the disregard such proposals manifest toward ordinary human beings. Sunstein claims, for example, that "a liberal government ought to be concerned with whether its citizens are experiencing satisfying lives" (1997: 21). I have argued that Sunstein would have no way of knowing what it would mean for any individual citizen to experience a satisfying life, and, indeed, there is no reliable way to know from afar whether alternative choices a person might make under other circumstances are to be preferred to her actual choices under her actual circumstances. Aside from that, however, it is not clear why Sunstein could justifiably override people's autonomy and independent judgment in the service of whatever conception of "satisfying lives" he offered because to do so would disrespect their equal moral agency. Respecting their agency means respecting their choices.

I focus on Sunstein not only because his argument is quite influential—President Obama appointed Sunstein his "Regulation Czar"—but also because Sunstein has doubled-down on his position: he extends the argument further and to more areas of human life in his book *Nudge,* which is already in a second edition. He has even gone so far as to argue that the government might be authorized to secretly infiltrate private organizations, clubs, online chat groups, and so on that it (the government) believes might pose "risks" to society; that the government might be justified in finding other ways to silently and secretly change people's minds about political, religious, and other matters; and so on.[9] Even more recently, Sunstein has argued that a government with substantially increased powers and authorities will make its citizens' lives "simpler" (Sunstein's term) by removing many of the daily personal decisions they would otherwise have to make (Sunstein 2013). Sunstein argues that by centrally managing the options available to people—in particular, limiting options regarding health care, education, workplace arrangements, personal and family finance, and so on—people's lives will be just that much simpler.[10] Many others have taken his position, and even extended it.[11] I suggest that it motivates and underlies much contemporary support for socialist-inclined policy, but it cannot be achieved without systematic and fundamental disrespecting of human moral agency.

Conclusion

Socialist-inclined policy conceives of people's group membership or class identity as more important than their individuality. But this is

---

[9] See Sunstein and Vermuele 2008.

[10] I note that Sunstein does not discuss what effects such policies might have on people's power of independent judgment.

[11] For example, Conly 2013 and Ubel 2009.

both a factual mistake—since people are, in fact, separate and discrete moral agents—and a moral mistake—since it is the historically relatively recent conception of all people as equal moral agents that has not only allowed us to condemn many previously common human practices as immoral, but also to elevate even the least among us to a level of dignity and respect that was previously reserved only to a few. As the example of John Lilburne shows, respecting people requires respecting them as individuals, and even when we suspect their choices are not the ones they would have made under different or idealized circumstances, they are still moral agents whose judgment we are bound to respect. We may, as Mill put it, remonstrate with them or try to convince them otherwise, but we must always allow them to still say "no" to us. We may not pressure, threaten, defraud, or coerce them without disrespecting the dignity that reflects their unique and precious value as individual—and equal—moral agents. We need to let them put locks on their doors.

8

Socialism's Great Mistake

Introduction

The disrespect socialist-inclined policy exhibits toward the equal moral agency of individual human beings rests, I argue, on a crucial factual mistake, namely, seeing people as essentially members of classes or groups, instead of as individuals. I do not claim that people do not form groups or associations; of course they do. I also do not claim that it is not fruitful and appropriate in some contexts to think of people as members of groups or classes, even to ascribe, again in the appropriate contexts, causal agency to the group. We can speak of people as Roman Catholics or Jews, as New Yorkers or as Americans; we can speak of the New York Giants as having won the 2011 Super Bowl, of Americans preferring football to soccer, and so on. When Margaret Thatcher said in 1987 that "there is no such thing as society," she was clearly mistaken, even if we understand the intent of her remark.[1] The great mistake that socialism makes lies not in its assumption that there are groups, that people can act jointly in groups, or that the existence of groups can influence its members and their relations to one another in various ways. Socialism's mistake is instead in its attempt to treat people as mere members of groups.

---

[1] She went on to say that there "are individual men and women, and there are families," which only clouded the issue: What reason could we give for disqualifying "society" but not "families"?

Individuals and Groups

Human beings are distinct, and discrete, consciousnesses. They associate with one another, influence one another, and coerce one another, but they do not, and cannot, coalesce into a single consciousness. Within their complex webs of connection and interdependence, each of them nevertheless remains a single, separate consciousness. They remain separate decision centers, with separate and unique reservoirs of knowledge and schedules of value. A married couple might pledge to one another never to make a decision again except jointly and unanimously: even if they kept this (surprisingly difficult) promise to one another, and even if in time they came to have largely overlapping reservoirs of local knowledge and schedules of value, they would still, in fact, remain separate and discrete consciousnesses. Consider members of the same voice in a choir, or members of a monastery, or residents of a kibbutz: Harmony of some specific purposes? Yes. Consonance of action or behavior in the service of these specific purposes? Yes. Reduction of separate consciousnesses into one? No.

When we speak of "the rich," for example, or of "the poor," our terminology can have sense if what we mean is generalizations or statistical categories—the top 1 percent versus the other 99 percent, say. The top 1 percent in income in the United States is a statistical category, but the people occupying it may have little or nothing else in common. Unlike even the groups discussed in the previous paragraph, they are not united in purpose or behavior or schedule of value. They have not had the same family lives, the same educations, the same opportunities; they do not have the same religion, the same politics, the same hopes and aspirations. They therefore are not fungible: one cannot substitute any of them for any other without substantial alteration and loss. This fact is reflected by the reality that "the rich" and "the poor" in the United States are almost never the same people over time. The usual course of people's lives in the United States has been to ascend from lower-income statistical groups into higher-income groups over time; and the individual people who are in the top income groups in any given year are likely no longer to be there within a decade. Thus, although the statistical groups remain, and will always remain, the individuals occupying them change all the time.[2]

---

[2] Data substantiating this claim is widely available. See, for example, United States Treasury Department 2008. See also Corak 2011's collection of studies. Bowlus and

Each person is captain of a unique world trajectory, possessing experiences and knowledge unlike that of any other, and connecting to others and to the rest of the world in ways that are irreplaceable and inimitable. No one before, no one now, and no one after will or could occupy the same place in the world as you. And the same is true for every other single human being. This is an effect of their autonomy and independent judgment—that is, of their moral agency—and it is a cause, I argue, of the dignity each of them possesses. Each human being is thus special and precious.

Yet it is one of the dark realities of human history that for most of it most people presumed anything but the unique preciousness of each individual. The ubiquity of slavery in human history is but one ugly, and unfortunately recurring, instance of this presumption: we matter more than you; therefore, we are your "natural masters" and you are our "natural slaves." That was Aristotle's language, but similar sentiments can be found in many times and places, including in modern times. Even John Stuart Mill, the great defender of individual liberty who argued that "the sole end for which mankind are warranted, individually or collectively, in interfering with the liberty of action of any of their number is self-protection," cannot resist immediately thereafter issuing the following qualification:

It is, perhaps, hardly necessary to say that this doctrine is meant to apply only to human beings in the maturity of their faculties. [...] Those who [like children] are still in a state to require being taken care of by others must be protected against their own actions as well as against external injury. For the same reason we may leave out of consideration those backward states of society in which *the race itself* may be considered in its nonage. (1997 [1859]: 9–10; my emphasis)

The last remark is particularly worrisome, evincing as it does exactly the mistake of socialist-inclined policy I have been pressing—even if for a person as brilliant as Mill it might seem perfectly reasonable (to Mill, no doubt almost everyone seemed to be in a state of nonage).[3] But the fitting and proper response to Mill's claim here was given by

Robins 2012 tracks not income classes but, rather, specific individuals throughout their lifetimes and discovers not only that there is great turbulence in composition of the income classes, but also, perhaps surprisingly, that inequality is actually less for people in the United States than for people in more socialist-inclined Western Europe.

[3] This is one aspect of Mill's argument in *On Liberty* that his critic James Fitzjames Stephen applauded. See Stephen 1993 (1872–3): chap. 1.

Lord Macaulay earlier in the nineteenth century, in an essay on the poetry of Milton:

There is only one cure for the evils which newly acquired freedom produces; and that cure is freedom. When a prisoner first leaves his cell he cannot bear the light of day: he is unable to discriminate colours, or recognise faces. But the remedy is, not to remand him into his dungeon, but to accustom him to the rays of the sun. The blaze of truth and liberty may at first dazzle and bewilder nations which have become half blind in the house of bondage. But let them gaze on, and they will soon be able to bear it. In a few years men learn to reason. The extreme violence of opinions subsides. Hostile theories correct each other. The scattered elements of truth cease to contend, and begin to coalesce. And at length a system of justice and order is educed out of the chaos.

Many politicians of our time are in the habit of laying it down as a self-evident proposition, that no people ought to be free till they are fit to use their freedom. The maxim is worthy of the fool in the old story, who resolved not to go into the water till he had learnt to swim. If men are to wait for liberty till they become wise and good in slavery, they may indeed wait for ever. (Macaulay 1825).

Sarah Conly argues that because people "don't reason very well," "can't really understand the facts they are presented with," and thus might "harm themselves," we need "simply to save people from themselves by making certain courses of action illegal" (2013: 1–4). Conly argues in favor of what she calls "coercive paternalism" on the grounds that individual autonomy along the lines of what I have defended is, in fact, "not all that valuable" (1). The alleged value of autonomy arises, she claims, from the assumption that people "are pre-eminently rational agents, each of us well suited to determining what goes in our own life" (2). But because we are, in fact, not very good reasoners and are often ill informed, the value of any autonomy our reasoning could justify is therefore diminished. As modern psychologists and behavioral economists have begun to identify mistakes we routinely make, Conly concludes that there is no reason not to "save people from doing things that are gravely bad for them when they do that only as a result of an error in thinking" (3). What are some of these "gravely bad" things? Conly offers familiar examples of smoking, not wearing seat belts, and not wearing motorcycle helmets, as well as stranger examples like mistakenly drinking antifreeze (3–6), but her main examples come from the field of health care (chap. 6).

I think Conly overestimates what she, or any other centralized authority, can know about what is good for any individual—although, curiously, she acknowledges her, and our, inability to know what is best for others in some particular cases, such as the selection of life mates and careers (chap. 7). I think she also underestimates the problems associated with creating centralized policies and agencies that will actually have the effects she desires. Moreover, Conly's position suffers from several by-now familiar fallacies. First is the Totalizing Fallacy: she asserts that "[w]e are too fat, we are too much in debt, and we save too little for the future" (1), when, in fact, only some of us are any of those things; yet from those premises she infers that "we" need to create centrally coordinated uniform solutions to these large problems. Nothing of the kind follows, however, since these are actually thousands, even millions, of different problems faced by thousands, even millions, of differently and uniquely situated persons. Her argument also repeatedly commits the fallacy of assuming that because something is possible it is therefore probable: because coercive paternalism might have good consequences, therefore it is likely that it will. And she commits the Great Mind Fallacy by simply assuming that experts in the government will be able to collect, assess, and act on all the knowledge required to prevent people from making bad decisions.

Putting those aside, however, she argues that a policy of respecting the equal moral agency of others by respecting the decisions—and their attendant consequences—they make actually "becomes a justification for inhumanity: the principle that those who fail deserve to fail isn't one that is geared to support equality and mutual respect" (2). On her argument, it is instead coercive paternalism that shows proper respect for people because it debars people from making decisions that would conflict with what they themselves would like to have chosen: "paternalistic action prevents you from doing something you want to do at that moment, but it does this for the sake of helping you obtain something you want more, something that your short-sighted action will make more difficult to achieve" (35). The moral objection to Conly's argument, however, is that its mandate to override people's decentralized decisions and choices—even if ostensibly out of respect for those individuals' true, authentic, ideal, or proper wishes—cannot take place without authorizing some group of people a scope of agency that is denied to others. Conly is not worried about the disrespect or potential dangers lurking behind such seemingly benevolent intentions, however, because she somehow claims to find no historical reason for suspecting that such power might be corrupted or abused (chap. 3). Yet because the paternalistic coercers have no actual knowledge of what individuals want, desire, or value, in practice their policies cannot but reflect only their own wants, desires, and values. The activities and behaviors they will restrict or prohibit will therefore be in the service of values that (they imagine) would apply to average, generic, and thus interchangeable persons.

But human beings are neither generic nor interchangeable. Each person is unique, special, and precious; each has a dignity in virtue of her moral agency that others are not entitled to infringe by invoking a self-appointed, even if well-intentioned, coercive authority. Socialist-inclined policy like Conly's mistakes ordinary human beings for the equivalent of poker chips or chess pieces, for members of classes with either a single personality, purpose, and motivation or with interchangeable personalities, purposes, and motivations. It is that assumption that enables the socialist to believe she is justified in moving those marbles from one urn to another, in rearranging the pieces on the chessboard, or in disregarding and overriding the autonomy of persons. Such coercive manipulation is appropriate to marbles and chess pieces; it is not appropriate to equal moral agents.

Conclusion

My argument is that our politics and economics should be informed by a conception of equal human dignity, that we should favor policies consistent with it, and resist policies inconsistent with it. If my reasoning has been sound, then the policies we should favor are those that are decentralized and capitalist-inclined, and those we should resist are centralized and socialist-inclined. Only the former are consistent with the conception of morality that sees each person as possessed of a dignity grounded in the uniqueness of each person's moral agency. Only the former accept all human agency as worthy of respect, and only the former build in that respect from the foundation up. However appealing the ideals of socialism may sound initially or in the abstract, as their practical implications are worked out it becomes clear that they violate the fundamental tenets of a morality worthy of free and responsible people.

9

Prosperity

Introduction

A central argument proponents of capitalist-inclined policy make is that it leads to increasing material prosperity. Few deny that claim any longer, even if people disagree about the relative extent to which markets by themselves, or markets combined with various government supports and restrictions, are responsible for that prosperity.[1] But proponents of socialist-inclined policy respond with two other claims. First, whatever capitalism's benefits, it also issues in costs—not only in the "destruction" part of its characteristic "creative destruction," but also in costs it imposes on unwitting third parties via various forms of externalities. Is it always clear that capitalism's alleged benefits outweigh these costs? Second, even if it transpires that socialist-inclined policy does issue in net costs—that is, that it reduces material prosperity overall—some goals might be worth the price. Sometimes sacrificing some of one's wealth is required, or justified, by allegiance to important moral goals, including perhaps fairness, equality, or community.[2]

---

[1] For competing views, see Forbes and Ames 2009 and Mackie and Sisodia 2013 (capitalism), and Holmes and Sunstein 2000 and Murphy and Nagel 2002 (capitalism plus government).

[2] There are other grounds on which one might argue for a justified tradeoff. One might press environmental concerns, for example: if decentralism led to overuse or despoliation of natural resources, one might argue that the putative tradeoff for increased material prosperity would not be worthwhile. It turns out, however, that decentralist economies score relatively better on "environmental performance" than do centralist

What exactly are the gains in prosperity that decentralist capitalism proposes, then, and what are the costs it imposes? Are the latter always justified by the former? And, if conflicts between material prosperity and moral goals that we share, or that we should share, do arise, is it clear that we should always find in favor of the former?

Decentralism's Gains

When people decide to trade, exchange, or otherwise cooperate with one another, they benefit—but not at each others' expense. Believing otherwise is falling prey to the *Zero-Sum Fallacy,* which holds that one person's gain must come at the expense of some other person. It is called "zero sum" for the simple reason that it maintains that if A benefits one unit, then it must happen at the expense of B: a "+1" for A is a "−1" for B, which, added together, equals zero. The claim is that when one person, or one group of people, accumulates more wealth than others—and here I use the slightly question-begging term *accumulate,* rather than, for example, *generate*—they can have done so only by taking that wealth from others. This is probably the unstated assumption behind the familiar objection to capitalism that in it "the rich get richer and the poor get poorer": the objection is not merely to some getting rich (or richer), but, rather, to some getting rich (or richer) *at the expense of others.* One hears this so often that for many of us it has become part of our unquestioned background worldview.

And yet it is a fallacy. Adam Smith articulated it over two centuries ago. He began by situating human beings in their empirical context. Other animals, Smith claimed, when they want "to obtain something either of a man or of another animal" have "no other means of persuasion but to gain favour of those whose service [they] require. A puppy fawns upon its dam, and a spaniel endeavours by a thousand attractions to engage the attention of its master who is at dinner, when it wants to be fed by him." The situation for human beings, however, is markedly different:

[M]an has almost constant occasion for the help of his brethren, and it is in vain for him to expect it from their benevolence only. He will be more likely

economies. See, for example, Anderson and Leal 2001, Bailey 2002, Emerson et al. 2012, Lomborg 2010, and McCloskey 2007.

to prevail if he can interest their self-love in his favour, and shew them that it is for their own advantage to do for him what he requires of them. Whoever offers to another a bargain of any kind, proposes to do this. Give me that which I want, and you shall have this which you want, is the meaning of every such offer; and it is in this manner that we obtain from one another the far greater part of those good offices which we stand in need of. (WN, 26)

There are several things to emphasize in this passage. Note, first, that Smith claims that this is the way we obtain the "good offices" that we need, not everything we need. That is important because the Smithian position is sometimes caricatured as the claim that markets can or should take care of everything. Nothing could be further from the truth. For Smith, we obtain *good offices* from market exchange, "good offices" being an old-fashioned term for what we would now call goods and services. Other important parts of a complete and happy human life—including friendship, affection, love, and the other effects of "beneficence"—properly fall, as Smith suggests, outside the scope of the dynamic described here.

Another important part of that passage is that the exchange is predicated on mutual benefit. We must show the other person that the exchange serves *his* purposes, whatever they are, not that they serve *ours*—even if the exchange does, in fact, also serve our purposes. Whether it serves our purposes is relevant to us, of course, because if it did not, we would not agree to the exchange; but when we make an offer of exchange to another person, we do not impose on him about its serving, or not, our purposes. Why not? Precisely because it is an imposition. It suggests that our purposes are more important than his, or that he should consider our purposes as outweighing his own. But if the potential trading partner is an equal moral agent, under normal circumstances we have no reasonable grounds on which to make such a suggestion. If we view his moral agency as equal to our own, then it follows that we must view his purposes as being just as important as our own. And it follows that we may not impose our purposes on him. Hence Smith's claim that in a proper voluntary transaction—one, that is, in which no coercion, fraud, invocation of special privilege, or other improper means were brought to bear—*both* parties' interests would have been served. Transactions undertaken freely in a decentralized system of political economy, therefore, are not zero-sum, but, rather, *positive*-sum.

There are several qualifications presumed in the preceding sentence. The first is that the transaction is truly voluntary, meaning not undertaken as a result of coercion or duress. This gets tricky, since although coercion is relatively easy to identify, people nevertheless may have good-faith disagreements about what counts as duress. As we saw in Chapter 5, there seems to be a relatively smooth continuum from, at one end of the spectrum, perfectly acceptable neutral providing information, to recommending, to exhorting, to pressuring, to threatening, to coercing at the other end. Although there would seem to be a threshold somewhere between "exhorting" and "pressuring" where one transitions from acceptable to unacceptable, the line is not always clear. This might lead one to think that there *is* no clear line between acceptable and unacceptable pressure, perhaps even that *any* pressure is unacceptable. But the existence of difficult cases about which people can in good faith disagree does not entail that there are not clear examples of each group—acceptable and unacceptable pressure—or that the distinction is not serviceable in the vast majority of cases. There will be hard cases at the margins, where no prior rule will settle things; in such cases, people have to rely on their judgment applied to the facts of the particular case at hand and employing criteria like "reasonable" and "prudent." Those are not infallible criteria by any stretch, but their sense arises via a mechanism that tends to accumulate the results of many people's experiences, and hence they are more powerful than it might initially be supposed. If we approach individual cases with the background assumption that coercion, fraud, and other unjustifiable pressure invalidate a transaction—and would, not coincidentally, make the transaction *zero*-sum instead of *positive*-sum— and that the transactions that are to be allowed and encouraged are instead those that are undertaken voluntarily by all parties directly involved,[3] then we understand the sense of Smith's discussion and we will allow ourselves to realize the mutual gains made possible by such exchanges in capitalist political economy.

The other important presumption in the sentence in question is the institutions that are involved in a "capitalist" political economy. For

---

[3] And those who are *in*directly involved? This question raises the issue of *externalities*, or those costs (and benefits) imposed on not-directly-involved third parties as a result of your and my exchange. This issue deserves separate discussion; I return to it momentarily.

Smith, what was required to allow these kinds of mutually beneficial transactions were two main things: property rights, since one has to own something (including perhaps oneself[4]) in order to sell or exchange it; and a "tolerable administration of justice," including courts and police to protect property and adjudicate disputes impartially. Beyond that, natural incentives would encourage "every man to apply himself to a particular occupation, and to cultivate and bring to perfection whatever talent or genius he may possess," resulting in a "universal opulence which extends itself to the lowest ranks of the people." Smith continues:

> Every workman has a great quantity of his own work to dispose of beyond what he himself has occasion for; and every other workman being in exactly the same situation, he is enabled to exchange a great quantity of his own goods for a great quantity, or, what comes to the same thing, for the price of a great quantity of theirs. He supplies them abundantly with what they have occasion for, and they accommodate him as amply with what he has occasion for, and a general plenty diffuses itself through all the different ranks of the society. (WN, 22)

This is Smith's bold prediction about commercial society: a hitherto unprecedented "universal opulence" and "general plenty" will ensue, extending itself through all the ranks of society. Note especially Smith's concern for people in the lower ranks. Smith was far less concerned with the welfare of people in the higher ranks, who manage to take care of themselves well enough in any case. It was rather the beneficial effects especially on the poor that made the institutions of capitalism eligible for Smith.

The positive-sum nature of the voluntary exchanges that take place in the free enterprise system is not altered by the existence, or not, of alternative possibilities. If you and I agree that I will complete a task for you for $100, that means that I valued the $100 more than the labor and forsaken opportunities it cost me, and you valued the completed task more than the $100 it cost you. Each of us benefits according to his respective schedule of value. Whether you or I had alternative opportunities and whether you or I would have respectively done or paid more or less, are irrelevant. So perhaps I had few other opportunities available to me other than to take your offer, and

---

[4] See Locke 1988 (1690): chaps. 1–5.

perhaps you would have been willing to pay me double that price: neither changes the fact that each of us, according to his own individual and unique schedule of value, judged that transaction as a net gain. It might also be the case that a third-party observer could imagine a different transaction you and I might have made—involving different people, different terms, or both—that would have benefitted either or both of us even more than we benefitted from our actual exchange. Not even that, however, alters the fact that each of us benefitted from this particular exchange, that each of us is at least marginally better off now than he otherwise would have been.

On the other hand, we sometimes come to regret decisions we made in the past. One might conclude from this common human experience that voluntary exchanges do not, in fact—or at least do not always—benefit all parties to the exchange. It may be true that, since the transaction was voluntary, all parties were sufficiently convinced *at the time of the transaction* that they were benefitting from the transaction, but it does not follow that (a) that they were right or (b) that they would not change their minds in the future, when other considerations or circumstances came to light. One might even conclude from these considerations that what I have called "voluntary" transactions were not actually voluntary, that subsequent regret or other later-revealed circumstances might invalidate the transaction's claim not only to being truly mutually beneficial but to being truly voluntary as well. I will address the criteria for 'truly voluntary' a bit later, but the response to the worry that a voluntary transaction might not be truly beneficial is to concede it. We are imperfect creatures who sometimes make mistakes; there is just no getting around that. The question, however, is: What can we do to minimize the number of inevitable mistakes and the damage they can do? The answer is, first, to rely as much as we can on the relevant local information to give the decisions people are making about what transactions to execute the best chance possible of being good decisions; and, second, to limit the reach of the consequences of the decisions to the decision makers themselves as much as possible. Both of those are accomplished by decentralism. Think of it this way: we can be sure that some of the decisions we will make we will later come to regret; but we cannot be sure *now* which ones we will regret—that is revealed only later, after the relevant decisions are made. Other people would have even less ability to know which decisions of ours we will come to regret, so empowering them to second-guess us in advance makes even less sense. Moreover, because under decentralism it is we ourselves who will tend to bear the consequences of our decisions, we have a strong and natural incentive not only to think carefully *before* making decisions but also *afterward* to revise our judgment accordingly once the consequences of our decisions become apparent. Third parties do not have such incentives.

A separate worry is that others who are not parties to our exchange might lose out. Others might have completed that task for you, but now cannot because I did; others, or even I myself, might have benefitted, or benefitted more, if I had worked for them instead of working for you. This happens all the time in a decentralized market economy. Perhaps even through repeated exchanges some people's losses accumulate to the point where they go out of business (if they cannot attract workers or customers) or they cannot find work at all (if they demand too much for their labor); these things, too, happen all the time in a market economy. Because no one is entitled to my labor, however, and because no one is entitled to your money, neither you nor I can claim any kind of injustice if I will not work for you or if you will not hire me.[5] We may be disappointed or frustrated or disconcerted, but if no promise was broken, if no one was defrauded, and of course if no one was assaulted, then no injustice was committed, and we cannot demand reparation. The good news, though, is that in market economies such disappointments tend not to last long, since other opportunities arise. Perhaps the other opportunities are not those we wanted (or thought we wanted)—I might have to take a job less preferable to me or with lower wages or benefits, for example—but consider, first,

---

[5] This conclusion is consistent with, and would perhaps follow from, a Lockean premise of self-ownership, but it does not require it. Entitlements are generated by contracts, agreements, and promises; we can even include "social" contracts and "tacit" promises as possibly generating entitlements. Absent some (broadly conceived) prior positive agreement, however, it is not clear how one could claim an entitlement either to another's labor or to another's money (assuming that the money was not unjustly obtained—that is, not through theft or fraud—and that the money derives from voluntary human labor). Even putting aside Locke's argument, then, our "natural" state would seem to be that of no prior agreement and thus no prima facie entitlements—a situation that would change only by specific positive actions. This position comports better not only with the conception of moral agency I defend, but also with our strongly held convictions about the undesirable possibilities opened up (coercive paternalism, legal privilege, forced labor, slavery, and so on) if we deny the claim.

that under no system of political economy will it ever be the case that everyone can get any job, or any worker, she wants, and, second, that other people are moral agents here too, not just you. In other words, if people do not want to work for you, or shop in your store, then that is their prerogative, just as much as it is your prerogative not to work for someone whose proffered terms do not suit you or to shop in some other store.

The other thing that helps mitigate our worries about the inevitable disappointments in market economies is that everyone benefits from living in such an economy. Capitalism proposes to expand the frontiers of possibility for mutually beneficial transactions, so that more and more people can work together in more and more—including unexpected—ways.[6] This expanding cooperation means increasing benefit, in new, unpredictable, and yes unequal, but nevertheless substantial ways. This is the core of the explanation for why capitalist economies have increased overall prosperity so dramatically. The gains to all of us—including *especially* the poorer among us—from allowing people to ply their time, talent, and treasure according to their own lights are considerable. Quoting Adam Smith once again, in a capitalist economy, "the most dissimilar geniuses are of use to one another; the different produces of their respective talents, by the general disposition to truck, barter, and exchange, being brought, as it were, into a common stock, where every man may purchase whatever part of the produce of other men's talents he has occasion for" (WN, 30).[7]

Externalities

The discussion so far has focused on the fruits of the freedom capitalism envisions for individuals, namely the freedom to cooperate—or, in Smith's words, "to truck, barter, and exchange"—with others according to each person's unique respective schedule of value and hierarchy

---

[6] This is the principal reason behind Matt Ridley's "rational optimism." See Ridley 2011.

[7] It does not follow from this that corporate goals are always served by individuals seeking to serve their own interests. See, e.g., Olson 1971. For small groups or those with a narrow range of goals (or both), achieving group goals requires individuals in the group to act from group-directed, not individual-directed, motivations. Smith's argument, by contrast, applies to large groups or those with broad, indeed indefinitely broad, ranges of objectives (or both).

of purpose. Yet a critic might claim that capitalism, in fact, impinges on freedom because of negative externalities. Suppose that A and B come to a voluntary agreement that benefits them both, as presumed on the capitalist model, but C, who was no party to the agreement, is harmed by it. Perhaps A and B pollute C's air; perhaps A and B divert some of C's water supply; perhaps A and B choke the road in front of C's house with new industrial traffic; and so on—we could think of any number of ways that C might be negatively affected by A and B's bargain, not even including the possibility that perhaps C was a business owner who now must close because A and B's bargain rendered C unable to compete.

The Smithian capitalist model reserves certain kinds of costs that negative externalities might impose as falling under the rubric of injustice. Property damage, violation of a contract, or fraud would all constitute a breach of the rules of Smithian justice and would therefore justify prevention, punishment, restitution, or some combination, as the case may be. Luckily, most cases like these are relatively easy to identify and therefore adjudicate by the impartial "administration of justice" that is a prerequisite of capitalist political economy. The relatively easy ones are when there is clear, measurable, or observable damage done to your property, to your contractual entitlements, or to your rights. Many cases of pollution can be adjudicated in this way since they will involve property damage; most fraud can be adjudicated in this way since it is a violation of your rights (if a promise, even a tacit one, made to you went unfulfilled); and most cases of nuisance can be adjudicated this way since they involve a violation of your reasonable expectations (say, for example, if you can no longer sleep at night or enjoy peace in your home from the noise). The exact actions to take to remedy these situations cannot be specified by any rule in advance because they will depend on the details of any particular case; but general common-law remedies have and could continue to develop enabling relatively peaceful resolution for many problems like these that inevitably arise in a community of diverse moral agents.[8] Indeed, we often underestimate the ability of localized

---

[8] See Epstein 2011. Some cases of pollution are harder for decentralized adjudication to handle well. Elinor Ostrom discusses some possibilities in Ostrom 2011; for a classic treatment, see Coase 1960.

people to discover mutually satisfactory resolutions to difficulties and conflicts that routinely arise.

Some cases of negative externality, however, are not so easy to address. The more difficult cases typically involve two kinds: people or firms that are forced out of business in capitalist competition, and externalities involving costs that are difficult, perhaps impossible, either to measure or to compensate monetarily. The former cases do not, as I argued in Chapter 8, call for restitution or reparation, even if they generate reasonable disappointment. They are part of the "destructive" part of capitalism's "creative destruction." But that is not as hard-hearted as it may sound, for at least two reasons. First, in such cases, people are merely not enjoying benefits they hoped they would. No one—no would-be customer, client, buyer, and so on—made their situation materially worse than it was before the hoped-for-but-unrealized exchange. Moreover, because they had no right to or claim on anyone else's labor or money, they can claim no injustice—only disappointment. Think of it this way: no single potential customer who decides to go to store A instead of store B has injured B, because she left B no worse off than B was before the customer came on the scene. When B opened its doors today, it had no customers; B's owner hoped to have some today, but if none come in, no one did any positive damage to B or left its owner worse off than he was when he opened. Only his hopes were dashed, not his person or property—and thus nothing to which he was *entitled*. To maintain otherwise, by contrast, would be to impose on those would-be customers by granting rights either to them or to their money. But they are equal moral agents too, and thus they are entitled to make decisions different from those that B's owner, or perhaps you and I, would have made or preferred. Perhaps you and I wish that B would stay in business, and so we patronize B in the hopes of helping; if other customers choose differently, however, on what legitimate grounds would we prevent or punish them for doing so?

Second, it turns out that everyone—even those who lose their businesses—are much better off overall, by virtually every measure, when people and firms are allowed to compete with one another without special favors or protections. The large-scale, or "macro," evidence for this claim comes in the form of studies that track the standards of living and prosperity of people living in relatively capitalist societies versus those living in societies that to varying degrees depart from that ideal. The evidence demonstrates that the citizens of the most economically capitalist countries enjoy, as compared to those at the other end of the spectrum, higher wealth, both as income and per capita gross domestic product; longer life expectancy; higher scores on the United Nations' Development Index; lower rates of infant mortality and child labor; higher rates of access to potable water, health care, and food production; even greater relative peace.[9]

Even more telling, countries' respective places on the continuum from decentralized or capitalist economies to centrally managed or socialist economies track all the way down on these criteria. With virtually each unit of distance from capitalist toward socialist, the score on these criteria ratchets down, to a high degree of correlation across all the criteria. Thus, places like Hong Kong, Singapore, New Zealand, Switzerland, and Australia—the top five most capitalist countries—also rank highest on the criteria of prosperity and well-being of citizens, across all their socioeconomic classes. By contrast, the Democratic Republic of Congo, Angola, Venezuela, Myanmar, and Zimbabwe—the five least capitalist countries, with the most closed and centralized economies[10]—also score at the bottom on scales of prosperity and well-being, with their poorest citizens faring disproportionately badly. Perhaps one of the most remarkable findings of this research, which is now quite systematic and has been conducted for decades, is precisely the relative effect on a given country's poor. It turns out that the benefits of capitalist institutions accrue to the poor disproportionately.[11] Moreover, the poor benefit from such institutions more than they benefit from direct aid transfers or from government welfare assistance (there is actually a negative correlation with these, meaning that the poor tend to be worse off the more of this there is); incredibly, the poor benefit from capitalist institutions even more than they do from increased formal education or from democratic political institutions.[12]

[9] See, e.g., Lawson et al. 2013.
[10] Lawson et al. (2013) do not rate North Korea or Cuba because they argue that trustworthy data on these countries is unable to be obtained.
[11] For this reason, McCloskey argues that the free enterprise society satisfies Rawls's difference principle—namely, that inequalities are justified to the extent they principally benefit the least advantaged of society—better than any centralized system of political economy. See McCloskey 2010: chap. 8.
[12] See, for example, Dollar and Kraay 2002.

In addition to innovation, however, capitalist economies do involve destruction. To succeed, firms must continually innovate and adapt to people's changing desires, and there will be continuous and regular success and failure: some firms will enjoy temporary success, contingent on continuing to serve the interests of their customers, while others will suffer failure, because they did not continue to serve the interests of their customers sufficiently. This is no day at the beach for either of them. Firms that are successful at any given time must constantly work and strive to remain so, and even then almost all of them either undergo significant transformations into totally different kinds of companies, as circumstances, opportunities, and people's interests change, or they, too, eventually go out of business. The only exception firms can get from the rigors of market competition is when they enlist the state to limit their exposure, by restricting competition, restricting entry, subsidizing losses, and so on. Although that goes on in otherwise "capitalist" countries, it is an abuse, not a use, of capitalism. It is, instead, "crony capitalism," and its relative presence in a country is one central factor at work in lowering a country's ranking on the "economic freedom" index—and, accordingly, lowering its score on indices of human prosperity.[13]

Reciprocal Rights of Agency

For those persons or firms going out of business, the displacement and disappointment can indeed be devastating. Some defenders of capitalism might wish either to deny that going out of business is in fact a "harm" borne by those going out of business, or alternatively to claim that although it may be a harm, it is not one we should worry about. Both those claims are wrong. Going out of business, like losing one's job, is a real harm, even if it is the result of entirely appropriate competition within the bounds of justice. If we care about people's well-being—which should, after all, be the main motivation driving political economy—then we should not simply ignore these harms or pretend they do not exist. They do. The question is: What should we do about it?

In Chapter 6, I raised the scenario of Jack and Jill, who, recall, have been dating for some time and both expect to marry. Yet right before

[13] See Zingales 2012.

Jack proposes to Jill, she meets Joe, with whom she falls in love and decides to elope. Jack, who had invested a lot of time, energy, and emotion into his relationship with Jill, had developed expectations that their relationship would continue indefinitely into the future. His disappointment at this sudden unlucky change of fortune is understandable and lamentable. I argued that despite the real pain Jack feels, there is nothing we or any other third party must do for him. Specifically, we should not attempt to prevent Jill from marrying Joe, prevent people like Joe from meeting or courting people like Jill, or allow Jack to sue for damages or demand compensation. Jack's disappointment at his undeserved bad luck is entirely understandable, but because Jill is a moral agent, too, he has no *right* to her affections or to her company. She has the right to say "no" if she chooses. Moreover, Jack has no grounds for preventing Joe from associating with her if he and she so choose, and he has no right to punish either of them, or anyone else, if they choose differently from what he wishes they would. The equal moral agency of Jill and of Joe entails that, in the absence of some prior promise or contract, Jack must reciprocally respect their decisions.

Or consider the relationship of a parent to his child. Because the child is still a child and dependent on her parent, the parent rightfully has the duty to provide and take responsibility for her and therefore the justified authority to impose (reasonable) restrictions on her activities and decisions. Suppose this means that a father raises his daughter as a Roman Catholic, which is his own religious faith and community. Perhaps the father develops expectations that his daughter will one day marry a Catholic and that their future family will become part of his Catholic community. But when the daughter becomes an adult, she decides to leave the faith and the community and marry someone who is instead an atheist. Perhaps the father becomes greatly distressed and pained at the prospect, and he deeply laments what he believes will be a real loss not only to his daughter, but also to his potential future grandchildren who now might not be part of the community organized by what he believes is the only true faith. Now ask the same question: What may he justifiably do about it? He may remonstrate with her, or try to convince her to change her mind, but if she persists in wishing to take her life in this new direction—a direction of which he disapproves—he is not entitled to stop her. He may decide not to associate with her; he may, perhaps with the heaviest of heavy hearts, disavow her; he may even threaten to or actually disavow her children as well. All of that remains within his authority as a moral agent. What he may not do, however, is coerce her, demand reparations from her, or call on a third party to punish her. As almost any parent can attest, children when grown frequently do not comport with parents' wishes. It may at times be painful, but it is part of the necessary transition of a child into an adult—and the respect for the equal moral agency that a parent is therefore required to grant to his grown children.

This example is based on religious belief, but similar conflicts obviously arise with any number of other issues. The moral to these stories is that equal moral agency requires reciprocal respect of each moral agent's decisions. Absent an injury arising from violation of some agreement, promise, or contract, potential disappointment and pain arising from others choosing to lead their lives in ways we disapprove is the price we are bound to pay for the principle of respecting equal moral agency. It is also the price we must pay for demanding, or expecting, that others respect our own agency.

The same applies to firms or endeavors, however beneficial or worthy we believe they are, that fail in decentralized capitalist economies. It is not enough that I would only be truly fulfilled by doing x. If I believe I can be happy—truly or authentically happy—by, say, writing mystery novels, I am entitled to pursue that activity. I am not, however, entitled to demand or expect that others must support my pursuit. If not enough people are willing buy my mystery novels to support me in that endeavor, however disappointing that might be to me, I am morally bound to respect their decisions. My happiness is not more important than anyone else's, because I am not more important than anyone else. The same holds true if I believe people would be better off if they read only what I consider to be worthy literature, or watched only those television programs I believe are worthy, or listened only to that music I believe is worthy: I may be right, but I may not cross the line from acceptable attempts at persuasion to (unacceptable) pressuring, threatening, or coercing.

Loss and Centralized Compensation

Because business success and failure usually entail inequality—the successful person or firm becomes wealthier, the unsuccessful person or firm, well, does not—the critic of capitalism may on that basis initiate an argument for some kind of corrective mechanism whereby a part of the former's success is redistributed to the latter. The argument often draws on the twin interests of equality and fairness. But the losses suffered are, even if compensated, still losses: they do not go away if they are redistributed. They are not converted into gains, because they cannot be. That means that redistribution does not prevent or alleviate any net cost; it only transfers it to someone else. It may be that it is transferred to many other people, so that it is less noticeable, but it is a loss nonetheless, and the gain to those to whom wealth is redistributed is illusory when viewed from the perspective of the society as a whole—like taking sand from one spot on the beach and piling it up in another spot.

Yet the loss is actually increased, however, beyond what it would have been absent outside interposition, for two reasons. First, the process of transferring entails costs: people must be paid to monitor, assess, extract, process, distribute, and so on. Thus the transfer from one spot on the beach to the other is via a "leaky bucket," as Arthur Okun (1975) put it. Second, this process of redistribution alters, even if only marginally, the rules of the game and thus the incentives involved. Consider the signal it sends if we protect relatively less-successful persons or firms with resources taken from relatively more-successful persons or firms. Making lack of success marginally less troublesome has at least three consequences: (1) it inclines persons or firms to be marginally less motivated to strive to be successful, resulting in marginal diminishment of benefit to others; (2) it makes it marginally less rewarding for persons or firms to be successful, again resulting in marginal diminishment of benefit to others; and (3) it makes others in society overall marginally less well-off than they might otherwise have been because they are now not benefitting from the effects of the invisible-hand mechanism present in capitalist political economy.

Redistribution intended to alleviate the pains suffered by failing firms, while perhaps resulting in isolated or concentrated benefit—this particular firm now remains in business—nevertheless leads to a net loss of benefit for everyone involved. This helps explain why those countries that undertake such redistribution have relatively lower overall productivity, thus relatively lower standards of living, and thus relatively lower scores on standard measures of prosperity and well-being in comparison to those countries that engage relatively less often in such redistributive activity. When we redistribute, we see before us the benefit—we save *this* business—and yet we do not see the loss to which that redistribution led, because a benefit not created is, in nineteenth-century economist Frédéric Bastiat's words, "unseen." But an unseen loss is no less real for being hidden, and, indeed, because it generates additional costs associated with procurement, transference, and monitoring, it may well have been greater than the visible gain.

Suppose, however, one suspects that the localized gains from wealth retrieved elsewhere either do, or at least might (if, say, managed properly or by the right people), equal or even exceed the "unseen" losses from those now-absent uses to which the redistributed wealth would otherwise have been put. Perhaps one believes that public "investment" in some localized projects or people might pay dividends later on that will compensate, perhaps even more than compensate, whatever loss it costs now. My argument does not deny that this is possible. But it does shift the burden of proof to the person making this claim: since every particle of capital one would redistribute must have been drawn away from some other potential use, and since its source must ultimately be the labor of some other persons, then for any redistribution one proposes, one will have to demonstrate that, taking all the costs into account—both the seen and the unseen—the gain to be realized outweighs, or will likely outweigh, the loss. That will prove far more formidable a task than one might initially suspect.

But even that underestimates the problem with such redistribution. That is, as we might say, an economic argument, regarding gains and benefits, losses and costs. There is also, however, a moral argument that applies, relating to the foundational conception of human beings as free moral agents deserving of equal respect. In decentralized market conditions, firms that succeed can do so only because they are relatively better at serving the relevant people's interests—that includes in the first place their customers, but in the second place their owners, stockholders, investors, or other stakeholders—than are their competitors. All those people are making individual decisions about where to spend or invest their time, talent, and treasure based on their respective unique schedules of value and hierarchies of purpose. As I have argued, the respect that their moral agency demands entails not only that they be afforded the freedom to make those decisions on their own, but also that they be held accountable for the results of those decisions. Centralized redistribution denies this accountability, and thus it denies moral agency. Centralized redistribution from successful firms to offset losses of unsuccessful firms is therefore undertaken on the morally dubious premise that some people's moral agency is more important than that of others, implying that the former are more deserving of respect than are the latter. But the default position of any creditable moral system is that all persons are equally moral agents, and thus equally deserving of respect for their free and responsible moral agency. Although we can imagine situations in which it is appropriate to consider a particular human being as either not yet (children) or no longer (mentally infirm) a full moral agent, those are exceptions that prove the rule. In any case, children and the mentally infirm are not what are at issue in discussions of the general principles informing political economy and redistribution of wealth. At issue here, instead, are the decisions of competent moral agents who are therefore deserving of the same respect of their decisions as are those who presume to disenfranchise their agency.

Positive Externalities

It is also the case that there are not one but two kinds of externalities— negative and positive. We have thus far discussed only the negative variety, since that understandably occupies theorists' attention. But consistency suggests that we treat both negative and positive externalities similarly, since they both involve involuntarily imposing on third parties the consequences of voluntary agreements between first and second parties. Yet "involuntary" does not equal or entail "unwanted," since many externalities—namely, the positive kind—are not only commonplace but make people better off and are thus desirable. So, for example, the fact that I maintain my yard has a marginal positive effect on other people's property values in my neighborhood. Or, the presence of a high-performing professor on a university campus may have a positive effect on other faculty and students, by marginally raising the chances that good students, or donor or grant support, and so on, might accrue to the campus. Or, an agreement between A and B might lead to improved goods or services, thereby giving others an incentive to improve their own goods or services, thereby making others better off. And so on: such examples multiply almost indefinitely. Indeed, almost every human being provides some uncompensated positive externalities to others.

That underscores the surprisingly extensive difficulties involved in trying to equalize, redistribute, or correct such externalities. Not only are they so pervasive that the job of the putative Bureau of Externality Correction (BEC) would continue indefinitely, but it would also *increase* indefinitely, since each attempted correction would itself give rise to further externalities, which would then have to be corrected, and so on. In addition, as shown in Chapter 5, the uncertainties introduced into people's lives by such a BEC would create disincentives for innovative, productive activities, since it would be almost impossible to know *ex ante* whether the results of anyone's activities would be curtailed, and if so to what degree, as a result of the BEC's decisions. Might the BEC decide that your university's so-called deadwood faculty actually constitute negative externalities that must therefore either be eliminated (how?) or made to compensate (how? to what extent?) others (whom?)? Might the BEC decide that, out of fairness, your university's superstar faculty need to be compensated (by whom? how much?) for their positive externalities? What a mess that would be. And the messiness itself is a disincentive to act, and therefore a real cost—not even including the direct costs involved in supporting the people who would be working in the BEC, as well as the "unseen" costs of forsaken benefit to the rest of us now that they are no longer engaging in otherwise productive activity.

Conclusion

While decentralism generates enormous benefits to everyone concerned despite the failures and disappointments that everyone will inevitably face in their lives, centralism generates costs both seen and unseen. For those of us lucky enough to have been born and lived in places and times of great wealth relative to other places and times, we can easily overestimate the robustness, even naturalness, of the institutions that have allowed the generation of the relative comfort we enjoy, and we can easily underestimate how desperately poorer people need these institutions. Our wealth can insulate us from feeling the consequences of altering these institutions or diminishing their effectiveness. Others, however, are not so lucky. Until the time comes when there are no more people suffering in the poverty that has been humanity's historical norm, it is their condition, and the potential benefit to them that such institutions promise, that should command our concern. Centralized redistribution to correct for inequality or in the service of other ends has, moreover, the effect of privileging the moral agency of some over that of others. The decentralized system has therefore the twin benefits of respecting everyone's agency equally and enabling growth in prosperity.

I0

Equality and Freedom

Introduction

One of the main values that supporters of socialism claim it fosters is equality, and one of the main values that supporters of capitalism claim it fosters is liberty. Supporters of socialism maintain, moreover, that the inequality to which capitalism leads is one of its primary flaws, whereas supporters of capitalism, for their part, often maintain that there is little or no individual liberty under socialism. This suggests a tension between freedom and equality. On the one hand, to the extent that we allow individuals to make decisions about how to direct their own lives without uninvited interference from third parties, the more people's individual diversity will result in differential outcomes. On the other hand, the more that we attempt to achieve equality, the more we will, in practice, have to limit the scope of people's individual liberty.

I argued in Chapter 9 that this is not a tradeoff worth making, or at least that we should err on the side of liberty rather than equality, so important is individual liberty to generating and maintaining moral agency and hence human dignity. But that leaves capitalism guilty of the charge of fostering inequality: if capitalism leads to both prosperity and inequality, it still leads to inequality. And indeed, capitalism does allow, even perhaps require, inequality. Because people's talents, skills, and values vary, because people's desires and attitudes and preferences vary, and because of sheer luck, some people will generate more wealth in a free enterprise system than others will. The question is whether we should worry about it—and, if so, what we should do about it.

In Chapters 7 and 8, I spelled out the reasons for holding individual liberty to be important—indeed, for holding it to be perhaps the cornerstone of a creditable conception of morality. In this chapter, let us review some of the reasons people worry about the inequalities that arise with the freedom allowed under capitalism, and see what we should make of them. It turns out that socialism also presents obstacles to equality, although in a way different from capitalism.

Smithian Equality

In Chapter 9, I argued that there are at least two general reasons why we should not be as worried about the inequalities to which capitalism can lead as we might initially suppose: one, everyone gains from allowing such inequalities, especially the poorest among us; and two, attempts to reduce these inequalities can result in the unintended but real consequence of jeopardizing prosperity. Yet it is also the case that capitalism itself presumes and promotes an important kind of equality, even as it allows material inequalities.

You have probably heard economics referred to as the "dismal science." The phrase comes from Thomas Carlyle, who objected to the late eighteenth-century and early nineteenth-century economists not, as one might suppose, because their discipline was dull, but because it was based on an assumption that was, to him, disheartening: namely, that all human beings were constructed and motivated in similar ways, hence evinced similar patterns of behavior and judgment, and hence were subject to the same set of political-economic policies.[1] How disheartening—what a "dismal" prospect—it was to Carlyle, who fancied himself a member of a superior race, to be told that the behavior of members of all races, even the allegedly "inferior" ones, was equally explicable according to the same set of political-economic axioms. It was even more distasteful to Carlyle because the early economists suggested that the "inferior" were capable of improving their own lives and bettering their own conditions—*without* the need for paternalistic

---

[1] We have David Levy to thank for recovering and recounting the actual history of the phrase. See Levy 2002; see also Peart and Levy 2005.

superintendence from "superiors." They were capable of responding rationally to incentives, of ordering their lives according to reasonable plans, and of improving their material condition through productive labor and exchange, just as others were, if only they were allowed the chance to do so. Early opposition to economics was motivated by a worldview holding that some groups were naturally superior to others, and that the former were naturally put in power over the latter to enable the latter to lead better lives than they would otherwise be capable of on their own. That people like Carlyle—and he was not alone—found the prospects of self-reliance and improvement on the part of the poor a "dismal" prospect gives some indication of the ugly, even racist, roots of some of the early opposition to capitalism, as well as the threat capitalism posed to their presumed superiority and authority.[2]

The early founders of what we today call economics did indeed make the "dismal" argument that people were by nature roughly equal in far more ways than their contemporaries were willing to allow, including in physical and mental ability, in motivation, and in response to incentives. Adam Smith was a pioneer here. In *The Wealth of Nations,* Smith writes: "The difference between the most dissimilar characters, between a philosopher and a common street porter, for example, seems to arise not so much from nature as from habit, custom, and education" (WN I.ii.4). He continues:

The difference of talents comes then to be taken notice of, and widens by degrees, till at last the vanity of the philosopher is willing to acknowledge scarce any resemblance. [...] By nature a philosopher is not in genius and disposition half so different from a street porter, as a mastiff is from a greyhound, or a greyhound from a spaniel, or this last from a shepherd's dog.

Thus, although people are different, their differences are less a result of natural limitations of their abilities than of their upbringing, experience, specialization, and training. From this Smith draws two important conclusions. First, people's natural endowments entitle them

---

[2] It should be noted that Carlyle was not interested in mere "nudging" or "paternalistic libertarianism," as Thaler and Sunstein, for example, are. In his 1849 essay, "Occasional Discourse on the Negro Question," he argued for reinstating racial slavery, partly on the basis of his odious belief that blacks were mere "two-legged calves"; see Levy 2002: chap. 1, as well as Levy and Peart 2001.

neither to privilege nor to limitation. Each person is an individual who should be treated according to her own contributions, not according to judgments about the class from which she comes. Second, people's "different geniuses and talents" are not only things to celebrate, since they are reflective of who each of us uniquely is, but they also constitute prima facie arguments for the free enterprise society. Since no one is by nature sufficiently superior to any other, no one is entitled by nature to supersede the judgment of any other. As Thomas Jefferson, who read Smith, wrote in 1826, "[t]he general spread of the light of science has already laid open to every view the palpable truth that the mass of mankind has not been born with saddles on their backs, nor a favored few booted and spurred, ready to ride them legitimately, by the grace of God." A society in which all individuals are accorded equal liberty to order their own lives according to their own judgment, without interposition from uninvited third parties, just is the decentralized free enterprise society.

The advocate of centralized planning, by contrast, holds that under such institutions bad decisions will be made because of bad information, false consciousness, improper socialization, weakness of will, insufficient education, irrationality, and so on. As Conly 2013 (to take a contemporary example) argues, we should therefore empower some group of elites—philosophers, experts, regulators, legislators—who will organize political and economic institutions so that they either coerce or nudge people to behave in ways that the nudgers prefer or judge best. Even assuming they do know best, nudgers assume a position superior to those whom they nudge. They interdict the decisions and behaviors people would otherwise have made or engaged in, and they redirect them, either coercively or manipulatively, often without either the consent or even the awareness of those whose decisions and behaviors they nudge.

The other reason Smithian political economy argues for the presumption of equal respect for individuals' schedules of value and purpose is because of the limitations third parties face in trying to assess those schedules. Each of us is in possession of unique knowledge of her own situation, including not only her values and purposes, but also her talents and shortcomings, the opportunities available to her, her desires and preferences, her loyalties and allegiances, her associations and agreements, her worries and concerns. Granting that we are not infallible observers of ourselves or our own situations—and that we often lie not only to others but also to ourselves[3]—still, typically no other person possesses this information to as great an extent as the individual does. The practical implication of this fact is that others are typically not in a good position to evaluate whether a person's actions are rational or not. The standard definition of rationality is that it is a faculty of determining actions or behaviors that conduce to one's goals. Thus one is rational if one is achieving, or making progress toward, one's goals, irrational if one's actions are taking one away from one's goals. But it follows that we can judge whether one is rational or not only if we know what one's goals are; more than that, we would also need to know what alternative means are available for achieving one's goals, how efficient or likely they are, what their trade-off points are, and so on.

Paternalism and Equality

Medical doctor Peter Ubel argues that obesity is irrational: since obesity is unhealthy, and no one wants to be unhealthy, it follows that anyone who is obese is acting contrary to his own goals and is thus acting irrationally.[4] Ubel's argument initially seems plausible, but scrutiny reveals its weakness: Ubel is presuming knowledge he does not, in fact, have. The equivocation comes with the term "healthy." Anyone who is asked whether he wants to be healthy or not will, of course, answer "yes." That is not the telling question, however, because it floats untethered to any context of reality that characterizes real life. The telling question is instead something like: What risks to your health would you be willing to accept to achieve your goals? Most people drive cars, for example, even though it is a leading cause of death, not because they do not value their health but rather because they value other things, too—and sometimes those other things require running certain risks. Similarly with obesity: it is entirely possible that an obese person continues to be obese not because he does not value his health but because he values other things, too—and sometimes those other things win out at the margins. As I argued in Chapter 3, there might, for example, be an obese person

---

[3] See, for example, Ariely 2010.
[4] See Ubel 2009. Leaving no doubt about his opinion of the people disagreeing with him, Ubel entitled his book *Free Market Madness*.

who is well acquainted with the risks he is running, but who values the pleasures of fine food now more than the risks he is running for diabetes or heart attack later. That does not make him irrational; it means he has a set of preferences—a schedule of value—that is different from what Ubel wants him to have. But as a moral agent, the rationally obese person is as entitled to his set of preferences as Ubel is to his—and just as disentitled to enforce his preferences on others as is Ubel. Hence Ubel is making both a factual mistake and a moral mistake. The factual mistake is presuming either that he knows what our rationally obese person's schedule of value is and can thus determine that he is acting irrationally or in contradiction to it, or that there is but one correct schedule of value applicable to all people that the rationally obese person is violating. Both of those are false. The moral mistake is in presuming that he is entitled—by dint of his expertise in health, perhaps—to assume a position of authority over others, thereby extending his own moral agency in such a way that it constricts theirs.

Ubel goes even further than Thaler and Sunstein 2009, dropping the "libertarian" part of the latter's position and embracing full and, when necessary, coercive paternalism. Similarly with Conly 2013, who argues explicitly for "coercive paternalism." One might thus see Ubel and Conly as contemporary Thomas Carlyles minus the racism: although Ubel and Conly display none of the racial animus Carlyle did, they nevertheless muster similar contempt for people they believe make bad decisions for themselves and therefore need superior experts like them to superintend their lives, coercively if necessary.

Ubel, Conly, and others who take positions similar to his are thus like the statesman Adam Smith calls a "man of system," who, according to Smith, acts as if people were not independent and free moral agents, overestimates the reach of his knowledge, and assumes that everyone's schedule of value either is or should be the same as his. But the man of system makes a moral mistake as well—namely, assuming that his fellow citizens are not his moral equal. Smith does not mince words in his condemnation of the legislator who denies this moral equality and who proceeds instead to implement his "ideal plan of government":

[T]o insist upon establishing, and upon establishing all at once, and in spite of all opposition, every thing which that idea may seem to require, must often be the highest degree of arrogance. It is to erect his own judgment into the supreme standard of right and wrong. It is to fancy himself the only wise and worthy man in the commonwealth, and that his fellow-citizens should accommodate themselves to him and not he to them. It is upon this account, that of all political speculators, sovereign princes are by far the most dangerous. This arrogance is perfectly familiar to them. They entertain no doubt of the immense superiority of their own judgment. (TMS, 234)

It is not only prudent for us to entertain doubts about the presumed superiority of our own judgment, owing to the limitations of human knowledge, but it is also morally required by the equal dignity and agency that people possess.

It is easy—indeed, all too easy[5]—for us to assume that our own set of preferences and our own schedule of values are the right ones, the ones others should have as well. Even the more generous of us can fall into a similar trap: we imagine ourselves in another's position and ask ourselves what we would desire or do in her position; then we compare what we imagine we would do to what the person is actually doing, and we judge accordingly. Although this imaginary change of place can often be a good proxy—indeed, Adam Smith argues that it is an integral element of human sociality—nevertheless, it is incomplete because we are not that other person: we do not have access to her situation the way she does, and ultimately we are directly aware of only our own thoughts, sentiments, and preferences. This consideration does not imply a moral relativism. Given one's goals, situation, and so on, there may indeed be objectively rational and irrational things for one to do. The consideration instead indicates the difficulty facing third parties when they try to acquire the knowledge necessary to make that determination about others.

The decentralized capitalist political-economic order is predicated on an equal respect for all human beings, regardless of race or station, recommending that the moral freedom often preferentially presumed by some instead be extended equally to all. Its set of institutions does not lead to equality in wealth, but they presume an equality of authority that is consistent with, and follows from, a profound moral equality.

[5] See Haidt 2012.

Moral Equality

Smithian economics presumed a rough equality in natural human ability, as well as a rough constancy in human motivation. Yet there was another feature of Smith's discussion of people's "different geniuses" that indicates not only a descriptive claim about the human condition, but a moral claim about how we ought to treat others. Recall that Smith wrote:

Among men [as opposed to nonhuman animals], the most dissimilar geniuses are of use to one another; the different produces of their respective talents, by the general disposition to truck, barter, and exchange, being brought, as it were, into a common stock, where every man may purchase whatever part of the produce of other men's talents he has occasion for. (WN, 30)

Part of what is at work in this passage is an early adumbration of Smith's Invisible Hand Argument, which holds that in a free-enterprise society, others can benefit from each individual pursuing his own interest in the market. The "dissimilar geniuses" can be "of use to one another" because when they cooperate or exchange or trade, they make each other better off; but their natural drive to better their own conditions leads them to discover ways to increase the value (to others) of what they do, which in turn leads to an increase in productivity, thereby increasing the "common stock" of goods and services from which all of us benefit.

We might call that an *economic* argument on behalf of capitalism. Capitalist societies expand the frontiers of cooperation among people, and the spreading of capitalist institutions over the last two centuries has led to the greatest increase of wealth and prosperity that humankind has ever known. But this economic argument implies a moral imperative when it is joined with a plausible moral premise. Let me adapt an argument from Peter Singer, who argues that: (1) poverty, and its attendant miseries, is bad; (2) if we can do something about it, we should; (3) we can do something about it; therefore, (4) we should.[6] My adaptation of the argument is: (1') poverty, and its attendant miseries, is bad; (2') if we can do something about it, we should; (3') we now know that decentralized capitalist institutions have alleviated

---

[6] See Singer 2009. Singer believes that his argument entails that we should give money to overseas aid agencies, but I do not think his argument actually implies that. See Otteson 2006: chap. 4.

more poverty than any other remedy ever discovered; therefore (4'), we should advocate decentralized capitalist institutions.

Yet there is another moral argument on behalf of capitalism lurking in that passage from Smith. Smith speaks of the "different genius" that different people possess, of the "dissimilar characters" they develop after "they come to be employed in very different occupations," of people's "different geniuses and talents" that he argues result more from their varying experience and training than from any "difference of natural talents," and of people's "dissimilar geniuses," which reflect their varying tastes, preferences, and specializations (WN, 28–30). What Smith is emphasizing is people's uniqueness despite their equality. This may sound paradoxical, but the nascent science of economics that Smith is working out is able to reconcile the two. People are roughly equal in their abilities to respond to incentives rationally (which sometimes also means irrationally!); they are also roughly equal in their motivations of expanded self-interest and limited benevolence, and in their capacity for organizing their lives around schedules of value and hierarchies of purpose. What makes them unique is the particular form these schedules and hierarchies take, the particular experiences and skills each of them accumulates and develops, and, just as important, the unique place they take in the various associations they join, including the unique relations they form with and bear to other people.

Allowing the material inequalities to which these differences among us can thus reflect a respect for individual dignity. Smith writes that "[i]t is not from the benevolence of the butcher, the brewer, or the baker, that we expect our dinner, but from their regard to their own interest. We address ourselves, not to their humanity but to their self-love, and never talk to them of our own necessities but of their own advantages" (WN, 26–7). That passage can sound as if Smith is suggesting either that human beings are motivated by nothing other than "self-love," or even that they should be motivated by nothing else. Since the former seems false and the latter seems repellent, this does not bode well either way for a system of political economy founded on it. But Smith saw in the dynamics of such exchanges not selfishness but *respect*. Consider the background assumptions required for such negotiations to be successful. Each party must hold—or at least behave as if she holds—that the other's life is her own to lead, and that each will respect and recognize, rather than try to trump, the other's schedule.

The nature of such proposals entails that A and B say, or assume, to each other: "I consider you a peer, so I propose terms on which we might cooperate to our mutual benefit, but you are free to say 'no.'" Consider the profound respect that assumes on each party's behalf. Consider, by contrast, the quite different assumptions involved when third parties C and D decide they should prevent A and B from engaging in what A and B themselves judge to be mutually beneficial voluntary cooperation. C and D say, or assume, to A and B: "You may make the wrong decisions, so we will review your proposals and then decide whether to allow you to proceed. You must obey our judgment." That assumes not a respect for A and B, but, rather, a distrust and suspicion of their judgment. But if A's and B's judgment is suspect, that must be demonstrated by particular reference to A and B; it may not be merely assumed without knowing anything about A and B particularly.

The kinds of equality that are compatible with beings possessing moral agency are *equality of jurisdiction* and *equality of respect*. What gives people dignity, what is admirable and noble in them, just is their capacity for moral agency. It is when people have the liberty to make free choices yet are required to take responsibility for those choices that they both *express* their uniquely moral natures and *become* moral beings. What I call *equality of jurisdiction* is the authority to which each moral being is entitled by virtue of this moral agency; because each moral agent is entitled to jurisdiction over her own actions, that means that each of us is equally entitled to the same scope of jurisdiction that is compatible with the same jurisdiction enjoyed by every other moral agent. Here is how Immanuel Kant summarized this point—and the political-economic policy it entails—in his *Metaphysics of Morals*: "Thus the universal law of right is as follows: let your external actions be such that the free application of your will can co-exist with the freedom of everyone in accordance with a universal law" (1992: 133). Kant makes a similar claim in his *Critique of Pure Reason*: "A constitution allowing *the greatest possible human freedom* in accordance with laws by which *the freedom of each is made to be consistent with that of all others*," he writes, is "a necessary idea, which must be taken as fundamental not only in first projecting a constitution but in all its laws."[7]

[7] Kant 1965 (1781): 312 (A316/B373); Kant's emphases. For discussion, see Otteson 2009.

But the other side of equality of jurisdiction is what I call *equality of respect*. It is when we not only give people the liberty to exercise their judgment but also hold them accountable for their decisions that we respect their moral natures. Kant was right that human dignity follows from one's ability to choose ends for oneself, and that the essence of humanity is as a freely choosing agent. He was also right, however, that that agency imposes an obligation on others to respect it. How do we respect others' agency? By recognizing their freedom to make choices—that is, by recognizing their jurisdiction as being equal to our own—but at the same time holding them responsible for the consequences of their decisions. This latter part is often either forgotten or softened, and it is easy to see why. Holding people responsible for their actions can often be unpleasant. When the consequences are bad, people often either do not wish to be held responsible for them, in which case we can risk confrontation (or worse) if we suggest otherwise, or the bad consequences might cause pain or difficulty—and we naturally wish to alleviate others' pain or mitigate the difficulties they face. Intervening can dissolve both of those sources of unpleasantness. But intervening has costs. There is the cost involved with our own time and scarce resources, and thus the opportunities we forsake to intervene; but, as Kant suggests, there is also the morally much more significant cost we impose on the person we undertake to help. Let me explain.

As I argued in Chapter 6, human beings have as part of their moral agency the skill that Aristotle called *phronesis,* or *judgment*—the skill of knowing what one ought to do. Aristotle was right to call judgment a skill, because, like other skills, to be effective it must be *developed;* and one develops judgment by, and only by, *using* it, which requires the freedom to make choices. Developing judgment in good directions requires receiving feedback: good feedback when one makes good choices, bad feedback when one makes bad choices. This feedback is the *accountability* that is the other side of the "freedom" coin. Its necessary role in developing good judgment is what not only expresses our Kantian dignity but might also, as Aristotle argued, enable true happiness. The cost we impose on others, then, when we intercede between their free decisions and the consequences to which those decisions lead is the denial of this opportunity to develop their judgment. Sometimes this cost is worth it, because the badness of the consequences is great enough to outweigh it. Our own judgment must be involved to know when we should and when we should not intervene. But intervening itself imposes not just a material but also a moral cost; hence a sound judgment about whether to intervene can be made only after these costs, too, have been considered.

This is clearly a delicate matter, and mistakes can be made in either direction—intervening too much or not enough. Yet because good judgment can develop—as well as maintain its robustness once developed—only by continual exercise, and because this exercise must include proper feedback, the default position should be to let the consequences of moral agents' decisions, whether good or bad, redound on them. Let persons enjoy their successes and let them suffer their losses—unless in a particular case there is clear and compelling reason to do otherwise. But those exceptions will have to be specially justified, and the justification will have to be sensitive to the particularities of time, manner, place, and person(s) involved. This has at least one immediate political implication: judging when an exceptional intervention in another's life is warranted will require extensive local knowledge, which cannot be had by people unfamiliar with the particular situation. That calls for decentralization, and a strong presumption against distant third-party interposition.

The claim made by some proponents of socialist-inclined policy that people often require positive help from others in order to fully realize their moral agency thus does not help the socialist's interventionist stance, even though it is true. To know when intervention is required, one needs to possess knowledge that no centralized decision makers could collect. But more than that, the intervention entailed by socialist-inclined policy proposals rely on resources and labor redistributed from other people. That is resources and labor that those others would have otherwise directed to other places had not the centralized agencies intervened to redirect it. Whatever benefit this may have provided for its intended recipient, as a matter of logic this redirection privileges the recipient above others by assuming that attending to the recipient's agency is more important, at least at the margins, than attending to theirs. But that assumption is inconsistent with their *equal* moral agency, and the equal respect that this principle demands for all agents.

In some cases one might argue that a specific person A actually suffers from diminished or corrupted agency, perhaps placing him at a level below the minimum threshold of actual agency altogether; moreover, one might claim that some specific B, C, and D are so comfortably above that minimum threshold that a relatively minor reallocation of their agency, or of the fruits of their agency, might bring A above the threshold and still leave B, C, and D safely above it as well. This argument seems initially plausible, and it might hold up even after scrutiny, but it must clear two significant hurdles before it could serve as the foundation of a general policy. First, because it is only rarely the case that an adult human being has such diminished capacities that he no longer qualifies as a moral agent, it could apply only to exceptional cases. Second, because knowing when an exception is warranted would require extensive particularized, and local, information, it would be difficult for centralized third parties to assess, for any specific case, whether the exception is warranted. In the vast majority of cases in which people possess full agency, even while they lack the means to fully realize in the world what their desires and goals might indicate, sacrificing their means to realize their own goals in order to increase the partial realization of others' goals entails disrespecting their agency in the service of others.

If the most compelling conception of human morality is the one that endorses and protects the principal moral aspects of humanity— freedom and accountability (which are really two aspects of the same feature), and the robust independent judgment we develop when allowed to exercise our freedom and accountability—then not holding people responsible for their decisions does them no favors. It is understandable, even admirable, when they are children, but it is inappropriate when they are adults.

An Unfortunate but Instructive Episode: Bernard Madoff

If people know, or believe, that others will take care of them if they make bad decisions, then they tend to relax their scrutiny and attention. Over time this can weaken their capacity of independent judgment. If they come to believe that *most* areas of their lives are safeguarded by others, they risk losing that capacity altogether. It can then become a self-fulfilling prophecy: treated as if they were not competent to make some decisions for themselves, they can begin to lose the ability to make good decisions in those areas for themselves, which we might take as further evidence of their incapacity and thus of the necessity for more extensive intervention in their lives; that then gives them yet less reason or need to exercise their judgment, leading to its further enervation; and so on. Consider a recent episode that illustrates the dangers to which such a policy can lead.

On December 11, 2008, federal authorities arrested Bernard Madoff on allegations of securities fraud. They were acting on information from his sons, who alleged that Madoff was—through his company Bernard L. Madoff Investment Securities, LLC—operating a multi-billion-dollar "Ponzi scheme" in which he falsified reports of gains and drew from principal to pay out alleged returns. On March 12, 2009, Madoff pleaded guilty to eleven felonies, and he was sentenced to 150 years in prison. The total wealth lost through Madoff's Ponzi scheme is estimated at $65 billion, involving some 13,500 investors.

Perhaps people should have known something was amiss. Madoff's reported returns averaged more than 10 percent per year—every single year, regardless of how the stock market performed. No one has returns like that. Indeed, some people *did* know something was amiss. Harry Markopolos, for example, who was working for a rival investment firm at the time, warned the Securities and Exchange Commission in 1999 and again in 2005 that Madoff could not actually have achieved the results he claimed—at least not legally. He also approached the *Wall Street Journal* in 2005, but the paper decided not to go forward with the story.

Many very smart people lost a lot of money with Madoff. Nobel Peace Prize winner and Holocaust survivor Elie Wiesel lost not only the endowment of his charity but also his personal life's savings. Other investors who lost money with Madoff included people like Steven Spielberg and Larry King, as well as institutions like the Royal Bank of Scotland and the Hong Kong and Shanghai Banking Corporation (HSBC). Madoff reportedly cultivated a "Wizard of Oz" personality: he often refused to meet personally with investors; many people's money he mysteriously refused to take; he boasted that his investment strategies were "too complicated" for most people to understand. Still, should it have taken a stock market crash or high-level statistical analysis to know that something strange was going on—that there was no real wizard behind the curtain? In retrospect, it is hard not to wonder why so many people failed to exercise a little skepticism. How could even highly educated people and sophisticated institutions like worldwide banking groups fall for such a seemingly obvious fraud?

Part of the answer might lie in a psychological phenomenon called *homeostasis,* or *risk compensation.* The idea is that the more that people believe that risks are minimized, the more likely they are to engage in dangerous or foolish behavior. Similarly, if they believe risks are heightened, they are more cautious than they otherwise would be. This phenomenon is called risk *compensation* because people tend to alter their behaviors to compensate for perceived risk. One consequence of the phenomenon of risk compensation—the one most relevant here—is that if third parties undertake to protect people from the undesirable consequences of their own bad decisions, then it gives them exactly the mental ammunition they need to *keep making bad decisions.*

Consider some examples. It turns out that the wearing of bicycle helmets has not decreased the incidence of significant head injury while cycling. This seems counterintuitive, but the explanation is that, feeling invulnerable under a helmet, cyclists take greater risks than they otherwise would. And cars, trucks, and buses around them do the same, passing cyclists wearing helmets at greater speeds and with less of a cushion than they do cyclists without helmets.[8] It also turns out that the increase in the proportion of people wearing helmets while skiing and snowboarding—now up to about 40 percent of all skiers and snowboarders—is not decreasing serious head injury. Why not? With helmets on, people take risks they otherwise never would have, thereby reducing whatever benefit the helmets might have provided.[9] Another example is antilock brakes. Studies conducted in Canada, Denmark, and Germany have demonstrated that the now nearly universal presence of antilock brakes in automobiles has made little measurable improvement in road safety. Researchers have found that drivers' main reaction to the presence of antilock brakes in their cars is to drive faster, begin braking later, and tailgate—thus neutralizing the beneficial effects of the antilock brakes themselves. Finally, it turns out, astonishingly, that there is little evidence that lives have been saved from the substantial worldwide increase in seat belting. According to one British study, "[i]n fact, after the passage of the

---

[8] For a review of a number of related studies, see Cook 2004.
[9] See, for example, Shealy et al. 2008.

[1983 British mandatory] seat-belt law more pedestrians and cyclists were killed as a consequence of belted motorists driving less carefully. And after seat belts became compulsory for children in rear seats, the number of children killed while travelling in rear seats increased, again almost certainly as a result of the false sense of security induced in the parent/driver." According to one researcher, "[t]here is no country in the world that has passed a seat belt law that can demonstrate that it has saved lives."[10]

Now return to Madoff. Why would people fall for schemes like his? No doubt many factors played roles, but perhaps part of the explanation was their knowledge that there are extensive expert watchdog government agencies whose central purpose is to prevent, ferret out, and punish frauds. People believed they were protected, which allowed them to relax their scrutiny and attention. The people conned by Madoff might have thought he was above suspicion because he operates in what is, after all, one of the most extensively and tightly regulated industries in the world. The United States Securities and Exchange Commission monitors, observes, and requires filing and reporting on every single transaction in which Madoff's company engaged; moreover, Madoff's activities also fall under the watchdog jurisdiction of several other governmental agencies, including the Federal Bureau of Investigation and the New York State's Attorney. Together, these agencies employ thousands of people and have annual budgets totaling billions of dollars. Would it not be reasonable for people to believe that they were protected by these agencies—that, surely, no one could get away with something as flagrant as a decades-long multibillion-dollar fraud?

No one wants what Madoff did to happen again. But creating a government agency—or indeed many of them—whose purported job is to take care of the risks to investors might be precisely the *wrong* thing to do. The phenomenon of risk compensation suggests that doing so might encourage people to be less scrutinizing and less skeptical, and thus fitter targets for future frauds. Imagine if what we said to people instead was: "You are on your own. If you invest foolishly and lose your money, too bad for you. So you'd better invest wisely." What would their reaction be? Perhaps people would begin to ask

[10] See Adams 2007.

their bankers, brokers, and advisors probing questions, shopping their money around, and bringing market pressures to bear on investment advisors—in short, being far more careful with their money than they otherwise would be—all of which would decrease the chances of their becoming subject to fraud attempts or increase the chances of early detection of such attempts.

The desire to protect people from the negative consequences of not exercising their judgment—or not exercising it well—is understandable and admirable. It is, after all, what good parents try to do for their children. But being a good parent also entails gradually releasing children from protection and tutelage as they grow into adults. It means that, except in extraordinary cases of actual, demonstrated incompetence, at some point good parents set their children entirely free—for good or ill. Doing otherwise is to imperil an essential part of their humanity—namely, *judgment*—and thus to disrespect what gives them moral dignity—namely, *accountability*. Not holding people accountable therefore not only disrespects their agency but also jeopardizes the conditions under which they can develop the judgment that is essential to their full humanity.

Objective and Subjective Liberty

The political and economic institutions that comport with what I argue are the proper conception of human morality call for the removal of obstacles to people's freedom. More specifically, they call for the removal of legal or other formal obstacles. They do not, however, call for the removal of influence. Thus they entail what might be called an *objective liberty,* or the elimination of coercive and artificial barriers to action. To qualify for removal under objective liberty, the relevant barriers must be *both* coercive and artificial. With acknowledgment that good faith disagreements can arise as to exactly when a barrier becomes coercive, this policy nonetheless applies to those that are coercive. The term "artificial" is meant to refer to those barriers that people erect or place in others' way, not whatever obstacles might "naturally" exist or occur.[11] So, for example, that we live in a world of scarcity, that I am

---

[11] Smith argues that injustice can properly occur only when the "pain" one suffers is produced "from design" (TMS, 96). See also Hayek 2011 (1960): chap. 1.

not seven feet tall, or that you inherited better genes from your parents than I did from mine might all limit the extent to which I can achieve all I would like to achieve, but because they are not the result of deliberate human agency aimed at limiting my freedom, they give rise to no obligation on any person's part to compensate me or refrain from or engage in any particular action. By contrast, a law preventing me from applying for a job because of my race, an ordinance not allowing me to offer my services as a hairdresser, or a restriction on what religious beliefs I may hold are all artificial—meaning they were created deliberately by other human beings—and are coercive insofar as they impose penalties—taxes, fines, or jail—on me if I fail to comply.

The political and economic institutions I argue human dignity implies calls for the elimination, to the extent possible, of all such artificial limitation on my action. Capitalist-inclined policy is distinguished in part by its tendency to comply with this maxim, conceiving of freedom as the absence of such obstacles. It is a "negative" conception, because it means that to be free does not require people to do things *for* me but rather to refrain from doing things *to* me.

Socialist-inclined policy, however, is often motivated by the belief that the *objective liberty* required by capitalism is insufficient. The norms, the reigning systems of beliefs, and the culturally entrenched background worldview in a community can all function as limitations on one's freedom, insofar as they might lead one to believe that one's options are constrained in various ways that they objectively are not.[12] So, for example, a community's beliefs about what lines of work are proper for men or for women might acculturate people to believe that certain occupations are improper, and thus off limits, for them when, in fact, they might be well suited to them. Other similar examples are easy to imagine. It might also be the case that the way options are framed for us can alter the choices we make. If school cafeterias, for example, put vegetables and fruits under bright lights near the front of the line, and fatty fried foods under dingy light near the back, they might encourage more people to choose fruits and vegetables instead of fried foods.[13] For reasons like these, some argue that public policy should strive to realize not only *objective liberty* but also

---

[12] See Sunstein 1997: esp. chaps. 1 and 2.
[13] See Thaler and Sunstein 2009.

what we might call *subjective liberty*—that is, the subjective feeling or belief that one is free to make a wide range of choices. We might, for example, using Thaler and Sunstein's language, ask policy makers to become "choice architects," using governmental authority and revenue to allow experts to arrange the way options appear to people in the hopes of either (1) increasing the likelihood that they will actually make choices we believe are better ones or (2) diminishing the power that negative or even pernicious influences have over people's choices.

In earlier chapters I examined several practical difficulties attendant on empowering centralized agencies with these kinds of mandates. The chief difficulties stem from the fact that we know far less than we might think about how to affect any given person's behavior, about what is actually a good choice for any given person, and about what unintended costs and other consequences might be associated with such mandates. Moreover, people's individual uniqueness makes it all but impossible to construct effective general policies. In addition to those practical difficulties, however, there is the principled one that *subjective liberty* cannot be achieved except by infringing people's *objective liberty*—and the latter takes lexical priority over the former. Only objective liberty is "compossible," meaning that all people can simultaneously enjoy it. By contrast, if a centralized authority could achieve subjective liberty at all, it could do so only selectively, by sacrificing some of the objective liberty of at least some people in the service of others. We know this because, first, the choice architects must be supported out of revenues that must be collected from others; that means that the produce of some people's labor will be put to uses to which they otherwise would not have put them. Additionally, however, if the choice architects are successful in getting people to alter their choices, it will only be by having taken positive steps to rearrange various aspects of people's circumstances. That entails the erection of barriers, inducements, and punishments that would constitute infringements, even if only small ones, on the objective liberty of those being induced.

The strongest objection to governmental attempts to establish subjective liberty, however, is the moral one that it entails a disrespecting of moral agency. Sunstein and others claim that people's choices are inevitably influenced not only by the laws but also the norms of society, and that hence it is impossible to have a government that exerts no influence on people. That may be true, but it does not follow that people cannot still make free and rational choices: *free* because it is their will, their own unique consciousnesses making the decisions, not those of others; and *rational* because they reflect their own personal schedules of value given the circumstances and opportunities they face. It may be true that I decided to enroll at Notre Dame in part because the Catholic high school I attended considered Notre Dame to be the greatest university in the world, perhaps even where God himself taught, all other colleges and universities following distantly behind. Nevertheless, it was I who made the decision. It might also be true that I therefore turned down other universities that were more highly ranked, but that does not mean that my decision to attend Notre Dame was not a rational one—indeed, the right one—for me. It follows similarly for any number of other decisions I have made and will make, for decisions you have made or will make, and so on for everyone else.

Conclusion

The institutions of capitalism do not second-guess the decisions you make, and they do not presume to know better than you what the right decisions are for you or what decisions you would have made had circumstances around you been different. Instead, they entrust you with responsibility for taking the proper factors into account correctly, even of determining what the proper factors are, and they have faith that you will not only seek out advice and counsel from the appropriate relevant others when it seems to you necessary or helpful, but also that you will learn from your inevitable mistakes. They remove artificial obstacles put in your way, and they grant neither special favors nor special privileges. They therefore treat you not like a child or an infirm person, but as a person of dignity and as the competent adult that you are. In so doing, they respect not only your moral agency, but that of everyone else as well. Therein lie both the equality and the freedom of capitalism.

11

Fairness

Introduction

One main argument in support of socialist-inclined policy is the alleged unfairness of outcomes that result from nonsocialist policies. Under capitalism, some will have more—indeed, some will have much more—than others, and the disparities will result, at least in part, from morally arbitrary reasons. This does not refer to theft or fraud, which are not allowed under capitalism, but rather to material factors affecting people's relative levels of success in life that none of the relevant people can claim to have deserved. Some people just get unlucky in the circumstances of their birth, for example. As Thomas Nagel asks, "How could it not be an evil that some people's life prospects at birth are radically inferior to others?" (1995: 28). John Rawls identifies three species of luck that substantially affect everyone's lives, in good and bad ways, but that he asserts cannot give rise to claims of moral desert because they were not chosen by the individual: "family and class origins," "natural endowments," and "fortune and luck" (1975: 95). The assumed premise is that one cannot claim to deserve something unless one freely chose to act in a way that created, generated, or contributed to it. This seems plausible: I cannot claim any moral credit (or blame) for my genes, for example, or for the education others provided for me. To the extent, then, that decentralized capitalist-political economy allows inequalities to result from these morally arbitrary factors, those inequalities are suspect.

Perhaps I could claim some credit for what I do with my native gifts (or burdens), but Rawls suggests that even there my role might be less than I might imagine since substantial parts of my personality also result from factors outside of my control: "it seems clear that the effort a person is willing to make is influenced by his natural abilities and skills and the alternatives open to him." Rawls continues, "[t]he better endowed are more likely, other things equal, to strive conscientiously, and there seems to be no way to discount for their greater good fortune. The idea of rewarding desert is [therefore] impracticable" (1971: 312).[1] Rawls concludes that it is unfair for some people to have been unduly benefitted by good luck, just as it is unfair for others to have been unduly burdened by bad luck, and thus a fair system of political economy—for Rawls, a *just* one, since for him justice is fairness—will take pains to correct for these unchosen and therefore undeserved advantages and disadvantages.

Socialist-inclined policy moves from plausible considerations like these to recommend the establishment of governmental institutions aimed at mitigating unfairness and promoting fairness, so conceived. Rawls claims that practical difficulties doom any attempt to reward desert, and he is no doubt correct if he means by that *centrally* rewarding desert—how could central authorities have any idea what you or I deserve? But the move to policy implied by his recommendation itself introduces substantial difficulties that may prove fatal to the attempt to realize fairness in our political-economic institutions. Let us look at three such difficulties: one arising from an incomplete and thus biased assessment of the benefits and liabilities involved, another from a perhaps surprising justification for a charge of unfairness directed at socialist-inclined policy, and a third relating to the connection between fairness and equality.

Fairness and Social Cost

The first problem with attempting to realize a conception of fairness through policy arises from an insight that Ronald Coase articulated in

---

[1] Whether the better endowed are, in fact, more likely to strive conscientiously is an empirical claim, one for which there is actually some doubt. See, for example, Eisenstadt et al. 1989 and Stanley and Danko 2010. For a classic statement, see Carnegie 2006 (1889): chap. 3.

his canonical 1960 paper "The Problem of Social Cost." Coase points out that many court cases alleging damages, and calling either for injunctions against the perpetrators of the damage or payment from the perpetrator to the victim to compensate for the damage, unjustifiably privilege one side of the costs and benefits—when, in fact, there is an additional set of costs and benefits that should, *in fairness,* also be reckoned. Coase discusses the case of *Sturges v. Bridgman* (1879) in which a medical doctor alleged he was unable to work in one of the rooms of his office because next door was a confectioner whose candy-making machinery caused disruptive vibrations and noise. The doctor sued for damages, and asked the court to issue an injunction against the confectioner. There were clear costs being borne by the doctor—revenue lost from unusable space, psychological anguish, and so on—as well as obvious benefit to the doctor if the confectioner stopped running those machines. But what was not taken notice of by the court was that such an injunction would itself have costs—namely, lost revenue to the confectioner, as well as lost benefit to the confectioner's employees and customers.

If the question is about costs, therefore, the matter is not simply whether costs are imposed on the doctor; of course they are. The question, rather, is which costs are greater—those generated by the injunction or those generated by continuing the status quo. The confectioner, after all, is benefitting from operating that machinery, and others—his employees, customers, family, and so on—are benefitting as well. The doctor would benefit from the cessation of operation of the machinery, but which is greater: the benefit to the doctor if the machines stop, or the benefit to the confectioner if he continues? Which is greater: the cost to the doctor if the confectioner's machines keep running, or the cost to the confectioner if he must stop them? Neither question can be answered in the abstract, and focusing only on (1) the doctor's costs if the machinery continues to run and (2) the benefits to the doctor if the machinery stops gives an incomplete picture of the situation. A judgment based on that partial picture is therefore biased in favor of the doctor.

Now apply Coase's reasoning to the worries about fairness. Suppose A believes that B is currently benefitting from some practice or situation that either does not benefit A, does not benefit A as much as B is benefitted, or makes A's situation worse than it might otherwise be if the practice or situation were different from what it is. If the situation is not what A voluntarily chose, or could reasonably have been foreseen by A when A made the relevant choices, then A claims the practice or situation is unfair and seeks injunction against B in the form of legal prohibition, tax correction (penalty on B or subsidy for A), or wealth transfer via damages. But any of those remedies would also impose costs not only on B but also on anyone dependent on or benefitting from B. That means that those options constitute the mirror image of A's grounds for complaint of unfairness, only now it is unfair to B. If we wish, therefore, to base a claim of unfairness on costs and benefits and do so on objective grounds, as opposed to grounds prejudicing one party to the dispute, then we would have to assess the respective costs and benefit of *both* courses of action, and then compare the two. It is not always clear which side will win.

The implication is that claims of fairness or unfairness often arise from privileging the perspective of one party to the dispute over that of the other party. Perhaps one party imagines it would profit more, or be happier, if things were different—and that may well be the case. If the contested status quo involves rights violations, such as the coercing or defrauding of unwilling others, then we have prima facie reason, on both socialist and capitalist grounds, for forbidding that aspect of the status quo or seeking reparations for the victims. But the kinds of cases typically invoked in claims of unfairness do not involve rights violations, coercion, or fraud. They involve instead accidents of fortune that benefit some more than others, that allow some to achieve more than others, and so on. The Coasean insight is simply that any imposed alteration to the status quo does not merely remove one set of costs or confer one set of benefits: it also imposes costs on and removes benefits to other parties, which can generate a plausible claim for them of unfairness on precisely the same grounds—because they, too, are not responsible for the same morally arbitrary elements involved in the status quo. Under the proposed reform of the status quo, they would be punished for accidents of fortune they did not cause and for which they are not responsible. Even though it might be true that those who (luckily) have better natural endowments, genes, or families will benefit from them—although this is by no means guaranteed—since such disparities do not arise from rights violations we cannot justify an imposed correction without first estimating the costs and benefits of both the status quo and of the imagined new social order and then demonstrating that the overall benefits of the latter outweigh those of the former. To justify the redistribution of costs and benefits, then, would require showing that the unfairness to one party, or set of parties, is greater or worse than it is or would be to the other party or set of parties.

How could one show that? Perhaps by claiming that inequality is, in and of itself, objectionable. Let us come back to that. Another way to justify a greater concern for the unfairness some face than for the unfairness others face is by claiming that some people's situations are *more deserving of consideration* than those of others. Perhaps the unfairness faced by the poorer among us deserves consideration before any unfairness faced by those not falling into that category. That seems at least initially plausible. But the grounds for believing that must, it would seem, be either (1) that the cost to them of the unfairness they face is greater than is the cost to the others of the unfairness those others face, (2) that the unfairness of being poor is inherently worse than other kinds of unfairness, or (3) that the situation of the poor is more important than is that of the nonpoor. Each of these seems insufficient. The first returns us to the discussion of Coase: one cannot merely assume that the costs and benefits applicable to one party exceed (or not) those applicable to other parties. Any proposed remedy or alteration to the status quo will entail costs on all concerned parties, and so must all be reckoned and compared in any creditable cost/benefit analysis.

For case (2): What reason is there to think this? Consider neglect, disrespect, misjudgment, and so on. Perhaps poverty compounds the unfairness of life; poverty itself might just be multiple unfairnesses. Fair enough. But that, too, refers us to the cost/benefit analysis applicable under Coasean reasoning.

Finally, for case (3): this seems a morally repugnant inequality. A foundational principle of morality is that all moral agents deserve equal respect qua moral agents. Privileging some—any group—over others violates that moral imperative, even if it sometimes serves ends we prefer. I therefore reject it on principled grounds.

If one wished to defend it selectively, however, one would face, in addition to the Coasean worries, an additional, potentially fatal problem: not all poor are alike. There is no obvious way to assess the unfairness faced by the poor as a group because that group includes people of radically different fortunes and on radically different trajectories. There are, for example, recently or only temporarily unemployed, recent immigrants, college students, Donald Trump during one of his bankruptcies, and so on—and there is no single way to accommodate them all appropriately. Hence, if this claim is to be based on the inherent unfairness of the situation of the poor, individual assessments of the relevant poor persons will be required. This will prove impossible to do centrally, and thus it would fail as a putative justification for any general policy.

Varieties of Fairness

One reason that disagreements about which political-economic policies are conducive to fairness often seem intractable is that people mean different things by "fairness." Jonathan Haidt has identified three separate conceptions of fairness that he finds animating the claims people press as being "fair" or "unfair." First is "procedural fairness," which Haidt describes as including concerns about "whether impartial and open procedures are used when affecting the well being of others are made"; it asks questions such as, "Is the decision-maker impartial? Is the game rigged?" A second conception is "distributive fairness," which "refers to how we distribute stuff—benefits as well as burdens." It asks questions such as, "Is everyone getting his fair share and doing her fair share?" Haidt argues, however, that distributive fairness has two "subtypes," namely, "equality," where everyone gets the same, and "proportionality," where everyone receives rewards in proportion to their inputs. So, according to Haidt, the three kinds of fairness are (1) procedural, (2) equally distributive, and (3) proportionally distributive. In Haidt's view, failure to distinguish these differing conceptions, the conflation of them, and the selective movement from one version to another, are what make arguments about fairness "interminable" because they allow people "to talk past each other" (2013: 43).[2]

---

[2] Haidt presents evidence suggesting that the differing conceptions of fairness fall along political lines. Although people on both the left and the right agree on procedural fairness, Haidt claims that the left "simultaneously endorses [distributive] equality, even when it is in tension with proportionality"; by contrast, "[c]onservatives prefer proportionality, even when it leads to massive inequalities of outcome" (Spring 2013: 43–4).

Perhaps the most influential twentieth-century treatment of fairness is that of John Rawls. According to Rawls, an institution is "fair" if, first, "it satisfies the two principles of justice," and, second, if "one has voluntarily accepted the benefits of the arrangement or taken advantage of the opportunities it offers to further one's interests" (1971: 111–12). His "two principles of justice" are: (1) "Each person is to have an equal right to the most extensive total system of equal basic liberties compatible with a similar system of liberty for all"; and (2) "Social and economic inequalities are to be arranged so that they are both: (a) to the greatest benefit of the least advantaged [...] and (b) attached to offices and positions open to all under conditions of fair equality of opportunity" (1971: 302). Rawls's full argument is quite complex, and we cannot hope to do it justice here. But its intuitive structure is clear: No one should be accorded more liberty than anyone else, at least not by society's basic legal institutions; and, while we start with equality as our social, economic, and moral "benchmark," we allow inequalities only insofar as they conduce primarily—although not necessarily exclusively—to the benefit of the least advantaged among us. Rawls believes that under proper deliberative conditions, substantially all of us would agree to these principles. That is what makes them "fair," and what provides their justification.

Rawls's first principle of justice is quite similar to the conception of equal moral agency for which I have argued, and which I claimed was reflected by both Adam Smith and Kant and thus captured in decentralist political economy. Rawls's second principle, however, takes him in the centralist direction. As I argued in Part I, this introduces substantial practical challenges—including difficulties with obtaining the required knowledge and the generation of significant costs—that Rawls opts not to consider but that might indeed imperil his project. But one potential objection to his second principle of justice that he does anticipate is itself based on a claim of unfairness. Some will claim that they *deserve* their relative success in life, and, as long as they have done no injury to anyone else, any attempt to penalize them or redistribute the fruits of their efforts is itself unfair. Rawls's answer: "No one deserves his greater natural capacity nor merits a more favorable starting place in society" (1971: 100); moreover, "It seems to be one of the fixed points of our considered judgments that no one deserves his place in the distribution of native endowments, any more than one deserves one's initial starting place in society" (1971: 104).³ If you concede that but still contend that you deserve whatever you do with your "native endowments," Rawls has an answer to that as well: "The assertion that a man deserves the superior character that enables him to make the effort to cultivate his abilities is equally problematic; for his character depends in large part upon fortunate family and social circumstances for which he can claim no credit. The notion of desert seems not to apply to these cases" (1971: 104). Rawls's argument is that the true unfairness involved here is when society's institutions allow some to reap benefit from fortunate but undeserved circumstances, while others benefit less or even suffer from unfortunate but equally undeserved circumstances.

John Tomasi has recently argued that there is another, third political-economic position one might take, one that combines the important moral insights from both the advocates of decentralism and the advocates of centralism. Tomasi calls his position "market democracy," and he argues that it prizes, on the one hand, both the material prosperity and the respect for individual moral agency reflected in decentralist political economy, while at the same time respecting the concern for the "great ills" that can befall people through undeserved misfortune that is reflected in centralist political economy. Tomasi's resolution of these claims—each, as he says, morally telling and yet pulling in different directions—is to sublimate them into a position that champions what he calls "free market fairness," according to which "a fair share is the largest possible bundle of real wealth that might be procured for (by!) the least fortunate, consistent with respecting the rights of other citizens" (2012: 268–9).

The argument I have made for decentralism's moral superiority to centralism has been based on the former's respect, and the latter's disrespect, of equal moral agency. Building now on an aspect of Tomasi's argument, I suggest that the moral principle underlying the demand

³ I note that Rawls is here bracketing out other plausible ways people might "deserve" their starting places in society. Perhaps one's parents worked to provide for their children an education they themselves did not enjoy; in that case, the children might deserve that education not because of anything they themselves did but because that was their parents' wish. Or perhaps someone might "deserve a chance," not because of anything she did in the past, but because of what promise she holds for what she might accomplish in the future. And so on. See Schmidtz 2002.

for equal moral respect implies an objection of "unfairness" to the Rawlsian position, although not like the unfairness objection Rawls himself addresses. As Tomasi rightly argues, respecting others' moral agency entails a general respect for the decisions they make about how to live their lives; that means it entails respect for their *economic* decisions just as much as it does their other decisions. Whereas centralists tend to be concerned, and justifiably, about other kinds of liberties— those associated with democratic voting rights, for example, with the creation and maintenance of human community, or with alleviation of poverty or misfortune—they tend to be less concerned about, for example, the liberty to allocate one's time, talent, and treasure according to one's unique and personal schedule of value. But this means that the centralist underestimates the degree to which these kinds of decisions are constitutive of our identities. People are not merely formal deciding machines; people are filled out, completed, and embodied by the decisions they make, the results of those decisions, the future decisions they make in light of the results, and so on. Respecting them as moral agents with a dignity equal to one's own entails, then, respecting all these decisions they make, and recognizing them as responsible for the resulting consequences.

Holding equality of results, along any dimension, to be the moral benchmark from which deviations must be specially defended thus gets the moral priority exactly backward. Indeed, we should expect that people will be unequal across these dimensions, because each of them is unique in all the substantive ways that matter. People's schedules of value, hierarchies of purpose, interests, preferences, goals, ambitions: these are the changing variables that integrate into the impossibly complex and dynamically evolving equation constituting each human being. Uniqueness plus liberty results in diversity. Thus, any material or substantive equality that any two persons share will likely be accidental, coincidental—and fleeting. Far from being the benchmark, then, substantive material equality among a population of unique moral agents should be the rare, even bizarre, exception. It follows that an attempt to create, or even approximate, such an equality cannot happen but by artificially restricting the decisions or actions (some) individuals can take, or by imposing artificial penalties on some actions or subsidies on others. This indeed is precisely what the centralist endorses, and thus what I argue inspires a charge of unfairness, because it fails to credit them as the unique moral agents they are.

Whatever else fairness might be, it does seem linked to the notion of moral desert: it is fair to get—and unfair not to get—what we deserve. Rawls's argument is that because we do not deserve our native endowments or the luck we experience, we cannot claim to deserve them; from there he argues that we can base no objection to centralized redistribution on unfairness. But if we are equal moral agents, and if the respect that that commands requires us to respect both people's liberty to make decisions and their responsibility for those decisions, then redistribution motivated to correct the signature of resulting effects constitutes a disrespect of people's equal moral agency. In light of their agency they *morally deserve* respect. Redistribution, as well as other methods of centralized restriction, denies them this respect. It is therefore unfair.

Fairness and Equality

Suppose we have two people, A and B, and A has much more wealth than B. Knowing nothing else about them, what if anything should we conclude about the fairness of their respective positions? A first question to ask is whether A got her wealth by violating any aspect of decentralism's conception of justice—did A steal or defraud anyone to get it? Let us stipulate that A did not: all of the transactions that led to A having that wealth were both voluntary and mutually beneficial. Let us further stipulate that all those transactions were "euvoluntary," Michael Munger's brilliant neologism that defines a proper transaction as having to meet all of the following six criteria[4]: (1) each party to the transaction had conventional (and uncontested) ownership of whatever was exchanged; (2) each party possessed the conventional (and uncontested) capacity to buy, sell, negotiate, and so on; (3) after the exchange (my addition: perhaps for a *reasonable period* thereafter), neither party regretted the exchange; (4) there ensued no uncompensated externalities (my addition: perhaps no *large, unreasonable,* or *uncompensatable* externalities); (5) no party to the exchange was coerced by human agency into exchanging (my addition: no party

---

[4] See Munger 2011.

experienced improper pressure of any kind from other human agents); and, finally, (6) no party to the exchange was coerced by circumstance, which Munger defines as meaning that the gap between the actual exchange and the next-best alternative to the negotiated agreement for the respective parties is not too large.

Now, are there any reasonable grounds to object to A's having more wealth than B? Perhaps your inclination is to say that if there was no theft or fraud and if the exchanges were all euvoluntary, then, no, there are no reasonable grounds to object. But suppose that A has *twice* as much wealth as B. Does that change your inclination? Suppose A has *ten* times as much wealth as B. Suppose that A has *100* times as much wealth as B. Is there something wrong with the situation now? Should we think it is unfair for this disparity to exist, even though no (negative) injustice took place and all transactions were euvoluntary? Perhaps we suspect that to occupy such a position of relative poverty B must be one of society's disadvantaged—disadvantaged, that is, by unfortunate accidents of (as Rawls puts it) "family and class origins," "natural endowments," "fortune and luck," or some combination of these. But suppose now I tell you that A is really Bill Gates, and B is really Michael Jordan. As of this writing, Gates is estimated to have a net worth of approximately $60 billion, whereas Jordan is estimated to have a net worth of a mere $600 million. So Gates has 100 times as much wealth as Jordan. But it is hard to imagine anyone thinking that Jordan must therefore be compensated for his unfortunate position. Indeed, even suggesting such a claim seems preposterous. But this suggests that the inequality of people's respective positions by itself does not generate any justifiable grounds for redistribution or reparation.

What matters is instead something else—not only how each of them got to the position he enjoys, but also the absolute position of the person in the inferior position. These are exactly the matters that the decentralized system of political economy addresses. Its insistence, first of all, that all transactions adhere to the rules of (negative) justice, which include that they are mutually voluntary and beneficial (which together roughly approximate Munger's euvoluntary criteria), addresses the first concern of how each of them attained his respective position.

Moreover, as I argued in Chapter 9, the wealth and prosperity that the decentralized system enables thereby also provides the only method we have yet discovered to raise people out of the poverty that has been the historical condition of human existence. The definition of "absolute" or "extreme" poverty that the World Bank offers is living at the level of $1.25 per day.[5] As Peter Singer puts it, "[t]his kind of poverty kills" (2009: 8). But that level of poverty is approximately the average of what all human beings throughout all human history faced—at least until about 1800 or so. Indeed, the average person alive in 1800 was no better off in terms of material prosperity than the average human alive 100,000 years ago.[6] Since then, however, as the global population increased from 1 billion (in 1804) to 7.1 billion (in 2013), approximately 6 billion people have ascended above those levels—and the rate of ascendence has been increasing, especially in the last few decades. The worldwide average today is $34 per day, a *twenty-seven-fold* real increase. (In the United States, the increase is even more dramatic: in 1800, the U.S. population was 5.3 million, the average life expectancy at birth was 39, and the real gross domestic product (GDP) per capita was $3.68 per day; in 2011, the population was 308 million, average life expectancy at birth was 78, and GDP per capita was $134 per day.) The wealth produced by decentralized capitalist exchange and innovation has now brought us to the point where, despite the septupling of the population, we can realistically imagine a time in the not-too-distant future where effectively *no one* lives at the historical levels of poverty. That is an astonishing prospect, all the more so when we realize just how unprecedented it is.

To put that into moral perspective, consider the following question: If you could solve only one social ill, either poverty or inequality, but not both, which would you solve? The evil of poverty lies not in the fact that some have less, even much less, than others. It lies instead in its absolute conditions. Decentralized capitalist-political economy has provided the only consistent and sustained means ever discovered to alleviate poverty, and its performance on this score, when viewed from the perspective of humanity's history, has been nothing less than spectacular. If it also allows inequality, however—as indeed it does—then the choice of poverty *or* inequality seems to be the actual choice we face. We cannot solve both.

---

[5] Here and throughout this discussion, I use constant 2009 U.S. dollars.
[6] See Clark 2007: chap. 1.

Thomas Nagel's question "How could it not be an evil that some people's life prospects at birth are radically inferior to others?" is not merely rhetorical. It turns out it has a serious answer: radically different prospects by themselves are not evil. When they obtain in the context of institutions allowing everyone to better his life prospects in real, substantial, and historically unprecedented ways, perhaps the true evil would lie in pursuing an equality that hinders this betterment.

Conclusion

The charge of unfairness underlies many calls for socialist-inclined redistribution. Yet discussions of such redistribution often take an incomplete view of the relevant costs and benefits. When a full view is taken, it is not always clear that the redistribution is warranted. Moreover, although there are several ways to conceive of fairness and unfairness, socialist-inclined policy itself generates an often unappreciated but nevertheless plausible charge of unfairness. Finally, socialist-inclined policy is motivated by worries of inequality, but if capitalist-inclined policy is alleviating poverty and leading to steadily fewer people suffering from its miseries, and at the same time instantiates a respect for equal moral agency of all individuals, then socialist-inclined policy is aiming at the wrong target. And if fairness as a moral category is to have a creditable political-economic import, then it will have to apply to the demand for respect of equal moral agency and the beneficial prosperity—especially for the poor—that its entailed decentralized political economy enables.

Conclusion

Grapes Sweet and Sour

Introduction

The two central questions facing socialism, as well as any other system of political economy, are whether it is *feasible* and whether it is *morally desirable*. As I have argued, these questions are lexical. The desirability of a system of political economy is, in part, a function of its feasibility, and before we can judge whether it is appropriate or desirable in itself, we must have a sense of the difficulties, challenges, and costs involved in implementing it. Investigation into the proper system of political economy must be motivated by a genuine concern for the prosperity and well-being of the people affected by the system—all of them, not only a subset of them. To warrant serious consideration, it must be a *complete* proposal, which requires addressing both of the aforementioned questions. A proposal addressing only one question does not yet rise to the level of a legitimate contender.

One of Aesop's fables, "The Fox and the Grapes," tells the story of a fox strolling through an orchard and coming upon a grape vine that has been trained over a high branch. That high branch has sweet, succulent grapes hanging from it. After repeated attempts, however, the fox simply cannot reach those grapes. In frustration, the fox finally gives up, declaring that the grapes were probably sour anyway. Aesop's moral: "It is easy to despise what you cannot get." Let us conclude our analysis of socialism by asking both the necessary questions: Is socialism unattainable, like the high grapes in Aesop's fable? And if it is, does that mean it is not morally desirable in itself—or is our condemnation of it just sour grapes?

The Feasibility of Socialism

Our examination has shown that socialism is not, in fact, feasible—at least not for any but very small groups, or without tremendous sacrifice in human well-being. Hutterites, Shakers, monasteries, kibbutzim, and other small-scale experiments have attempted to centrally organize their economies, with varying levels of success.[1] But their examples are inapplicable to larger communities like cities, states, or countries because what success they can achieve depends on (1) their small size, (2) their narrow ultimate aims, (3) their unity of schedules of value of their members, and (4) their members' willingness to accept substantially lower standards of living—none of which is present in larger communities. For socialism to achieve its goals on larger scales it would require centralized planners to organize the production of goods and services, to allocate scarce resources, and to coordinate people's decisions, associations with others, and productive activities. As our analysis has demonstrated, however, the knowledge required to accomplish these tasks is both vast and constantly changing, and for those reasons is unable to be gathered, assessed, and acted upon by any group of centralized planners. Thus any attempt to achieve the ends of socialist-inclined policy on larger scales will require narrowing the possibilities of innovative cooperation, and each step in that direction entails reduction of prosperity. As the frontiers of open cooperation approach zero, prosperity will approach collapse.[2]

But socialist policies face the further problem of introducing massive costs and disincentives. The gathering and assessing of knowledge will require centralized apparatuses staffed by people no longer engaged in wealth-producing labor; the execution of the decisions

---

[1] I thank Jason Sorens for a helpful discussion on this point.

[2] For discussion of various historical experiments on both small and large scales, see Bethell 1998, esp. chaps. 9 and 10; Muravchik 2002; and Pipes 2000, esp. chap. 5. Ridley (2010) provides several historical examples illustrating the process. One particularly striking instance is that of Tasmania, which suffered severe regressions in prosperity when it attempted to achieve self-sufficiency about 10,000 years ago. Ridley writes: "The archaeologist who first described the Tasmanian regress, Rhys Jones, called it a case of the 'slow strangulation of mind'" (2010: 79).

the central authorities make will also require apparatuses staffed by people similarly unengaged in wealth-producing labor; and both sets of apparatus will require continuous monitoring, just as the results of the decisions and the behaviors of citizens in reaction to those decisions will have to be monitored as well. The costs associated with these efforts, including the costs in forgone production—what these people would have produced had they not been engaged in these efforts—are not inconsiderable.

It is not only the cost of these required agencies, however, that must be reckoned, but also the disincentive they provide to productive labor. As has been demonstrated by numerous historical examples,[3] people often respond adversely when they believe that others will decide how much of the fruits of their labors they themselves will be allowed to keep, and what the disposition will be of that portion the centralized group takes from them. Their impulse is often to slacken their efforts, not only out of resentment and spite—although these are not to be underestimated—but also, especially as the proportion taken for redistribution increases, on the increasingly rational realization that laboring is not worth the effort. If some people, including perhaps those reasoning this out themselves, receive payment from the common pool whether they labor or not, then the calculation is not only simple but coldly straightforward: the fruits of my own efforts are divided among many people, and hence make a negligible difference to any one person; on the other hand, ceasing my efforts makes a significant difference to me by saving my own energy. The rational conclusion is for me to stop working and to live off others' labor. This tragedy-of-the-commons logic becomes all the more compelling the more that equality is sought by greater redistribution of wealth. As this dynamic unfolds, with each iteration of redistribution there is, hence, marginally less to redistribute, owing both to decreasing production by laborers and to the increasing proportion of wealth consumed by the centralized planners and their agents required to effect and monitor the redistribution. This process will continue with ups and downs, but with downwardly sloping trend lines, until wealth production can effectively cease. Unfortunately, there is no escape from this tragic trajectory—except by abandoning the drive toward

---

[3] See, for example, Acemoglu and Robinson 2012.

centralization. What has happened in every attempt to implement socialist policy on any scale larger than a family or very small group— namely, regression—has happened not by accident or chance, then, and not because of contingent local circumstances, but as the inexorable result of socialism's unfolding centralist logic.

Reaching Socialism's Grapes

Some might argue that the infeasibility of socialism by itself completes the case against it. What more, one might ask, needs to be said about a proposed system of political economy if it has been demonstrated that its ideal is impossible for any large or diverse community to establish in practice? But socialism's infeasibility does not defeat it *as an ideal.* It might, as an ideal, still be desirable in itself, or preferable to other ideals, which might, after all, also turn out to be impossible to instantiate in practice perfectly. In Plato's *Republic,* Socrates responds thus to the objection that his ideally conceived city, organized and planned centrally by philosopher-kings, might not be possible to instantiate in practice:

> [SOCRATES:] Do you think that someone is a worse painter if, having painted a model of what the finest and most beautiful human being would be like and having rendered every detail of his picture adequately, he could not prove that such a man could come into being?
> [GLAUCON:] No, by god, I don't.
> [SOCRATES:] Then what about our own case? Didn't we say that we were making a theoretical model of a good city?
> [GLAUCON:] Certainly.
> [SOCRATES:] So do you think that our discussion will be any less reasonable if we can't prove that it's possible to found a city that's the same as the one in our theory?
> [GLAUCON:] Not at all.
> [SOCRATES:] Then that's the truth of the matter.[4]

A similar dialogue could be run with respect to socialism. Hence the examination—and alleged refutation—of socialism is not yet complete.

Almost all moral ideals are impossible to instantiate perfectly in practice. Consider, for example, this Kantian categorical imperative:

---

[4] Plato 1992, bk. 5, 472d–e, pp. 147–8.

"Act only according to that maxim whereby you can at the same time will that it should become a universal law."[5] Putting to one side the difficulties in interpreting this imperative's exact meaning (not to mention the difficulties involved in determining how to apply it to various concrete cases), it is probably safe to say that no one, including Kant himself, imagined that anyone could flawlessly live her entire life in accordance with this maxim. We are imperfect creatures—for Kant, who was a Christian, we are *fallen*—and thus perfection is not possible for us; as Kant writes, humanity is fashioned from "crooked timber" from which "nothing straight can be made" (1992: 46–7). What can be hoped for instead, and against which we may indeed properly be judged, is the degree to which we are able to approximate this ideal in our lives. Some people come nearer to the ideal than others; at some points in our lives, we ourselves approached it more nearly than at other times; and at some points others, and we ourselves, clearly fell short. Kant's categorical imperative can serve, therefore, as an ideal toward which we can aspire. It can also serve as a measuring stick against which we can judge both ourselves and others, and it can provide a relatively fixed standard against which we can determine whether a proposed behavior is morally acceptable. In these ways Kant's categorical imperative is useful and applicable to human life, even if we concede from the outset that it is impossible to attain fully.[6]

Other moral ideals can function in a similar way. Consider the phrase "WWJD?" It is shorthand for "What Would Jesus Do?" and was popular in some parts of the United States for some time on wristbands, t-shirts, and so on. According to the Christian view, Jesus was, although human, also fully divine, and hence His example could be assumed to be perfect. By the same token, however, it means that no other human beings (who are not also divine) could be expected to fully live up to His example. The Christian believes instead that he is called to incorporate, to the extent possible given his "fallen" nature, Jesus's example into his own life, and to use Jesus as a regulative standard against which he judges both himself and others.

[5] Kant 1981, Ak. 421, p. 30.
[6] I do not claim that it is the correct standard of morality, only that the impossibility of realizing it perfectly in our lives does not by itself defeat it.

Hence emulating Jesus can become for the Christian a moral duty, even while fully knowing that no one will be able to do so consistently or perfectly.

Similarly for other moral ideals—including Aristotle's *phronemos* or "virtuous man," Adam Smith's "impartial spectator," the "joint verdict" of David Hume's "true judge[s]," and John Stuart Mill's "competent judges."[7] Each of them involves evaluating an actual person or behavior from the imagined perspective of an ideally situated judge. How each of them understands what it is to be an ideally situated judge might differ, but probably none of them believed that actual living human beings could fully or perfectly become such a judge. The ideal judge would require near-perfect knowledge of the relevant situations and details, near-perfect reasoning or calculating abilities (including the ability to perfectly discount the future), and near-perfect goodness—all of which remain beyond the competence of actual human beings. Nevertheless, each model can serve important functions that give us good reason to adopt and use them in our lives.

The fact that these standards, or any others, cannot be perfectly met in practice therefore does not by itself defeat the standard as an ideal, since it may still be the case that striving to approximate the standard as best as one can is *the right thing to do* regardless of the difficulties involved. Hence, more is required to warrant rejection of an ideal standard. Specifically: one would have to show in addition that the ideal does not merit attaining even if one could. That raises the question of whether the grapes, as it were, are sweet in themselves, even if the fox cannot reach them. So our question is: Are the socialist grapes sweet?

Socialism's Fruits. Yet before addressing that question, one other aspect of the feasibility concern must be broached. What if the attempt to achieve the ideal involved not only various kinds of costs—which, after all, one might judge worth paying in light of other considerations—but, in fact, issued in evils? Let us not use the word *evil* lightly. The fact that under one system of political economy there are "too many" or "not enough" kinds of toothpaste, for example, does not rise to the level of an evil, even if people might plausibly claim in either case that

---

[7] See, respectively, Aristotle 1985, bk. 6, esp. chaps. 5–13; Adam Smith 1982b, bk. 3, chap. 2, paras. 31–2; David Hume 1987: 241; and John Stuart Mill 2012, chap. 2.

the situation is less than ideal.[8] Let us instead reserve the epithet "evil" for things like human-caused starvation or deliberately preventing people from innocently bettering their own conditions of poverty. As miserable and horrific as starvation is, for example, it would not qualify as an evil under this definition unless it was deliberately inflicted by other people. Since for most of human history such poverty was part of humanity's default—even "natural"—condition, even absolute poverty, as bad as it is, would not qualify as evil unless one was either forced into it by other people or someone else actively prevented one from attempting to ascend out of it. If it turned out that the attempt to achieve a moral or political ideal led predictably to evil so defined— the clear and dramatic worsening of people's conditions, or the clear and dramatic prevention of people bettering their own conditions, by means of deliberate human action—then the ideal becomes not only infeasible but potentially vicious as well.

What, then, have attempts to instantiate socialism wrought? The historical empirical record here is both clear and consistent: as socialist-inclined policy is implemented, prosperity decreases and overall quality of life diminishes; whereas when capitalist-inclined policy is implemented, prosperity increases and overall quality of life improves. This pattern holds true for virtually every criterion we have been able to measure or study to gauge human well-being[9]:

- It holds for *wealth,* both in per-capita income and in gross domestic product (GDP) per capita.
- It holds for the *United Nations Development Index,* which is a combined measure of life expectancy, adult literacy rates, levels of school enrollment, and per-capita income.
- It holds for both *life expectancy* and *infant mortality* rates.
- It holds for *child labor* rates, with the more capitalist-inclined countries having a lower proportion of children working than in socialist-inclined countries.

---

[8] This example comes from Schwartz 2005.

[9] For data substantiating these claims, see Lawson et al. 2013, available at: http://www.freetheworld.com/reports.html (accessed December 30, 2012). See also Brooks 2012, McCloskey 2010, Sirico 2012, and Tomasi 2012. Filip Spagnoli has assembled dozens of correlations between GDP and different measures of human prosperity at: http://filipspagnoli.wordpress.com/stats-on-human-rights/statistics-on-gross-domestic-product-correlations/ (accessed July 17, 2012). Numerous other sources for similar data exist.

- It holds for *environmental performance,* including environmental stresses and ecosystem vitality.
- It holds for *literacy* rates.
- It holds for *food production* rates, as measured by yield per hectare.
- It holds for rates of access to *health care* and to *potable water.*
- It holds for proportion of GDP dedicated to *research.*
- It holds for relative *political stability* over time.
- It holds for *peace* over time.
- It holds for *gender equality.*

Implementation of socialist-inclined policy leads to worsening of human conditions on each of these variables and indices; implementation of capitalist-inclined policy leads to improvement on each. Indeed, a new meta-study of 402 separate studies conducted over the last 15 years on the connection between capitalist-inclined policy and human welfare concludes: "the balance of evidence is overwhelming that [capitalist-inclined] economic freedom corresponds with a wide variety of positive outcomes with almost no negative tradeoffs."[10]

Particularly concerning is the condition of the poorest in the each of the respective populations. The difference in life prospects for the poorest citizens of the world's countries varies dramatically depending on the degree to which their country is socialist-inclined or capitalist-inclined, with poor citizens in the latter faring significantly better than poor citizens in the former. For example: the average real income of the poorest 10 percent in the most capitalist-inclined countries is some *ten times* as high as that of the poorest 10 percent in the most socialist-inclined countries, and their share of their country's total wealth is higher as well. A World Bank study that looked at data from 137 countries to determine which policies seemed to help the poor and which seemed to hurt them, concluded: "private property rights, fiscal discipline, macro stability, and openness to trade increases the income of the poor to the same extent that it increases the income of other

---

[10] Hall and Lawson 2013. Their study reviewed 402 papers published in 211 different peer-reviewed journals during the period of 1996–2011. The range of variables studied in the papers included not only those listed earlier, but even things such as "telephone lines per capita, numbers of supermarkets, biodiversity, and numbers of magazines" (2013: 7).

households in society," specifically adding that this appears not to be a "trickle-down process," but that the benefits to both rich and poor accrued "contemporaneously."[11] The study also concluded that these capitalist-inclined institutions helped the poor *more than* did "government social spending, formal democratic institutions, primary school enrollment rates, and agricultural productivity," adding that overall centralized government spending negatively and disproportionately affected the poor, regardless of how it was spent.

Consider also the comparison of per-capita purchasing power parity in the following places, each pair of which is linked both culturally and historically. The number in parentheses is their 2012 ranking on the Economic Freedom Index, which approximates decentralized capitalist institutions (the higher the ranking, the more decentralist-capitalist the country is; the lower the ranking, the more centralist-socialist).[12]

- Hong Kong (#1), $45,900 vs. China (#82), $7,600.
- Taiwan (#22), $35,700 vs. China (#82), $7,600.
- South Korea (#37), $30,000 vs. North Korea (n/r),[13] $1800.
- Miami, Florida (n/r), $33,712. vs. Cuba (n/r), $9,700.

Correlation does not entail causation, but the fact that so many variables, from so many sources, across so many countries and cultures and peoples, converge on similar conclusions strongly suggest that the decentralized capitalist or centralized socialist institutions themselves either promote or impede, respectively, human prosperity.

[11] Dollar and Kraay 2002. A selection from the large literature on this topic: Acemoglu and Robinson 2012; Easterly 2008: esp. "Introduction" and chaps. 9, 12–14, and 17–20; Ferguson 2011; Kling and Schulz 2009; Kraay 2006; and Landes 1999.

[12] Here is how Lawson et al. (2013) define "economic freedom": "Individuals have economic freedom when property they acquire without the use of force, fraud, or theft is protected from physical invasions by others and they are free to use, exchange, or give their property as long as their actions do not violate the identical rights of others. An index of economic freedom should measure the extent to which rightly acquired property is protected and individuals are engaged in voluntary transactions." A comparable but not identical source is Heritage Foundation/*Wall Street Journal* 2012. Another source is the *CIA World Factbook*.

[13] Neither North Korea nor Cuba is ranked by Lawson et al. (2013) because, in their judgment, the reported data from those countries is not sufficiently reliable. Lawson told me that he believes both countries would probably be "at or near the bottom" of the rankings, but because they cannot independently verify the data they have, they will not make a formal placement.

Thus, capitalist-inclined policy has outperformed socialist-inclined policy on virtually every criterion that can be measured, and the contest has not been close. Moreover, attempts to implement socialist-inclined policy have led, to varying degrees, to difficulties in people's lives that it is reasonable to assume they otherwise would not have suffered. That is the point of comparing, for example, North Korea to South Korea: two countries with substantially the same people, culture, language, history, and natural resources, but artificially divided and subjected to quite opposed systems of political economy—with standards of living that have taken very different trajectories.[14] One might make similar comparisons of, for example, Haiti and the Dominican Republic; or Hong Kong before its capitalistic reforms in the early 1960s, and subsequently; or China before its small capitalistic reforms beginning in the late 1970s, and subsequently; and so on.

Robert Lawson, one of the economists who has been compiling and analyzing this data for many years, reports that it has actually made him less, not more, ideological in his politics—because "the results are in," as he puts it.[15] Lawson's analogy: imagine two chemists arguing about whether a given compound emits an odor of roses or of vinegar. The obvious way to solve the problem is not to search for a priori arguments about how the compound *should* smell, but rather to check and see. The same holds true for systems of political economy. People have long argued about whether capitalist-inclined or socialist-inclined policy is more conducive to human prosperity; in the past, when there existed insufficient empirical evidence to resolve the issue, the arguments made little headway and were largely unproductive. Today, however, the large and growing evidence puts us in a very different position. If the question is which system of political economy leads to more prosperity, or under which system of political economy the poor in particular fare better, there is no longer any real dispute. Moreover, and more to the point here, if the question is which system of political economy either makes people worse off or reduces their

---

[14] In addition to the stark differences in per-capita income and GDP, one statistic is especially both grim and telling: people in North Korea are apparently on average about three inches shorter than people in South Korea, owing principally to malnutrition. See Newson 2012.

[15] Remarks given in a lecture at Yeshiva University in New York on September 1, 2010.

opportunities to make themselves better off—the criteria we offered for calling a policy "vicious"—then this evidence constitutes a significant challenge that the socialist must face.

The End of the Argument?

The discussion is not required to end there, however. One strong argument on behalf of socialism is based on Marx's argument about our "species being."[16] Marx argued that under capitalism workers work not for themselves but for others; because workers do not own the means of production, both their labor and the product of their labor also belong to others, specifically to the capitalist proprietors who own the means of production. This fact has further significant consequences according to Marx. First, workers no longer use nature as a "means of life" properly understood because the natural materials on which they work they do not put to their own "life" uses. It is instead taken away in exchange for mere "means of subsistence," thus "alienating" workers from the external natural world. Second, workers become alienated from others around them: their coworkers become not colleagues but competitors; their employers become not their fellow human beings but their masters. And third, when part of the individual—one's labor—is taken from the individual and sold by the bourgeoisie, that part of the individual becomes "commodified"; the result is that one becomes not only degraded to the level of a mere commodity, but one's very self disintegrates as one loses ever more of one's nature and identity. One can even come to see oneself as a commodity.

Here is how Marx describes mankind's "species-being": "Man is a species-being not only in that he practically and theoretically makes his own species as well as that of other things his object, but also—and this is only another expression for the same thing—in that as present and living species he considers himself to be a *universal* and consequently free being" (1994: 62, emphasis in the original). Part of what Marx has in mind here is that, unlike other creatures, human beings are capable of envisioning themselves as part of a group, or species, and that this self-understanding helps fill out an important

---

[16] See Marx 1994: 58–68.

part of each individual. Our identity is integrally bound up with understanding ourselves not only as individuals but also as parts of a larger species-being. This explains why we often act not only out of our own narrowly conceived self-interest but also in the interest of others—even when so doing jeopardizes our own individual well-being. If economic or political institutions induce us to see ourselves rather in an antagonistic or adversarial relationship with others, they rob us therefore of an important part of our humanity. Insofar as capitalism alienates us from our natural species-being, then, it reduces us to a fraction of what we actually are, or could be. As Marx states, "By degrading free spontaneous activity to the level of a means, alienated labor makes the species-life of man a means of his [mere] physical existence" (1994: 64).

Marx argues that private property is at the root of this problem because that single institution, perhaps more than any other institution, inclines people to look inward ("What do I have?") rather than outward ("What can we become?"). Marx argues that "overcoming" private property is thus a first, necessary step toward enabling the proper kind of human association that sees the integrated community, not the isolated individual, as the principal object of its concerns (1994: 68–79). For Marx, communism represents "the *genuine* resolution of the antagonism between man and nature and between man and man; it is the true resolution of the conflict between existence and essence, objectification and self-affirmation, freedom and necessity, individual and species" (1994: 71, emphasis in original). Although equality plays a role in Marx's argument, it is not its centerpiece. Community is— harmonious, balanced, integrated, and equal community. And capitalist-inclined policy does indeed focus people's attention elsewhere. If there is no private property, then there is no market exchange or trade; in such conditions, people do not look to make a profit—indeed, the notion of making a profit has no place in such conditions. Instead, people rely on the personal bonds they establish within their communities, which makes them keenly interested in their community as such and less interested in either themselves or other members of their community as individuals.

In capitalism, by contrast, Marx sees the fomentation of class struggles—the propertied versus the propertyless—and the introduction of associated conflicting class interests—those of the "bourgeoisie" versus those of the "proletariat," respectively. The former exploit the latter, who believe they have no choice but to comply, both because their wages have been driven down so low by the former that they have no real wherewithal to say "no," and because they have become so convinced by the ideology of capitalism that they have come to believe erroneously that it actually serves their interests. If one had observed London in the 1850s and seen the disparities of wealth between the richest (who lived in mansions and had butlers wearing white gloves) and the condition of the laboring poor (who huddled together in windowless apartments without running water), it would have been easy to conclude that something must be very wrong—and that any poor person who professed to approve of this system had to be suffering from false consciousness. The revolution for which Marx and Engels called in their 1848 *Manifesto of the Communist Party* would have been easy to understand.[17]

Putting aside all strictly economic questions now, this concern for human beings' true, social nature and for the deleterious effects that capitalism might have on it constitute perhaps the strongest argument in favor of socialism, but they also constitute its downfall. Human beings are members of classes only metaphorically, not literally. The classes into which we group them—"rich" and "poor," "bourgeoisie" and "proletariat"—have class purposes and class interests only metaphorically, not literally. On the contrary, human beings are literally individuals. Their purposes and interests are literally only their own. They work in concert with others, they form and dissolve and reform associations with others, they interact and exchange with and learn from others. Their relationships with others are real, and the benefits they get from them are real; but their consciousnesses remain their own. Their reservoirs of knowledge, their peculiar and changing signatures of association with others, and their processes of decision making are uniquely and individually their own. Even when people agree on a decision—millions of people buy iPads or shop at Wal-Mart

---

[17] Some of the disparities Marx would have seen were caused not by capitalism but by crony capitalism: legalized economic privileges and restrictions, legalized eminent domain and other takings, legally enforced class restrictions, and so on. Even so, however, by 1850 Britain had "the most sophisticated economy in the world" (Mokyr 2009: 476), and its poor enjoyed perhaps the highest average standard of living of any poor in the world. See Mokyr 2009: esp. chap. 19.

or voted for President Obama—and, further, even when the reason some of them did so is *because* others did, still, the decision to act the way they did was their own, was the effect of decision-making processes within only themselves, and was based on reasons of their own. Thus each of them freely made the decision and each of them bears personal and individual responsibility for it.

Socialist-inclined policy tends to view human beings as if they were literally members of classes, and as if the purported purposes and intentions of the classes either organized them somehow into a single collective actor or were the purposes and intentions of every single individual in the class. But neither of those is true. It is true that we may share many motivations or goals. For example, we all wish to better our conditions, however each of us understands what bettering our condition means; perhaps we also all strive for status and status-signaling, as Rousseau suggested in his 1755 *Discourse on the Origins of Inequality* and as has been corroborated by some modern research.[18] Yet despite these similarities, it is nevertheless the things that distinguish us that make all the difference. Consider all the things about each of us that are separate, distinct, and indexed uniquely to each individual. They include our values, our goals, our ambitions. They include what each of us would, and would not, do to earn money, and what each of us would, and would not, do with money. They include what counts as success in life, what counts as raising or lowering status, what counts as bettering our condition. They include with whom each of us would, and would not, associate. They also include who *decides*. Sometimes we decide to let others decide for us—what we will have for dinner tonight or whether we will go to a movie—and sometimes we decide not to let others decide even when we have done so before. In each of these cases, however, and in all the countless others like them, about matters big and small, we retain both the ability to decide whether to let another decide, and we retain the discretion to do so as well—*unless* someone else exerts force or fraud to supplant his (or their) will (or wills) for ours.

This last point implicates what I believe is a grave moral mistake socialism makes. If the factual mistake is to view human beings as something other than unique individuals, then the moral mistake that

---

[18] See, for example, Podolny 2008.

follows from it is to deny to them the dignity that their individual moral agency and subsequent equal respect demand. Think of the tremendous moral progress humanity has made in its relatively recent history as it has systematically ruled as immoral formerly ubiquitous practices such as slavery and forced labor, genocide and ethnic cleansing, summary execution and imprisonment, torture and mutilation, forced marriage and concubinage. Living comfortably today in the West can enable us to forget just how widespread and pedestrian such practices have been throughout human society, and how prevalent they remain today in some parts of the world.[19] But where progress has been made in combating these evils, it has been made precisely by asserting the unique preciousness of every human being, and denying the class or group membership that otherwise can serve as moral cover for such atrocities. They are not Africans or kulaks or women or homosexuals or Christians or Jews or Irish or Tutsis or Hutus: they are unique, individual, precious human beings—each and every one of them. It is precisely that understanding of human beings that has enabled us to construct both arguments and moral sentiments opposing the atrocities that human beings have perpetrated against other humans whom they viewed as mere members of enemy classes or disfavored groups.[20] Notions like human rights and equality before the law, which Americans and many other Westerners today simply take for granted, are actually quite rare in human history, and not only do they make little sense applied to groups instead of individuals, but they would thereby lose most of their moral power.

Socialism addresses, then, not *individual dignity* but *class membership,* and it confers rights and privileges according to that membership. This is consistent with the Marxian theory that capitalism—and indeed, all previous human history—is characterized by class conflict and that communism's ultimate victory is a resolution of these class conflicts by means of socialism's necessary intermediate steps of centralizing authority in privileged groups who will guide the transition. Marx understood the Communists to "represent the interests of the movement as a whole," to be "the most advanced and resolute section

[19] See Pinker 2011.
[20] For an eye-opening discussion of how many different groups have perpetuated atrocities and been subject to similar atrocities in human history, see Sowell 1999.

of the working-class parties of every country, that section which pushes forward all the others," and to be those who possess "the advantage of clearly understanding the line of march, the conditions, and the ultimate general results of the proletarian movement"; these are the people whom we entrust to make "despotic inroads on the rights of [private] property" and to whom we entrust "the forcible overthrow of all existing social conditions": "In place of the old bourgeois society, with its classes and class antagonisms, we shall have an association, in which the free development of each is a condition for the free development of all" (1994: 169, 175–6, and 186). Note the centrality of the notion of class membership—on all sides, both that of the "bourgeoisie" and of the "proletariat"—in Marx's argument. The classes are what identify us; the classes are what give us purposes and what have interests; the classes are what conflict with each other, requiring resolution by one defeating, and then assimilating, the other.

Socialism rightly emphasizes the importance of community and its central role in human flourishing. Human beings are social creatures who need the companionship of others to lead fulfilled and ultimately happy lives. But respect for the sacredness of each individual requires that we respect the choices they make regarding what communities to form or leave, with whom to associate or dissociate, and how to cooperate with others in what they perceive to be mutually beneficial ways. This is also a *prudent* moral principle: the moment we begin to think of some others as belonging to a group we dislike, it only all too quickly can lead us to depreciate them, to consider them as less than equal in status to us, perhaps even as less than fully human. That way atrocities lie, as the twentieth-century showed in horrifying and graphic vividness.[21] The simple right to *opt out*—to say "no, thank you" and go elsewhere—is, all by itself, a shining and powerful manifestation of respect for each person's individuality. And it is precisely what socialist-inclined policy disallows. G. A. Cohen writes: "The market, one might say, is a casino from which it is difficult to escape" (2009: 33). And yet no one has ever built walls to keep citizens in capitalist countries.

---

[21] See, for example, Courteois et al. 1999, Pinker 2011, Pipes 2001, Revel 2009, Rummel 1994, Scott 1998 and 2009, Snyder 2010, and White 2011.

The End of Socialism

Socialism thus faces grave difficulties. Its requirements are difficult to reconcile with plausible descriptions of human nature and the human condition. Its implementation requires knowledge that its central planners do not have and cannot collect. Its large-scale attempts have imposed significant costs, have left people worse off than they otherwise would have been, and have prevented them from bettering their own conditions. Its conception of humanity as essentially communal is in a crucial sense empirically incorrect and then also morally flawed. Its concerns for community, equality, and fairness are initially plausible, but turn out on examination to be in each case misplaced. It thus proposes, as both a theory and in practice, decreasing prosperity, declining quality of human life, and disrespecting of the dignity each of us should enjoy as equal moral agents.

Now, it is surely the case that there is some tipping point—some threshold beyond which we cannot stop these problematics, but yet before which socialist-inclined policies of centralized intervention, restriction, and redistribution *can* be absorbed with marginal but not fatal loss. As Adam Smith said, there is "a great deal of ruin in a nation." But we cannot know where that point of no return is. What we can know is that although the principal values to which socialism appeals—community, equality, and fairness—may continue to resonate with us, its logic will nevertheless drive us inexorably toward impoverishment, selective privilege, and inequality of moral agency. That is the end that socialism proposes, and at the limit it spells the end of socialism because it spells the end of free and prosperous human civilization.

The socialist grapes, therefore, seem impossible to harvest, have nevertheless induced numerous but destructive attempts, and yet seem sour in their moral core. Perhaps it is time, then, to give up on the socialist grapes.

Bibliography

Acemoglu, Daron and James A. Robinson. 2012. *Why Nations Fail: The Origins of Power, Prosperity, and Poverty*. New York: Crown Business.

Acton, Lord (John Emerich Edward Dalberg). 1985. "The History of Freedom in Antiquity" and "The History of Freedom in Christianity." In *Selected Writings of Lord Acton*, vol. 1. J. Rufus Fears, ed. Indianapolis: Liberty Fund.

Adams, John. 2007. "Britain's Seat Belt Law Should Be Repealed." *Significance* 4, 2: 86–9.

Alchien, Armen A. June 1950. "Uncertainty, Evolution, and Economic Theory." *The Journal of Political Economy* 58, 3: 211–21.

Anderson, Elizabeth. 1999. "What Is the Point of Equality?" *Ethics* 109, 2: 287–337.

Anderson, Terry L. and Donald R. Leal. 2001. *Free Market Environmentalism*, rev. ed. New York: Palgrave Macmillan.

Ariely, Dan. 2010. *Predictably Irrational*, rev. ed. New York: Harper Perennial.

    2012. *The Honest Truth about Dishonesty: How We Lie to Everyone—Especially Ourselves*. New York: Harper.

Aristotle. 1985. *The Politics*. Trans. Carnes Lord. Chicago: University of Chicago Press.

Arneson, Richard. 1989. "Equality and Equal Opportunity for Welfare." *Philosophical Studies* 56, 1: 77–93.

    2000. "Luck Egalitarianism and Prioritarianism." *Ethics* 110, 2: 339–49.

    2004. "Luck Egalitarianism: An Interpretation and Defense." *Philosophical Topics* 32, 1 and 2: 1–20.

Bailey, Ronald, ed. 2002. *Global Warming and Other Eco Myths: How the Environmental Movement Uses False Science to Scare Us to Death*. New York: Prima Lifestyles.

Bastiat, Frédéric. 1848. What Is Seen and What Is Not Seen. In *Selected Essays on Political Economy*. Irvington, NY: Foundation for Economic Education.

Baumslag, Naomi. 2005. *Murderous Medicine: Nazi Doctors, Human Experimentation, and Typhus*. Westport, CT: Praeger.

Beinhocker, Eric. 2007. *The Origin of Wealth: The Radical Remaking of Economics and What It Means for Business and Society*. Cambridge, MA: Harvard Business School Press.

Bennett, William J. and David Wilezol. 2013. *Is College Worth It? A Former United States Secretary of Education and a Liberal Arts Graduate Expose the Broken Promise of Higher Education*. Nashville, TN: Thomas Nelson.

Bethell, Tom. 1998. *The Noblest Triumph: Property and Prosperity through the Ages*. New York: St. Martin's Press.

Bloomberg, Michael. "National Salt Reduction Initiative." Available at: http://www.nyc.gov/html/doh/html/cardio/cardio-salt-initiative.shtml.

Boettke, Peter. 2012. *Living Economics: Yesterday, Today, and Tomorrow*. Oakland, CA: Independent Institute.

Bowlus, Audra J. and Jean-Marc Robin. 2012. "An International Comparison of Lifetime Inequality: How Continental Europe Resembles North America." *Journal of the European Economic Association* 10, 6: 1236–62.

Brennan, Jason. 2011. *The Ethics of Voting*. Princeton, NJ: Princeton University Press.

Brooks, Arthur C. 2012. *The Road to Freedom: How to Win the Fight for Free Enterprise*. New York: Basic Books.

Buchanan, James M. 1999 (1964). "What Should Economists Do?" *Southern Economic Journal* 30 (January): 213–22.

   2005. "Afraid to Be Free: Dependency as Desideratum." *Public Choice* 124: 19–31.

Caplan, Bryan. 2011. *Selfish Reasons to Have More Kids: Why Being a Great Parent is Less Work and More Fun than You Think*. New York: Basic Books.

Carlyle, Thomas. 1849. "Occasional Discourse on the Negro Question." *Fraser's Magazine for Town and Country*, vol. XL.

Carnegie, Andrew. 2006 (1889). *The "Gospel of Wealth" Essays and Other Writings*. David Nasaw, ed. New York: Penguin Classics.

Clark, Gregory. 2007. *A Farewell to Alms: A Brief Economic History of the World*. Princeton, NJ: Princeton University Press.

Clark, Henry C., ed. 2003. *Commerce, Culture, and Liberty: Readings on Capitalism Before Adam Smith*. Indianapolis, IN: Liberty Fund.

   2012. "Violence, 'Capitalism,' and the Civilizing Process in Early Modern Europe." *Society* 49, 2: 122–31.

Coase, Ronald. 1960. "The Problem of Social Cost." *Journal of Law and Economics*, 3 (October): 1–44.

Coase, Ronald and Ning Wang. 2013. *How China Became Capitalist*. New York: Palgrave Macmillan.

Cohen, G. A. 1989. "On the Currency of Egalitarian Justice." *Ethics* 99, 4: 906–44.

1995. *Self-Ownership, Freedom, and Equality.* New York: Cambridge University Press.

2000. *If You're an Egalitarian, How Come You're So Rich?* Cambridge, MA: Harvard University Press.

2008. *Rescuing Justice and Equality.* Cambridge, MA: Harvard University Press.

2009. *Why Not Socialism?* Princeton, NJ: Princeton University Press.

Conly, Sarah. 2013. *Against Autonomy: Justifying Coercive Paternalism.* New York: Cambridge University Press.

Cook, Adrian. 2004. "Mind Your Head: The Data and Debate on Bicycle Helmet Effectiveness." *Significance* 1, 4: 162–3.

Coolidge, Calvin. 2001. *The Price of Freedom: Speeches and Addresses.* Amsterdam, The Netherlands: Fredonia Books.

Copp, David. 1988. "Equality, Justice, and Basic Needs." In *Necessary Goods: Our Responsibilities to Meet Others' Needs.* Gillian Brock, ed. New York: Rowman and Littlefield.

Corak, Miles, ed. 2011. *Generational Income Mobility in North America and Europe.* New York: Cambridge University Press.

Courtois, Stéfane et al. 1999. *The Black Book of Communism: Crimes, Terror, Repression.* Cambridge, MA: Harvard University Press.

Crawford, Matthew. 2011. *The Case for Working with Your Hands, Or, Why Office Work Is Bad for Us and Fixing Things Feels Good.* New York: Penguin Viking.

Cullity, Garrett. 2004. *The Moral Demands of Affluence.* New York: Oxford University Press.

Darwall, Stephen. 2009. *The Second-Person Standpoint: Morality, Respect, and Accountability.* Cambridge, MA: Harvard University Press.

Dawson, John W. and John J. Seater. 2013. "Federal Regulation and Aggregate Economic Growth." *Journal of Economic Growth* 18, 2: 137–77.

Demsetz, Harold. 1969. "Information and Efficiency: Another Viewpoint." *Journal of Law and Economics,* 12, 1: 1–22.

Dollar, David and Aart Kraay. 2002. "Growth Is Good for the Poor." *Journal of Economic Growth* 7, 3: 195–225

Dworkin, Ronald. 2003. "Equality, Luck, and Hierarchy." *Philosophy and Public Affairs* 31, 2: 190–8.

Eagleton, Terry. 2012. *Why Marx Was Right.* New Haven, CT: Yale University Press.

Easterly, William, ed. 2008. *Reinventing Foreign Aid.* Cambridge, MA: MIT Press.

Economist, The. 2012. "Sweden: The New Model." October 13. Available at: http://www.economist.com/node/21564412.

Eisenstadt, Marvin, Andre Haynal, Pierre Rentschnick, and Pie De Denarclens. 1989. *Parental Loss and Achievement.* Madison, CT: International Universities Press.

Emerson, John W., Daniel C. Esty, Mark A. Levy, and William Dornbos 2012. *2012 Environmental Performance Index.* New Haven, CT: Yale Center for Environmental Law and Policy. Available at: http://www.epi.yale. edu/.

Epstein, Richard. 1995. *Simple Rules for a Complex World.* Cambridge, MA: Harvard University Press.

2011. *Design for Liberty: Private Property, Public Administration, and the Rule of Law.* Cambridge, MA: Harvard University Press.

Ferguson, Niall. 2011. *Civilization: The West and the Rest.* New York: Penguin.

Fleischacker, Samuel. 1999. *A Third Concept of Liberty: Judgment and Freedom in Kant and Adam Smith.* Princeton, NJ: Princeton University Press.

Forthcoming. 2015. "Adam Smith and the Left." In *Princeton Guide to Adam Smith.* Ryan Patrick Hanley, ed. Princeton, NJ: Princeton University Press.

Forbes, Steve and Elizabeth Ames. 2009. *How Capitalism Will Save Us: Why Free People and Free Markets Are the Best Answer to Today's Economy.* New York: Crown Business.

Frank, Robert. 1988. *Passions within Reason: The Strategic Role of the Emotions.* New York: W. W. Norton.

2011. *The Darwin Economy: Liberty, Competition, and the Common Good.* Princeton, NJ: Princeton University Press.

Friedman, Milton. 2002. *Capitalism and Freedom,* 40th anniv. ed. Chicago: University of Chicago Press.

Gaus, Gerald. 2010. *The Order of Public Reason: A Theory of Freedom and Morality in a Diverse and Bounded World.* New York: Cambridge University Press.

Glaeser, Edward L. 2011. *Triumph of the City: How Our Greatest Invention Makes Us Richer, Smarter, Greener, Healthier, and Happier.* New York: Penguin.

Haidt, Jonathan. 2012. *The Righteous Mind: Why Good People Are Divided by Politics and Religion.* New York: Pantheon.

2013. "Of Freedom and Fairness." *Democracy Journal* (Spring): 38–50.

Hall, Joshua C. and Robert A. Lawson. 2013. "Economic Freedom of the World: An Accounting of the Literature." *Contemporary Economic Policy* (March): 1–19.

Hanushek, Erik A. and Steven G. Rivken. 1997. "Understanding the 20th Century Growth in U.S. School Spending." *Journal of Human Resources* 31, 1: 34–68.

Hardin, Garrett. 1968. "The Tragedy of the Commons." *Science* 13: 1243–8.

Harris, Judith Rich. 2006. *No Two Alike: Human Nature and Human Individuality.* New York: W. W. Norton.

Hayek, Friedrich. 1945. "The Use of Knowledge in Society." In *Individualism and Economic Order.* Chicago: University of Chicago Press. Pp. 77–91.

1948 (1935a, 1935b, and 1940). "Socialist Calculation I, II, and III." In *Individualism and Economic Order.* Chicago: University of Chicago Press. Pp. 119–208.

1976. *The Mirage of Social Justice*. Chicago: University of Chicago Press.

1978. "The Atavism of Social Justice." In *New Studies in Philosophy, Politics, Economics, and the History of Ideas*. Chicago: University of Chicago Press. Pp. 57–68.

1988. *The Fatal Conceit: The Errors of Socialism*. Chicago: University of Chicago Press.

2007 (1944). *The Road to Serfdom*. Chicago: University of Chicago Press.

2011 (1960). *The Constitution of Liberty: The Definitive Edition*. Chicago: University of Chicago Press.

Heritage Foundation/*Wall Street Journal*. 2012. *2012 Index of Economic Freedom*. Available at: http://www.heritage.org/index/default.

Heyes, Cressida. 2012. "Identity Politics." *Stanford Encyclopedia of Philosophy*. Available at: http://plato.stanford.edu/entries/identity-politics/.

Holmes, Stephen and Cass Sunstein. 2000. *The Cost of Rights: Why Liberty Depends on Taxes*. New York: W. W. Norton.

Hume, David. 1987 (1741). "Of a Standard of Taste." In *David Hume: Essays Moral Political and Literary*. Eugene F. Miller, ed. Indianapolis, IN: Liberty Fund.

1988. *Dialogues Concerning Natural Religion*. Indianapolis, IN: Hackett.

2000 (1739–40). *A Treatise of Human Nature*. David Fate Norton and Mary J. Norton, eds. New York: Oxford University Press.

Johnson, Robert J., Jasper E. Shealy, and Carl F. Ettlinger. 2009. "Do Helmets Reduce Fatalities or Merely Alter the Patterns of Death?" *Journal of ASTM International* 17, STP1510: 39–43.

Kahneman, Daniel and Amos Tversky. 2000. *Choices, Values, and Frames*. New York: Cambridge University Press.

Kant, Immanuel. 1965 (1781). *Critique of Pure Reason*. Norman Kemp Smith, trans. New York: St. Martin's Press.

1981. *Grounding for the Metaphysics of Morals*. James W. Ellington, trans. Indianapolis, IN: Hackett.

1992. *Kant: Political Writings*. Hans Reiss, ed. New York: Cambridge University Press.

Kekes, John. 2010. "The Right to Private Property: A Justification." *Social Philosophy and Policy* 27, 10: 1–20.

Kling, Arnold and Nick Schulz. 2009. *From Poverty to Prosperity: Intangible Assets, Hidden Liabilities and the Lasting Triumph over Scarcity*. New York: Encounter.

Knight, Frank. 1997 (1935). *The Ethics of Competition*. New Brunswick, NJ: Transaction Publishers.

Kraay, Aart. 2006. "When Is Growth Pro-Poor? Evidence from a Panel of Countries." *Journal of Development Economics* 80, 1: 198–227.

Kymlicka, Will. 2002a. *Contemporary Political Philosophy*, 2nd ed. New York: Oxford University Press.

2002b. "Marxism." In *Contemporary Political Philosophy*, 2nd ed. New York: Oxford University Press.

Landes, David S. 1999. *The Wealth and Poverty of Nations: Why Some Are So Rich and Some So Poor*. New York: W. W. Norton.

Lawson, Robert, Joshua Hall, and James Gwartney. 2013. *Economic Freedom of the World Report*. Vancouver: Fraser Institute.

Levy, David M. 2002. *How the Dismal Science Got Its Name*. Ann Arbor: University of Michigan Press.

Levy, David M. and Sandra Peart. 2001. "The Secret History of the Dismal Science." Available at: http://www.econlib.org/library/Columns/LevyPeartdismal.html.

Locke, John. 1988 (1690). *Two Treatises of Government*. Peter Laslett, ed. New York: Cambridge University Press.

Lockwood, Benjamin B. and Matthew Weinzierl. 2012. "*De Gustibus non est Taxandum*: Heterogenity in Preferences and Optimal Redistribution." Cambridge, MA: Harvard Business School. Available at: http://hbswk.hbs.edu/item/6940.html.

Lomborg, Bjørn. 2010. *The Skeptical Environmentalist: Measuring the Real State of the World*. New York: Cambridge University Press.

Macaulay, Thomas Babington. 1825. "Milton." *The Edinburgh Review* (August): 1–60.

Mackie, John and Raj Sisodia. 2013. *Conscious Capitalism: Liberating the Heroic Spirit of Business*. Cambridge, MA: Harvard Business Review Press.

Macpherson, C. B. 2011 (1962). *The Political Theory of Possessive Individualism: Hobbes to Locke*. New York: Oxford University Press.

Maddison, Angus. 2007. *Contours of the World Economy: 1–2030 AD*. New York: Oxford University Press.

Marks, Steven G. 2012. "The Word 'Capitalism': The Soviet Union's Gift to America." *Society* 49, 2: 155–63.

Marx, Karl. 1994. *Karl Marx: Selected Writings*. Lawrence H. Simon, ed. Indianapolis, IN: Hackett.

McChesney, Fred S. 1987. "Rent Extraction and Rent Creation in the Economic Theory of Regulation." *Journal of Legal Studies* 16: 101–18.

McCloskey, Deirdre. 2007. *The Bourgeois Virtues: Ethics for an Age of Commerce*. Chicago: University of Chicago Press.

  2010. *Bourgeois Dignity: Why Economics Can't Explain the Modern World*. Chicago: University of Chicago Press.

Mill, John Stuart. 1997 (1859). *On Liberty*. Stefan Collini, ed. New York: Cambridge University Press.

  2002. *Utilitarianism*, 2nd ed. George Sher, ed. Indianapolis, IN: Hackett.

Mises, Ludwig von. 1990 (1920). *Economic Calculation in the Socialist Commonwealth*. Auburn, AL: Mises Institute.

Mokyr, Joel. 2009. *The Enlightened Economy: An Economic History of Britain 1700–1850*. New Haven, CT: Yale University Press.

Muller, Jerry Z. 2003. *The Mind and the Market: Capitalism in Western Thought*. New York: Anchor.

Munger, Michael C. 2011. "'Euvoluntary' Exchange and the 'Difference Principle.'" Available at SSRN: http://ssrn.com/abstract=1904035.

Muravchik, Joshua. 2002. *Heaven on Earth: The Rise and Fall of Socialism.* New York: Encounter.

Murphy, Liam and Thomas Nagel. 2002. *The Myth of Ownership: Taxes and Justice.* New York: Oxford University Press.

Murray, Charles. 2009. *Real Education: Four Simple Truths for Bringing America's Schools Back to Reality.* New York: Three Rivers Press.

2012. *Coming Apart: The State of White America, 1960–2010.* New York: Crown Forum.

Nagel, Thomas. 1995. *Equality and Partiality.* New York: Oxford University Press.

Newman, Michael. 2005. *Socialism: A Very Short Introduction.* New York: Oxford University Press.

Newson, Tomiko. 2012. "Journey into the Heart of North Korea." *The Independent* (UK). Available at: http://www.independent.co.uk/news/world/asia/journey-into-the-heart-of-north-korea-7640702.html.

Nozick, Robert. 1974. *Anarchy, State, and Utopia.* New York: Basic Books.

Nussbaum, Martha. 1988. "Aristotelian Social Democracy," In *Necessary Goods: Our Responsibilities to Meet Others' Needs.* Gillian Brock, ed. New York: Rowman and Littlefield.

2000. *Women and Human Development.* New York: Cambridge University Press.

2006. *Frontiers of Justice: Disability, Nationality, Species Membership.* Cambridge, MA: Belknap.

2011. *Creating Capabilities: The Human Development Approach.* Cambridge, MA: Belknap.

Okun, Arthur. 1975. *Equality and Efficiency: The Big Tradeoff.* New York: Brookings Institution.

Olsaretti, Serena, ed. 2003. *Desert and Justice.* New York: Oxford University Press.

2004. *Liberty, Desert and the Market.* New York: Cambridge University Press.

Olson, Mancur. 1971. *The Logic of Collective Action: Public Goods and the Theory of Groups.* Cambridge, MA: Harvard University Press.

Ostrom, Elinor. 2011. *Governing the Commons: The Evolution of Institutions for Collective Action.* New York: Cambridge University Press.

Otteson, James R. 2002a. "Adam Smith's First Market: The Development of Language," *History of Philosophy Quarterly* 19, 1: 65–86.

2002b. *Adam Smith's Marketplace of Life.* New York: Cambridge University Press.

2003. *The Levellers: Overton, Walwyn, and Lilburne,* 5 vols. Bristol, UK: Thoemmes Press.

2006. *Actual Ethics.* New York: Cambridge University Press.

2009. "Kantian Individualism and Political Libertarianism." *The Independent Review* 13, 3: 389–409.

2010. "Adam Smith and the Great Mind Fallacy." *Social Philosophy and Policy* 27, 1: 276–304.

2013. *Adam Smith*. New York: Bloomsbury.

Forthcoming. 2015. "Adam Smith and the Right." *Princeton Guide to Adam Smith*. Ryan Patrick Hanley, ed. Princeton, NJ: Princeton University Press.

Peart, Sandra J. and David M. Levy. 2001. "The Secret History of the Dismal Science." Available at: http://econlib.org/library/Columns/LevyPeartdismal.html.

2005. *The "Vanity of the Philosopher": From Equality to Hierarchy in Post-Classical Economics*. Ann Arbor: University of Michigan Press.

Pinker, Steven. 2002. *The Blank Slate: The Modern Denial of Human Nature*. New York: Penguin.

2011. *The Better Angels of Our Nature: Why Violence Has Declined*. New York: Viking.

Pipes, Richard. 1999. *Property and Freedom*. New York: Vintage.

2001. *Communism: A History*. New York: Modern Library.

Plato. 1992. *Republic*. Trans. G. M. A. Grube, rev. C. D. C. Reeve. Indianapolis, IN: Hackett.

Podolny, Joel M. 2008. *Status Signals: A Sociological Study of Market Competition*. Princeton, NJ: Princeton University Press.

Putnam, Robert D. 2000. *Bowling Alone: The Collapse and Revival of American Community*. New York: Simon and Schuster.

2007. "E Pluribus Unum: Diversity and Community in the Twenty-First Century." *Scandinavian Political Studies* 30, 2: 137–74.

Rawls, John. 1971. *A Theory of Justice*. Cambridge, MA: Harvard University Press.

1975. "A Kantian Conception of Equality." *Cambridge Review* 96, 2225: 94–9.

Revel, Jean-François. 2009. *Last Exit to Utopia*. New York: Encounter.

Ridley, Matt. 2011. *The Rational Optimist: How Prosperity Evolves*. New York: Harper Perennial.

Robbins, Lionel. 2000 (1932). *A History of Economic Thought*. Princeton, NJ: Princeton University Press.

Röpke, Wilhelm. 1998 (1960). *A Humane Economy: The Social Framework of a Free Society*. Wilmington, DE: ISI Press.

Rose, David. 2011. *The Moral Foundation of Economic Behavior*. New York: Oxford University Press.

Rousseau, Jean-Jacques. 1988a (1754). Discourse on the Origin of Inequality. In *Jean-Jacques Rousseau: The Basic Political Writings*. Donald A. Cress, trans. Indianapolis, IN: Hackett.

1988b. Social Contract. In *Jean-Jacques Rousseau: The Basic Political Writings*, Donald A. Cress, trans. Indianapolis, IN: Hackett.

2003. "Luxury, Commerce, and the Arts." In *Commerce, Culture, and Liberty: Writings on Capitalism before Adam Smith*, Henry C. Clark, ed. Indianapolis, IN: Liberty Fund.

Rummel, R. J. 1994. *Death by Government: Genocide and Mass Murder in the Twentieth Century*. New Brunswick, NJ: Transaction.

Sandel, Michael. 2010. *Justice: What's the Right Thing to Do?* New York: Farrar, Straus and Giroux.

2012. *What Money Can't Buy: The Moral Limits of Markets*. New York: Farrar, Straus and Giroux.

Satz, Debra. 2010. *The Moral Limits of Markets: Why Some Things Should Not Be for Sale*. New York: Oxford University Press.

Scheffler, Samuel. 2003. "What Is Egalitarianism?" *Philosophy and Public Affairs* 31, 1: 5–39.

2005. "Choice, Circumstance, and the Value of Equality." *Politics, Philosophy, and Economics* 4, 1: 5–28.

Schmidtz, David. 2002. "How to Deserve." *Political Theory* 30, 6: 774–99.

2008. "The Institution of Property." In *Person, Polis, Planet*. New York: Oxford University Press.

2011. "Nonideal Theory: What It Is and What It Needs to Be." *Ethics* 121, 4: 772–96.

2012. "Friedrich Hayek." *Stanford Encyclopedia of Philosophy*. Available at: http://plato.stanford.edu/entries/friedrich-hayek/.

Schumpeter, Joseph. 1947. *Capitalism, Socialism, and Democracy*, 2nd ed. New York: Martino.

Schwartz, Barry. 2005. *The Paradox of Choice: Why More Is Less*. New York: Harper Perennial.

Scott, James C. 1998. *Seeing Like a State: How Certain Schemes to Improve the Human Condition Have Failed*. New Haven: Yale University Press.

2009. *The Art of Not Being Governed: An Anarchist History of Upland Southeast Asia*. New Haven: Yale University Press.

Seabright, Paul. 2010. *The Company of Strangers: A Natural History of Economic Life*, rev. ed. Princeton, NJ: Princeton University Press.

Simmons, A. John. 2010. "Ideal and Nonideal Theory." *Philosophy and Public Affairs* 38, 1: 5–36.

Singer, Peter. 2009. *The Life You Can Save: How to Do Your Part to End World Poverty*. New York: Random House.

2011a. *The Expanding Circle*. Princeton, NJ: Princeton University Press.

2011b. *Practical Ethics*, 3rd. ed. New York: Cambridge University Press.

Sirico, Rev. Robert A. 2012. *Defending the Free Market: The Moral Case for a Free Economy*. Washington, DC: Regnery.

Skidelsky, Robert and Edward Skidelsky. 2012. *How Much Is Enough? Money and the Good Life*. New York: Other Press.

Skousen, Mark. 2009. *The Making of Modern Economics*, 2nd. ed. New York: M. E. Sharpe.

Smiles, Samuel. 2002 (1859). *Self-Help*. New York: Oxford University Press.

Smith, Adam. 1980. *Essays on Philosophical Subjects*. W. P. D. Wightman, ed. Indianapolis, IN: Liberty Fund.

1981 (1776). *An Inquiry into the Nature and Causes of the Wealth of Nations*. R. H. Campbell and A. S. Skinner, eds. Indianapolis, IN: Liberty Fund.

1982a. *Lectures on Jurisprudence*. R. L. Meek, D. D. Raphael, and P. G. Stein, eds. Indianapolis, IN: Liberty Fund.

1982b (1759). *The Theory of Moral Sentiments*. D. D. Raphael and A. L. Macfie, eds. Indianapolis, IN: Liberty Fund.

1987. *Correspondence of Adam Smith*. E. C. Mossner and I. S. Ross, eds. Indianapolis, IN: Liberty Fund.

Snyder, Timothy. 2010. *Bloodlands: Europe between Hitler and Stalin*. New York: Basic Books.

Sowell, Thomas. 1999. *Conquests and Cultures: An International History*. New York: Basic Books.

2007a. *A Conflict of Visions*, rev. ed. New York: Basic Books.

2007b. *Basic Economics: A Common Sense Guide to the Economy*, 3rd ed. New York: Basic Books.

Stanley, Thomas J. and William D. Danko 2010. *The Millionaire Next Door: The Surprising Secrets of America's Wealthy*. New York: Taylor Trade.

Stephen, James Fitzjames. 1993 (1872–3). *Liberty, Equality, Fraternity*. Stuart D. Warner, ed. Indianapolis, IN: Liberty Fund.

Stigler, George J. 1971. "The Theory of Economic Regulation." *The Bell Journal of Economics and Management Science* 2, 1: 3–21.

Stiglitz, Joseph. 2012. *The Price of Inequality: How Today's Divided Society Endangers Our Future*. New York: W. W. Norton.

Strange, Marty. 2009. *Family Farming: A New Economic Vision*. Winnipeg: Bison Books.

Sumner, William Graham. 1883. "The Forgotten Man." In *On Liberty, Society, and Politics: The Essential Essays of William Graham Sumner*. Robert C. Bannister, ed. Indianapolis, IN: Liberty Fund.

Sunstein, Cass R. 1997. *Free Markets and Social Justice*. New York: Oxford University Press.

2002. *Risk and Reason: Safety, Law, and the Environment*. New York: Cambridge University Press.

2013. *Simpler: The Future of Government*. New York: Simon and Schuster.

Sunstein, Cass and Adrian Vermeule. 2008. "Conspiracy Theories." Harvard, Public Law Working Paper No. 08–03; University of Chicago, Public Law Working Paper No. 199; University of Chicago, Law & Economics Olin Working Paper No. 387.

Taylor, James Stacey, ed. 2005. *Personal Autonomy*. New York: Cambridge University Press.

Thaler, Richard and Cass Sunstein. 2009. *Nudge: Improving Decisions about Health, Wealth, and Happiness*, rev. and updated ed. New York: Penguin.

Tomasi, John. 2012. *Free Market Fairness*. Princeton, NJ: Princeton University Press.

Tullock, Gordon. 2005. *The Rent-Seeking Society*. Indianapolis, IN: Liberty Fund.

Ubel, Peter. 2009. *Free Market Madness: Why Economics Is at Odds with Human Nature—And Why It Matters*. Cambridge, MA: Harvard Business School Press.

United States Treasury Department. 2008. "Income Mobility in the United States from 1996 to 2005." Available at: http://www.treasury.gov/resource-center/tax-policy/Documents/incomemobilitystudy03–08revise.pdf.

Vallentyne, Peter. 2002. "Brute Luck, Option Luck, and Equality of Initial Opportunities." *Ethics* 112: 529–57.

White, Matthew. 2011. *The Big Book of Horrible Things: The Definitive Chronicle of History's 100 Worst Atrocities*. New York: W. W. Norton.

Wilson, David Sloan. 2011. *The Neighborhood Project: Using Evolution to Improve My City, One Block at a Time*. New York: Little, Brown.

Woolf, Virginia. 1989 (1929). *A Room of One's Own*. New York: Harcourt.

World Factbook. Central Intelligence Agency. Available at: https://www.cia.gov/library/publications/the-world-factbook/.

Zak, Paul J. 2012. *The Moral Molecule: The Source of Love and Prosperity*. New York: Dutton.

Zamyatin, Yevgeny. 1970 (1923). "On Literature, Revolution, Entropy, and Other Matters." In *A Soviet Heretic: Essays by Yevgeny Zamyatin*. Mirra Ginsburg, trans. Chicago: University of Chicago Press.

Zingales, Luigi. 2012. *A Capitalism for the People: Recapturing the Lost Genius of American Prosperity*. New York: Basic Books.

Index